MADNESS
AND
LUST

MADNESS
AND
LUST
A Psychoanalytical Approach
to Don Quixote

CARROLL B. JOHNSON

UNIVERSITY OF CALIFORNIA PRESS
Berkeley   Los Angeles   London

University of California Press
Berkeley and Los Angeles, California

University of California Press, Ltd.
London, England

Library of Congress Cataloging in Publication Data

Johnson, Carroll B.
　　Madness and lust.

　　　Includes bibliographical references and index.
　　　1. Cervantes Saavedra, Miguel de, 1547–1616. Don
Quixote.　2. Cervantes Saavedra, Miguel de, 1547–1616—
Characters—Don Quixote.　3. Cervantes Saavedra,
Miguel de, 1547–1616—Knowledge—Psychology.
4. Psychoanalysis and literature.　I. Title.
PQ6353.J63　　　1982　　　863'.3　　　83-10916
ISBN 0-520-04752-4

Printed in the United States of America

for Leslie

CONTENTS

ACKNOWLEDGMENTS

I wish to express publicly my gratitude to several people and institutions without whose intervention this book would never have been. My interest in *Don Quixote* was and continues to be stimulated by the students I have been fortunate enough to teach at UCLA. It was for them that I first began to think seriously about Cervantes's text, and it is they who keep me honest in my critical appraisals of it. My interest in psychoanalysis and therefore in the theoretical basis of this study is owing to the indirect and perhaps unwitting stimulus of my first wife, Carmen. In retrospect, my debt to her is enormous. Dr. James Rosenblum led me—not without massive resistance on my part—to whatever knowledge of the human psyche I possess. I would also like to thank my colleagues in the Department of Spanish & Portuguese, for making me their chairman from 1975 to 1981 and thereby thrusting upon me the necessity to use time efficiently. The National Endowment for the Humanities provided a generous grant in support of those portions of the study that deal with sixteenth-century Spanish theories of personality. James Kubeck of the University of California Press took a benevolent interest in this study and guided it skillfully around the bureaucratic shoals. Finally, my wife Leslie has been patient and supportive through the gestation and elaboration of theories and countertheories, helpful with the contribution of some acute observations, and responsible for the preparation of the manuscript. My debt to her is greater than I can say.

If there is something of value in these pages, we may all be grateful to the foregoing. For the rest, the responsibility is mine.

C. B. J.

Culver City
March 1982

INTRODUCTION

"Don Quichotte ne se démode pas, porté qu'il est par la psyché éternelle."
Gilbert Durand

In 1891 Paul Gauguin left a good job as a Paris stockbroker and sailed off to Tahiti to paint bare-breasted women. He was forty-three years old. In 1977 two businessmen in Beverly Hills gave up comfortable lives and high standards of living to open a shop specializing in obsolete wood-carving equipment. They were fifty-five and fifty-nine years of age.[1] A prominent attorney of my acquaintance abandoned his law practice in order to devote himself to an import business specializing in cardboard binoculars and electric Tee-shirts. He was forty-nine. And somewhere in La Mancha, an anonymous, fiftyish *hidalgo* gives up his life as a country gentleman, changes his name to Don Quixote, and rides off one July morning into the life of a fifteenth-century knight-errant, to battle giants and right wrongs.

All these men—four real and one imagined—have in common the fact that somewhere around age fifty they abandoned comfort, stability, and routine and threw themselves into consuming new projects that may without undue violence be characterized as foolish, crazy, or, most precisely, quixotic. The presence of this last adjective in our language, together with its startling applicability to the lives of at least four real men whose actions are a matter of public record, suggests that life imitates art, that my lawyer friend and Gauguin and the wood-carvers were all inspired to embark on their new lives by the example of

1

Don Quixote. In fact, as Aristotle suggested long ago, the reverse is true. It is because Don Quixote acts the way real men act that his story is so easily assimilable to those of Gauguin and the others. That he acts like real people of a certain age act in real life invites us to take the fiction of *Don Quixote* seriously, to consider Don Quixote as though he were a real person, to trace his actions back to their unspoken motivations. What I shall be proposing here is a psychological, or more precisely, a psychoanalytical reading of the novel, by means of which I can present Don Quixote as a complex, verisimilar, eminently believable—in short, novelistic— literary personage. In this way I hope to strike a blow for humanism and humanity in an intellectual climate suffocated by sterile theories of economic determinism and pseudoscientific structuralist mystification. And, not incidentally, I hope to enrich the twentieth-century reader's possible experience of one of the classics of our occidental tradition. I do not expect to exhaust the interpretive possibilities of either the character or the work. Criticism of a masterpiece evolves necessarily through an accretion of individual studies of particular aspects.

Don Quixote has been presented in many aspects, determined by wildly differing critical tastes, artistic preferences, and political, religious, and economic ideologies. Let me offer a few relatively recent examples. We have had Don Quixote as a fictionalized spokesman for the Counter-Reformation theology adopted by the Council of Trent.[2] We have seen Don Quixote presented as a clandestine Hebrew prophet whose adventures and pronouncements constitute a surreptitious continuation of the Zohar.[3] As the regime of General Franco neared its inevitable end and Spanish political and intellectual life began to be liberalized, it was only mildly surprising to learn that Don Quixote had been a left-wing liberal democrat all along.[4]

What we have not seen is Don Quixote as a man who is about fifty years of age and, furthermore, insane. In the succeeding pages I should like to consider Don Quixote in light of these two factors. The enterprise seems fairly straightforward, but in fact it is fraught with difficulties. I must say that no one to my knowledge has made a particular issue of Don Quixote's age. Everyone accepts him as a fifty-year-old (*cincuentón* in Spanish), and only a few critics, notably Luis Andrés Murillo and Juan Bautista Avalle-Arce, have actually pondered the implications of our hero's age.

It is more difficult, apparently, to accept Don Quixote as a man and to believe that he acts the way real men act. His adventures are so absurd, his acts of insanity so mechanical and so divorced from his cogent discourses on the Golden Age, arms and letters, love and marriage, that it becomes impossible to detect any coherent pattern of cause and effect, motivation and behavior. It is temptingly easy to view Don Quixote as an allegorical figure or as a satirist's puppet.

Even more serious are the difficulties presented by our hero's madness. There are two basic questions involved here, each with different possible answers. The first is simply the question of whether Don Quixote is in fact insane at all. Mauro Olmeda, for example, considers that Cervantes causes Don Quixote to exhibit behavior associated with madness simply as a front for his own critical commentary.[5] Salvador de Madariaga, Mark Van Doren, and, most recently, Arturo Serrano Plaja all consider that although Don Quixote does act crazy, somewhere in his heart of hearts (or psyche of psyches) he knows that he is really engaging in an enormously sophisticated and exhilarating game. Serrano Plaja in particular compares his playacting to a child's ability to project himself into fantasy and operate as though fantasy were reality. F. Sánchez Castañer is willing to admit that Don Quixote really is crazy but asserts that his madness and its symptoms are derived entirely from preexisting literature and are therefore inverisimilar and not to be taken seriously.[6] Opposing this is the view of a string of clinicians, beginning in 1848, who insist that Don Quixote is crazy and, furthermore, that his symptoms are described in perfect accord with the symptomatology of modern clinical psychiatry.[7]

The second important question concerning Don Quixote's madness springs from the division we have just observed. Assuming Don Quixote really is crazy, Cervantes could have based his description of symptoms only on such rudimentary sixteenth-century concepts of madness and sanity as were available to him, and it is therefore foolishly anachronistic to attempt to analyze Don Quixote through the prism of twentieth-century knowledge of mental processes and disorders. One of the most eloquent spokesmen for this point of view is the distinguished Cervantine scholar, Juan Bautista Avalle-Arce. "The use of the discoveries of Freud, his disciples and detractors, to penetrate the psychic secrets locked away in the minds of bygone epochs attuned to different issues and values is a useless and dangerous anachronism. The application of sixteenth-century Spanish psychological texts to the analysis of the mentalities of that period is, in contrast, valid and effective."[8]

Professor Avalle's observation seems rooted in the conviction that mental processes in the sixteenth century were different from mental processes in the twentieth century because the issues that concerned men were different then. This in turn suggests that what is psychically real is limited to what is visible and overt or, phrased another way, that in the sixteenth century, unconscious processes such as we know them today either did not exist or were concerned entirely with sixteenth-century issues such as religious orthodoxy and bullion from America. This view was stated much more directly by Cesare De Lollis many years ago when he affirmed simply that all psychological profundity in the description of characters is lacking in Cervantes. Américo Castro remarked by way of response that although Cervantes does not linger in reflexive self-analysis, "every character in his best works reveals an unprecedented inner complexity."[9] This insight is easily associated to Freud's thought and to the study of literature from a psychoanalytical point of view in general, although Castro himself is certainly no Freudian.

Two practicing analysts, both Freudian, offer a particularly succinct account of the relation between imaginative literature and the inner lives of real people.

> We treat the novels as if they were the life histories of real people. This goes back to Freud himself, as this is exactly what he did. In 1907 Freud remarked concerning the creative writer: "The description of the human mind is indeed the domain which is most his own. He has from time immemorial been the precursor of science, and so too of scientific psychology." Our own studies have more than convinced us of the deep similarity between what is discovered in the analysis of patients and what authors and storytellers have been describing "from time immemorial." A great novel does form a psychologically consistent pattern, and its author succeeds repeatedly in portraying events which are true derivatives of unconscious nuclear substrates in its fictional characters. We have also assumed that the reader's unconscious resonates harmonically, as it were, with the unconscious of the characters (or resists resonance), so that only those works which tell us something deeply human and important can earn the vicarious identification of generations upon generations of readers.[10]

These ideas are not entirely new. The literary criterion of verisimilitude, so central to Aristotle's poetic theory and so dear to the sixteenth-century Aristotelians, simply demands that literary characters look, talk, act, think, and experience life as real people do. This in turn necessitates a psychic (that is, an unconscious) dimension, the "interior man" posited by Augustine. This basic identification of real people and literary characters has been part of the grand tradition of occidental thought since Aristotle, and of occidental literature since Sophocles. Ernst Kris insists on this fact in terms that have a special relevance for the study of *Don Quixote*.

> The very fact that certain themes of human experience and conflict are recurrent wherever men live or where, at least, certain cultural conditions prevail (best known from the tradition of Mediterranean civilizations)—the fact that from Sophocles to

Proust the struggle against incestuous impulses, dependency, guilt and aggression has remained a topic of Western literature—seems, after almost half a century, as well established as any other thesis in the social sciences.[11]

It is interesting to note that Kris's affirmation is much truer with respect to humanistic studies in general than with specific reference to Hispanic and especially Cervantine studies, although Maurice Molho has already made valuable contributions along these lines, and a controversial new book by Louis Combet may signal the beginning of a new awareness among Cervantine scholars of the importance of the recurring themes enumerated by Kris.[12] I am a Hispanist by profession, and so my psychoanalytical reading of Cervantes's text will be relieved from time to time by such historical, contextual, and linguistic insights as my training affords, in the hope that the general reader's experience of the novel will be incidentally enriched. The psychoanalytical bases of this study are the product, first, of lengthy clinical experience that led to the acquisition and systematization of theory. My orientation is emphatically not theoretical. I have approached the analysis of Don Quixote in the spirit of the clinical practitioner whose work is grounded in Freud, but Freud modified by the work of other investigators and tested in the crucible of clinical experience. For this reason I quote Erik Erikson and even C. G. Jung, among others, on the general phenomenon of the stages of human growth, and Emil Gutheil rather than Freud on the analysis of dreams. In short, instead of relying on a "French Freud" or a "Yale Freud," I have attempted to base my study on the reality of contemporary psychoanalysis as practiced in this country.

For all that, I do not mean to lose sight of the fact that the object of this study is a character in a novel, whose only objective, verifiable existence is circumscribed by the covers of a book. What we study is a text. The text poses certain questions. I have been intrigued in particular by those that refer to the apparent lack of motivation for Don Quixote's behavior. It has already been discovered, for example, that he does not go mad because he reads too many romances of chivalry, but that his madness is motivated by a need to escape from the monotony of his humdrum existence. But what is it about this existence that produces a sudden, massive crisis capable of precipitating a flight into psychosis? How could a sensitive man like Don Quixote fall in love with a loud, coarse, vulgar girl like Aldonza Lorenzo? Why does he mention Aldonza by name to Sancho in Part I, chapter 25, thus endangering the myth of Dulcinea by revealing its prosaic underpinnings? What happens to Aldonza between Parts I and II, and why is she not a character in Part II? What explains Don Quixote's repeated erotic fantasies in paradoxical coexistence with a pathological terror of normal sexual relations? How is it possible for him to recover his sanity so quickly and so thoroughly at the end of this third sally? Why does the recuperation of sanity coincide with a decision to abandon life altogether?

If there are no convincing explanations for these anomalies, if Don Quixote's actions are found to be unmotivated, then his character lacks verisimilitude, and the generations of readers and critics who have identified this work as the first modern novel have all been wrong. The questions of behavior and motivation raised in the text are psychological questions and can only be answered with the aid of what modern science has taught us about the workings of the human mind.

This study, I repeat, is not meant to be definitive. How could any study of any work of genius be anything but partial and incomplete? I have attempted simply to take Don Quixote seriously as a verisimilar fictional character—a fifty-year-old hidalgo, bachelor, voracious reader, the only man in a household dominated by women, living in La Mancha toward the end of the sixteenth century—and to proceed in consequence.

I want first to establish a general context within which the mental life of a sixteenth-century literary character may be studied, by reviewing the theories of personality and the psychi-

7

atric texts that Cervantes had at his disposal. These are both
varied and interesting, as we shall see. We turn next to the insights
of modern clinical psychiatry and observe the precision with
which Don Quixote's malady has been diagnosed by competent
physicians in the nineteenth and twentieth centuries. It is clear
that Cervantes was abreast of the theories of his contemporaries,
and that he anticipated with uncanny accuracy many of the discoveries of modern clinical psychiatry.

Putting the right label on our hero's madness, or establishing that Cervantes had read certain sixteenth-century physicians,
is interesting and even important, but it does not fully establish
the scientific context in which Don Quixote's character may be
studied. We must have recourse to the insights of psychoanalysis
for the general phenomena or behavior and motivation, and in
particular we need to acquire some knowledge of the psychodynamic processes operative in fifty-year-old men. The phenomenon of "mid-life crisis" has lately been a fashionable subject of
both popular and academic discourse, and the anecdotes related
at the beginning of this introduction can be placed in the context
of several recent empirical longitudinal studies of men in mid-life
by sociologists, psychologists, and psychoanalysts.

Having established the extraliterary standards by means of
which the sixteenth-century fictional representation of a middle-
aged psychotic may be studied and judged, we can proceed to the
analysis of our text. This is divided into two phases. The first
describes Don Quixote's situation and offers what I believe is the
only plausible, verisimilar explanation for his sudden and dramatic flight into psychosis. The second phase traces his relations
with the women he meets throughout Parts I and II of the novel
and attempts to answer the questions I posed above, culminating
in a consideration of Don Quixote's sudden recuperation of sanity and simultaneous decision to abandon life. This phase of the
analysis springs from Barchilon and Kovel's statement that "the
aesthetic experience emerges from the working through of the

themes, not necessarily from the themes themselves."[13] A brief concluding statement contains some observations on Don Quixote's character from the point of view of his success or failure as a human being and some further literary remarks on the structure of the novel and its generic characteristics.

I do not expect this book to be received with enthusiasm by most of my fellow Hispanists. I ask only that it be received with an open mind and taken as seriously as I have attempted to take Cervantes and Don Quixote.

1
PSYCHIATRY
AND DON QUIXOTE

Let us begin on the familiar terrain of English literary history and observe the evolution of twentieth-century scholarly interest in Elizabethan theories of personality and psychology as keys to understanding character and motivation in Elizabethan literature. Two influential studies, an article by Edward Dowden in *Atlantic Monthly* (1907) and a book by P. Ansell Robin (1911), introduced modern readers to a number of sixteenth-century treatises on the subject of human personality which were widely read in Shakespeare's England. These include Continental works in translation—among them Juan Huarte de San Juan's *Examination of Men's Wits*, from Spain—and such English studies as Thomas Wright's *The Passions of the Mind*, Timothy Bright's *On Melancholy*, and the one best known today, Robert Burton's *Anatomy of Melancholy*.

The suggestion that Elizabethan dramatists were familiar with these treatises and based their conception of literary character upon what was known, or believed to be known, about real character led to a series of studies, the most notable of which is Lilly Bess Campbell's classic *Shakespeare's Tragic Heroes: Slaves of Passion* (1930). Since then, and especially with the rise of what we might call postformalist contextual criticism, it has come to be natural and normal to consider contemporary theories of character as part of the cultural-social-intellectual and economic context in which a literary work is conceived by its author and apprehended by its public. Francis Johnson observes that "in a loose, wholly unclinical fashion every Elizabethan dramatist invoked the contemporary science and terminology of psychology in depicting characters on the stage," and that "the audience of 1600 had a general knowledge of the psychological framework inherited from Antiquity, just as we in 1950 have a vague acquaintance with the general doctrines of modern psychiatry and psychoanalysis which we bring with us to a performance of *Mourning Becomes Electra* or *The Cocktail Party*."[1]

All this is eminently reasonable, and analogous observations have been made with respect to Spanish literary history. Franz Alexander and Sheldon Selesnick, for example, remark that Cervantes's grasp of the psychology of mental illness as revealed in *Don Quixote* is even more striking than Shakespeare's. Besides the psychotic fantasies, Cervantes also demonstrates and exploits in artistic terms the principle that the mentality of the psychotic includes the essential qualities of normal thinking.[2] That is, Cervantes is concerned simultaneously with normal mental processes and with mental disorders. His interest is rooted in an extraordinarily rich and fertile subsoil, as his countrymen for some two hundred years prior to *Don Quixote* had been dealing both theoretically and practically with the phenomenon of personality and with the insane and their care. This tradition has won for Spain the sobriquet "cradle of psychiatry."[3]

It is customary to consider Ospitalis Ignoscencium, established at Valencia in 1409, as the first European facility devoted entirely to the care of mental patients. Recently, however, it has been argued that the Hospital of Santa Cruz in Barcelona (1401) was the first facility in which the mentally ill were actually cared for and therapy practiced by trained personnel, and that the Valencia operation, while established specifically for vagrant and antisocial mental deviates, was in fact a kind of glorified soup kitchen, where care was limited to confinement and physical nourishment.[4] Whatever the relative merits of patient care at these two facilities may have been, the fact remains that in the first years of the fifteenth century Spain, and specifically the Crown of Aragón, took the lead in Europe in the estabishment of centers for the mentally ill. The mental hospital in Zaragoza was founded in 1425, that of Palma de Mallorca in 1456. Within the domain of the Crown of Castile, the oldest facility was the "Hospital de Inocentes" established at Sevilla in 1436. This is probably the madhouse Cervantes refers to in the barber's story of the patient who believed he was Neptune (*Don Quixote* II, 1).[5] (The Sevilla institution was followed by those at Toledo [the "Casa del Nuncio" in 1483] and Valladolid [in 1489].) By the beginning of the sixteenth century, a full hundred years before *Don Quixote*, Spain possessed a widespread network of facilities devoted to the care of the insane, and it is reasonable to suppose that Cervantes was personally acquainted with at least one institution.

More to the point for our purposes, the practical care of mental patients during the sixteenth century was accompanied by a series of more or less theoretical treatises on human personality and on the causes and suggested cures for personality disorders. Cervantes, as we know, was an avid reader. His father was himself a surgeon and may have possessed a library that included some of these works. There is every reason to suppose, before we take up his fiction at all, that Cervantes had access to and was familiar with this body of material. When we consider that his own work is peppered with mentally disturbed characters, of whom Don Quixote is merely the most fully developed and best known, it becomes both arrogant and foolish to assume that Cervantes was not abreast of current thinking in the field. With this in mind, it might be profitable to pass some of these treatises in review and offer some comments on their possible relation to or influence upon Cervantes in general and Don Quixote in particular.

One of the more original and prescient of these, the *Nueva filosofía de la naturaleza del hombre* [New philosophy of the nature of man] (1587), attributed to Oliva Sabuco de Nantes Barrera, is actually the work of her father, the Bachiller Miguel Sabuco. He considers the human neurological system to have the form of an inverted tree, with the roots in the brain, the trunk in the spinal column, and the foliage in the other members, especially the stomach. Man possesses two "harmonies," whose relationship controls his health. The first resides in the brain and the second in the stomach. When the cerebral harmony is altered in some way, cerebral moisture is lost and illness results. This alteration may arise from two causes: internal factors, which Sabuco calls the *affects*, and external causes such as plague, the evil eye, poison, changes in habitat, diet, and the like. Sabuco considers the affects more important than all other causes in the psychogenesis of disease. "The harm caused to the secondary harmony of the stomach," he writes, "is nothing compared to that caused by anger, grief and other affects in the primary harmony of the brain." The therapeutic technique he proposes consists first in reestablishing the overall harmony between body and soul, stomach and brain, and to this end he advises "words and acts which in adults engender happiness and hope. Then the harmony of the stomach should be seen to, with comforting foods and medications to soothe it."[6]

One has the impression, upon reading Sabuco, of a disquieting modernity. He understands that emotional states—grief, anger, frustration, even an excess of joy—can have disastrous physical effects, to the point of causing death. His therapeutic formula consists of four sequential phases. First, learn to recognize when you are becoming angry or distraught (or when your friend is becoming so). Second, talk yourself out of it (or, help your friend by talking him out of it). Sabuco insists again and again on the efficacy of the spoken word as medicine for these emotional disorders. Third, support the spoken word with pleasant and harmonious surroundings—music, country rest with the movement of trees and the splashing of fountains. Fourth, calm the stomach with bland foods and suitable medication. In modern terminology we might describe his approach as *holistic*, the insistence on the interdependence of psyche and soma, emphasizing positive thinking and supportive psychotherapy in combination with surroundings, diet, and medication conducive to the reduction of tension. This is in fact the normal routine in most mental hospitals today.

Another treatise, also disturbing in its ready assimilation to at least one aspect of the most current thinking, is that of Jerónimo de Mondragón, *Censura de la locura humana, y excelencias della* [Censure and excellencies of madness] (1598).[7] A translation of this work's extensive subtitle will suffice to indicate its orientation: "In whose first part is demonstrated that those who are considered by the world to be sane are mad, and therefore deserve no praise. In the second part it is demonstrated how those commonly held to be mad are worthy of great praise. With a great variety of pleasant and curious histories, and other things no less useful than delightful." Mondragón's tongue-in-cheek praise of folly recalls, besides Erasmus, the relationship between the presumably sane Duke and Duchess and the certifiably mad Don Quixote as delineated by their resident chaplain (II, 32). The equation of madness and sanity with public opinion anticipates an important aspect of the thought of R. D. Laing, for whom madness is defined as whatever society decrees it to be, sanity being the reverse. This brings us back to the events of I, 45, where a barber's basin is transformed into Mambrino's helmet by the imposition of the will of the majority of those present.

The works of Sabuco and Mondragón, suggestive though they be, are not really representative of the mainstream of sixteenth-century medical thought. Sixteenth-century medicine is still basically medieval humoral medicine, with Galen and Avicenna the principal authorities, and mental disorders are overwhelmingly considered to be caused by some humoral imbalance or alteration. Before proceeding, we might pause to review the principal tenets of humoral theory as it was current in the late sixteenth century. Briefly, the human body is composed of four humors: yellow bile, blood, black bile, and phlegm. Each person's physical characteristics and personality are controlled by the particular mixture of the four humors within him. The predominance of one over the others results in personality types whose names and characteristics are still familiar to us: the choleric, the sanguine, the melancholic, and the phlegmatic. Now, a complex system of correspondences had been established between the four bodily humors, the four elements of the earth, and the characteristics of the latter (hot, cold, dry, moist). These, in turn, are all related to the body organs that secrete the four humors. Thus, for example, Don Quixote's choleric temperament is determined by his liver, which produces yellow bile (choler) associated with the element air, whose primary characteristic is its dryness. Indeed, dryness is an essential part of our hero's psychophysical constitution, as we shall see.[8]

An important treatise that Cervantes might well have known is that of Andrés Velázquez, *Libro de la melancolía* (1585). The term *melancholy* appears here in its generally accepted sixteenth-century sense: a disturbance or alienation of the faculties of understanding or reason, without fever. Velázquez distinguishes two varieties of melancholy, which are in fact differences of degree and not of kind: melancholy proper, and mania. Within the category of melancholy proper, fear and sadness are by no means the only possible manifestations. In fact the symptoms are extremely variable. "One patient may believe he is a rooster, flap his arms as though they were wings, and attempt to crow. Another may think he is a brick, and refuse water because he is afraid of melting."[9]

16

A particularly interesting humoral treatise, especially pertinent for the study of Cervantes, is that of Alfonso Ponce de Santa
Cruz, *Diagnotio et cura affectum melancholicorum* (1622). It is interesting as an example of humoral theory in general, and for one
astounding case history in particular. Dr. Ponce was the personal
physician of Philip II and was thus a contemporary of Cervantes;
his son Antonio published the treatise on melancholy post-
humously. The author affirms that the "melancholy humor" is
the product of black bile, which attacks the brain in its several
faculties. When this humor affects the memory, for example, it
produces fear, forgetfulness, and sadness. He also offers some
case histories, among which the following merits special comment. A patient believed he had been transformed into a glass
vase and consequently avoided contact with people for fear of
being broken. He was covered with straw and locked inside a
room. A fire was set, whereupon the patient began to bang on the
door and scream to be let out. Upon his release from the burning
room, he was asked how it was that he had not broken himself
while pounding on the door, to which he replied that he was no
longer made of glass but was simply an unfortunate man.[10] The
parallels with Cervantes's *El Licenciado Vidriera* are so striking as to
suggest something beyond coincidence. Cervantes surely must
have known this patient or have heard of him from Dr. Ponce or
another source. The etiology and the cure, of course, are quite
different. In Cervantes's story the melancholy delusion is induced by poison (as Sabuco suggests), and the cure is effected not
by endangering the patient's life in a fire but by lengthy and
persistent supportive psychotherapy, also following the model
suggested by Sabuco.

By far the most important humoral theorist, for the modernity of his thought as well as for his obvious affinities with Cervantes, is Dr. Juan Huarte de San Juan. He wrote a treatise of
great influence, both in Spain and elsewhere in Europe, entitled
Examen de ingenios para las ciencias [Examination of mental facul-

ties for the sciences]. It was published at Baeza in 1575 and reprinted five times before the Inquisition placed it on the *Index* in 1583. The *Expurgatorio* of 1584 specified forty-four passages to be eliminated. Huarte prepared the required expurgated edition but decided not to publish it, and it was not until 1594, when his son authorized publication, that his work became available in the form in which we have known it until recently. It is possible that Cervantes met Huarte's son in Baeza in 1591 through Don Diego de Benavides and Don Juan Vilalta, two old prison companions from Algiers he happened to run into there.[11]

Huarte's original contributions are two. First, he develops the existing relationships between the four humors and the four characteristics (hot and cold, wet and dry); in fact, he is concerned more with the latter than with the former. A perfect equilibrium, he asserts, produces an individual whose principal characteristics are dullness and unsuitability for any occupation involving the use of the mental faculties. This is what he defines as the first level of *ingenio*: passive receptivity, limited to absorbing what is transmitted through the senses and by teachers. Huarte's next level, that of normal human intelligence, is produced by some imbalance among the humors and the characteristics. Most people fall into this group, as medieval tradition suggests. Normal human intelligence as defined by Huarte is capable of acquiring knowledge through its own resources, utilizing the data provided by sense perceptions and formal instruction, but in addition is able to develop cognitive systems, concepts, and principles on independent grounds. Furthermore, normal human intelligence is capable of generating new thoughts and of finding appropriate expression for them. Finally, Huarte posits a third level of intelligence which he calls *ingenio superior* and which is frequently accompanied by dementia. This level occurs only rarely and, in humoral terms, is the result of a massive, radical imbalance among humors and characteristics. It is capable, without particular study or apparent effort, to "speak such subtle and surprising things, yet true, that were never before seen, heard or writ, or even so much as thought of."[12]

Huarte's thought here coincides in great part with the prevailing medical theory of his time, expressed in the subtitle of Andrés Velázquez's 1585 treatise on melancholy: "In which is discussed the nature of this disease called melancholy, and its causes and symptoms, and if the rustic can speak Latin or philosophize while in a frenetic or manic state, without having first studied these subjects." What makes Huarte particularly interesting for us moderns is not so much the humoral basis of his thought, which he shares with virtually every physician of his time, but his second—and most original—contribution: his definition of the three levels of mental faculties in terms of the ability to generate new ideas and concepts. That is, for Huarte, intelligence (ingenio) is a generative faculty, and indeed he derives the Spanish *ingenio* from Latin *ingenerare* 'to engender.' An important corollary of this is his association of the superior ingenio with madness, thus inverting the usual value judgments brought to bear on the individual so constituted or affected. What for Andrés Velázquez exists negatively, as a curiosity—the rustic speaking Latin—is for Huarte a positive manifestation of intellectual superiority.

The relationship between Huarte's application of humoral theory—his concept of the superior intelligence (ingenio) touched with madness—and Cervantes's character (*el ingenioso hidalgo*) is obviously a suggestive one, and since the turn of this century a body of scholarship has grown up which seeks to define and clarify it. In 1905 Rafael Salillas published a book entitled *Un gran inspirador de Cervantes: el Dr. Juan Huarte y su "Examen de ingenios"* (Madrid: Victoriano Suárez), in which he relates pertinent passages in Cervantes's first work (the pastoral *La Galatea* of 1585), the exemplary novel *El Licenciado Vidriera* (1613), and the posthumous *Trabajos de Persiles y Sigismunda* (1617), as well as the *Quixote*, to different aspects of Huarte's doctrine. For Salillas, *ingenioso* comes to be a synonym of *loco* (insane), and the description of Don Quixote's character is developed accordingly. Huarte's own thought was further studied by Mavricio de Iriarte, who pointed out its importance as a theory of personality in 1948 and who elaborates the relation between Huarte's *ingenio* and Cervantes's *ingenioso hidalgo*.[13]

In 1954, Vicente Peset offered a summary of Huarte's doctrine on the combination of hot and dry. Although Dr. Peset does not apply these characteristics directly to the study of Don Quixote, they are worth noting for their power both to elucidate and to confuse our analysis of the mad knight's character. In Huarte, heat is associated with imagination. Since the words spoken in delirium are a product of the individual's imagination rather than of memory or understanding, and "since frenzy, mania and melancholia are hot passions of the brain, there is a strong argument in favor of the imaginative faculty consisting in heat." Dryness, however, is associated with understanding, as Huarte states: "Old men possess great understanding because they are dry, and for the same reason, because they lack moisture, their memories fail them." Huarte's *mapa mentis*, it appears, is not without some shoals.

Passing to Huarte's third (superior) level of intelligence, Peset offers the following table of the physical and personality traits which result from the combination of hot and dry.

1. *Intelligence and ability*: sharpness of imagination.
2. *Habits and personality*: courageous, arrogant, generous, shameless, witty.
3. *Voice*: heavy and somewhat coarse.
4. *Flesh*: lean, hard, tough, made of sinews, extremely broad veins.

5. *Color*: dark, tanned, dark greenish, ashen.
6. *Body hair*: a great deal, black and thick, especially from the thighs to the navel.[14]

It will be observed that by no means do all these characteristics correlate with Don Quixote (no one was ever less shameless, for example) and that some of them—color, for instance—are internally inconsistent. Others, however, offer remarkable similarities with the Cervantes character.

The best-known rapprochement of Huarte and Don Quixote is that proposed by the American Hispanist Otis H. Green in a now-classic article published in 1958.[15] Green applies Huarte's doctrine systematically to Don Quixote, from the etiology of his madness to his cure and death. At the beginning, the anonymous hidalgo is naturally choleric, the result of a predominance of yellow bile in combination with heat and dryness. This temperament is aggravated beyond the point of sanity by the drying out caused by lack of sleep, for instead of sleeping our man stays up reading romances of chivalry. The narrator reports, in fact, that "from so little sleeping and so much reading, his brain dried up and he went completely out of his mind."[16] At the end of each sally Don Quixote sleeps, which partially restores his humoral balance by introducing moisture, although not in sufficient amount to cure him until the end of the third sally. In fact, on the eve of that sally his friends visit him and find him particularly dried out. What allows the cure to finally occur is that beginning in II, 58 Don Quixote begins to experience attacks of melancholy, which in terms of humoral medicine is the opposite of choler, being cold and dry to choler's hot and dry. Melancholy restores judgment, at the expense of imagination. The cold of melancholy, in combination with the moisture induced by sleep, finally effects the cure. It brings Don Quixote's death as well, for melancholy has the unfortunate side effect of constricting the heart.

21

Green's study has the merit of suggesting in the strongest possible terms the direct relation between Huarte's medical doctrine and its artistic exploitation by Cervantes, which in turn places Cervantes near the forefront of the most advanced versions of sixteenth-century personality theory based on traditional humoral medicine.

More recently, Carlos P. Otero has returned to the general relation between Huarte and Cervantes and their contemporary, the grammarian Fernando Sánchez de las Brozas ("El Brocense"), locating all of them within what we might call the "rationalist out-group" of sixteenth-century Spanish intelligentsia, whose minoritarian ideology brought them into conflict with the official policy in matters scientific and religious.[17] In view of Huarte's association of superior intelligence with dementia, and considering what we know now about Cervantes and El Brocense and their society thanks to Américo Castro's masterful analyses, Otero's comments suggest an interesting hypothesis—namely, that in the repressive, conformist atmosphere of late sixteenth-century Spain, a person of superior intelligence had to be a little bit crazy merely in order to exist. We shall return to this line of thought when we consider Don Quixote's household in chapter 3.

I do not think there can be any doubt that Cervantes was acquainted with Huarte's work and that he consciously incorporated various of Huarte's ideas into the *Quixote*. The *ingenio-ingenerare* relation, for example, giving rise to the concept that one can generate oneself, with its obvious "precocious existentialist" appeal, is of course fundamental. When Cervantes remarks in his prologue to Part I that Don Quixote is "dried up, shriveled and eccentric, . . . and filled with various thoughts that never occurred to anyone else" (p. 11), he is obviously paraphrasing Huarte's own description of the third or superior level of intelligence: "to speak such subtle and surprising things . . . that were never before seen, heard or writ, or even thought of." When Don Quixote shows his hand to Maritornes and the innkeeper's

22

daughter in I, 43, calling attention to "the contexture of the sinews, the network of the muscles, the breadth and spaciousness of the veins" (p. 393), he seems to be paraphrasing Huarte's summary of the flesh of the hot-dry type: "hard, tough, made of sinews, extremely broad veins." When the narrator tells us that Don Quixote lost sleep, the restorer of moisture, that his brain dried out, and that his personality altered as a result, he is already dealing with Huarte's ideas, in their more traditional form, as studied by Green. Similarly, the genesis of the exemplary novel *El coloquio de los perros* [The dogs' colloquy] in its author's delirium, which is induced by a similar drying-out process—he is taking the sweats as treatment for venereal disease—seems also to be based on Huarte's theory of mechanical changes in the humors and their psychic effects. When Cervantes in the prologue to *Ocho comedias y ocho entremeses* remarks offhandedly that the dramatist Lope de Rueda is buried in the cathedral of Córdoba, next to the famous madman Luis López, he is referring to a case history related by Huarte in the *Examen de ingenios*. López had lost his reason, was attacked by a sudden fever, and suddenly rose to Huarte's third or superior level of intelligence.

Although invoking Huarte allows us to understand the contemporary scientific theoretical basis for a number of concrete behavioral manifestations, *Don Quixote* is clearly much more than a fictionalized version of the *Examen de ingenios*. The most glaring discrepancy between the two lies in Cervantes's conception of character as based on acts of will, on throwing oneself into situations and entering into a dialectical relationship with one's circumstance—in short, all the features we consider "novelistic"— and Huarte's, which is based on preformed characteristics that determine aptitudes and even reactions to stimuli. Iriarte called attention to this in 1948 when he remarked that "it seems that Huarte sees only temperamentally determined reactions in an agent's actions."[18] With respect to the passage of time, Cervantes shows Don Quixote changing—and becoming more himself—

23

because of his accumulated experience, while Huarte considers temperamental changes across time to be the result of mechanical alterations in the relationship of wet and dry and hot and cold. Thus, for example, youths have retentive memories because their brains are still nice and moist, while old men have superior intellect, but cannot remember things, because their brains have dried out over the years. Curiously enough, although Cervantes obviously rejects these mechanistic concepts at the level of consciousness, the idea of capabilities and behavior appropriate to certain ages is obviously of fundamental importance to him. Don Quixote does not act like a man of twenty-five or thirty, but like one of fifty. These considerations will form the basis of chapter 2. For the present it is sufficient to conclude that Cervantes must have been acquainted with Huarte and that he consciously exploited parts of his doctrine. At the same time, he appears to have consciously rejected other parts.

Provocative as he is, Huarte de San Juan is not the total of sixteenth-century psychiatry. As we have seen, he is a contemporary of, and shares a common orientation with, Andrés Velázquez and Alfonso Ponce de Santa Cruz, both of whom wrote influential treatises on melancholy. It is to this subject that I must now return, and to a specific manifestation known by the name conferred upon it by the French physician Jacques Ferrand in his *Traité de l'essence et guerison de l'amour, ou de la melancholie erotique* (1610). I refer to the phenomenon of erotomania, the symptoms associated with the courtly love syndrome—loss of appetite, insensitivity to anything that is not the beloved, alienation, and the like. The "lover's malady," an idea already discussed by Plato, the symptoms of which had been current in romance literature since the troubadours, was put on a scientific footing by Ferrand's treatise.

As Green remarks, melancholy is usually associated with the humor blood and with cold-dry characteristics, and it should therefore be opposed to Don Quixote's hot and dry choleric temperament. Nevertheless, Ferrand considers that hot and dry humors, as well as blood, may incline one to love, and he specifically states that choleric persons are amorous. Now in Ferrand's theory, if love remains unsatisfied, melancholy humors and attendant symptoms can develop. Love, if thwarted, cools and dries the body in various ways. It does so first through the continual mental activity it provokes. By thus busying the mind with thoughts of love, moisture is consumed, drying out results, and a humoral imbalance is produced. The hot passions which assail the lover— desire, hope, joy, anger—may also bring on melancholy by burning the humors. In addition, Ferrand mentions unevacuated seed as a possible cause of erotomania.[19] As to the symptomatology, we should remember that for Cervantes and his contemporaries melancholy was not simply a form of depression, as we think of it today, but referred to any disturbance or alienation not accompanied by fever. Symptoms could either be depressive or manic, as Dr. Velázquez observed in 1585. An alternation of the two sets of symptoms was perfectly possible. Indeed, this is the case of Cardenio in I, 23 and Basilio in II, 20.

It is customary to consider Don Quixote's brush with erotomania, the willful imitation of Amadís *cum* Orlando suggested by his recent encounter with Cardenio, as a brilliant parodic tour de force on Cervantes's part, wherein a genuine madman deliberately becomes a counterfeit madman without abandoning his own madness.[20] His behavior thus offers a contrast to both Cardenio—a genuine erotomaniac—and Basilio—a trickster who feigns erotomania in order to win the girl he loves. This is true, of course, but we should remember that Don Quixote, like all knights-errant, is a man in love. Being in love, as Vivaldo points out in I, 13, is an essential constituent feature of the profession of knight-errantry. Don Quixote's love for Dulcinea comes by II, 59 to define his existence as Don Quixote. The readers of the apocryphal second part of his adventures by Alonso Fernández de Avellaneda inform him that in that spurious work Don Quixote is no longer in love with Dulcinea. Our hero seizes the opportunity to demonstrate who he is by invoking his undying love. Don Quixote is nothing if not a lover. It is reasonable, then, to suppose that in spite of the contrasts between himself and Cardenio and Basilio, the combination of unrequited love and mental disorder should function in a serious, nonparodic way in Don Quixote's character. I shall investigate this important subject in chapter 3.

Until now we have been concerned with sixteenth-century theories of mental disorders to which Cervantes might have had access, his possible familiarity with them and artistic exploitation of them. We have observed that the mind and its disorders consti- tuted an important area of theoretical investigation and clinical practice in Cervantes's society. Besides the network of mental hospitals begun in 1401, with which Cervantes was at least par- tially familiar, a considerable body of scholarly writing on the subject had grown up by his time. Cervantes's works certainly demonstrate his interest in the phenomenon of mental disorders. They attest as well to his general familiarity with the doctrines then current: the notions of humoral imbalance, general symp- tomatology (both manic and depressive) of the disorder known as melancholy, and the like. Cervantes's works also reveal precise and particular knowledge of specific texts—for example, the patient made of glass reported by Dr. Ponce de Santa Cruz, or the effects of drying out studied by Huarte. I might summarize by saying that Cervantes was certainly abreast of current theory and practice, he may actually have been ahead of it, and he was clearly not enslaved to any one particular medical authority. Cervantes had certainly read and assimilated Huarte, for example, but Huarte (or Sabuco, or Velázquez, or Ponce) did not invent Don Quixote.

Nor did all of them together. Cervantes's intuitions go far beyond contemporary medical theory, and his description of symptoms has been shown to anticipate perfectly the discoveries and classification of mental disorders made by clinical psychiatry beginning in the nineteenth century. This remarkable aspect of Cervantes's creativity has been the subject of a series of studies by practicing clinicians, the majority Spanish, beginning with Antonio Hernández Morejón, *La historia clínica de Don Quijote* (1848), and continuing practically to the present. The most recent such work is that of the Spanish psychiatrist Antonio Vallejo Nágera, who resumes the tradition of modern clinical discussions of mental disorders in Don Quixote and other Cervantine characters.[21]

The nineteenth-century physicians—Hernández Morejón and Emilio Pi y Molist—consider Don Quixote a case of monomania, perfectly in accord with the concepts of mental illness then current. In 1905, doubtless inspired by the centenary of the publication of *Don Quixote*, a new, double tradition was initiated. I have already mentioned the work of Rafael Salillas, which inaugurated the Cervantes-Huarte studies. Another line of studies was begun by Ricardo Royo Villanova, a professor of medical pathology, who applied the most recent psychiatric doctrines to the symptoms exhibited by Don Quixote and concluded that his illness should be diagnosed as a "chronic paranoia or partial systematic delirium of the expansive type, the megalomaniacal form and the philanthropic variety." This is an important point of departure, for it incorporates the description of paranoia as defined by Kraepelin, which is still current in clinical psychiatry. Most succeeding studies of Don Quixote's disease consider it from this perspective. They tend to assume a somatic basis for the disease and take special care for the accurate and precise description of symptoms as the basis for an accurate diagnosis. The doctoral thesis of Lucien Libert, *La folie de Don Quichotte* (1909), and the studies of Dr. J. Goyanes, *Tipología del Quijote* (1932) and *De la biotypologie de Don Quichotte et de Sancho Panza* (1934), are representative.

By all odds the most important manifestations of this tendency are those of the Peruvian psychiatrist Carlos Gutiérrez

Noriega in the 1940s and the Spaniard Vallejo Nágera, whose first "Cervantine pathography" appeared in 1950.[22] Both these authors are practicing psychiatrists—that is, physicians who are trained in the diagnosis and treatment of certain mental illnesses (basically those defined by Kraepelin: paranoia, manic-depressive psychosis, schizophrenia) and whose effort is concentrated on isolating the symptoms and describing them with the greatest possible accuracy, for the treatment depends on the diagnosis. When a clinical psychiatrist approaches a literary text, he focuses exclusively on instances of clearly pathological behavior, which he notes and then attempts to relate to a recognizable syndrome associated with a real mental disease. Since a cure is obviously impossible, literary criticism as practiced by the clinicians becomes exclusively a matter of diagnosis, or put inelegantly, making sure that the correct label is applied to the symptoms exhibited by a particular character.[23] Both Gutiérrez Noriega and Vallejo Nágera, as well as others, are convinced that in Don Quixote Cervantes has created in fiction a perfect representation of paranoia as defined by Kraepelin. Vallejo Nágera reports, in fact, that he used to give a class to medical students in which he offered Don Quixote as a model of paranoia, Tomás Rodaja as a model of deliriant schizophrenia, and Felipe Carrizales as a model of psychopathic jealousy, remarking that Cervantes achieved, "without consciously attempting to, the description of prototypes of mental illnesses which can serve as examples for psychiatric nosography, anticipating their classification and study by centuries."[24]

Both Pi y Molist in the nineteenth century and Vallejo Nágera in the twentieth coincide in the conclusion that Cervantes was in fact considerably in advance of current medical theory in his description of madmen. Obviously, he could not have invented his clinically accurate characters out of nothing, nor did he receive advanced training at some as yet undiscovered secret institute. His characters are rather the result of an interest in people and years spent observing them in jails and mental hospitals, taverns and inns, *plazas* and *paseos*. To this I would only add that Cervantes's interest in people, like that of all great writers, was so consuming as to constitute an obsession, and that he was obsessed not only by people but by the way they interact with each other and with their circumstances—in a word, by the phenomenon of life as a process.

Before proceeding to a couple of final observations, I should pause to remark that the "clinical psychiatry" approach to our novel is severely limited. It has the merit of demonstrating a great author's magnificent intuitions, but because it is static and not dynamic (in this sense akin to a definition of literary genre on the basis of accumulated formal characteristics), it cannot illuminate the structure of the work of art, nor can it elucidate for us the process of life unfolding, which of course is the business of the novel as a genre. As readers and literary critics, we are only marginally interested in having the name of Don Quixote's disorder; we are preoccupied instead with the web of relationships established between this particular madman and the particular objects and people with whom he comes in contact, how these relationships affect each other, how the world affects Don Quixote, and how he affects the world—and ourselves. We are much more concerned, in short, with the total phenomenon of verisimilitude—artistic re-creation of plausible reality, as defined by Aristotle—than we are with the particular detail of it encompassed in the clinical name for the hero's malady. Martine Bigeard, in her excellent study of madmen in Spanish literature of the Golden Age, after summarizing the contributions of Hernández Morejón, Kirschner, Vallejo Nágera, and Gutiérrez Noriega, concludes: "En assimilant le *Quichotte* à une fiche clinique et Cervantès à un génial psychiâtre, les études réduisent un chef-d'oeuvre aux dimensions d'un roman d'anticipation médicale et rebaissent son auteur au niveau d'un Jules Verne de la pathologie mentale."[25]

The foregoing begins to suggest how clinical psychiatry as a tool of literary criticism differs from psychoanalysis. Clinical psychiatry is static, concerned with the accumulation of examples of pathological behavior, which are in turn translated into symptoms, a syndrome, the name of a disease. This is an operation performed by the clinician on someone else; that is, the literary character exists for the clinician not as an artistically created complex human being but as an object without consciousness, a "fiche clinique" in Bigeard's graphic phrase. By contrast, psychoanalysis, like the novel, is concerned with process, with questions of motivation and behavior, cause and effect. These are literary questions, the bases for any discussion of plot and character. Psychoanalytical literary criticism treats literary characters as though they were real people; and people, as Ortega and Sartre (among others) have taught us, are distinguished by the possession of a history—an evolution through time—as opposed to an essence, and a consciousness of the fact of their existence in and through time. We are also characterized by complex mental processes that exist below the level of consciousness (as Freud, among others, has taught us) and that frequently determine our behavior. In psychoanalysis, the analysand comes gradually to perceive, consciously, the unconscious motivation for his sometimes bizarre and almost always self-destructive behavior. Through psychoanalytical literary criticism, the reader comes gradually to perceive the unconscious motivation for the character's behavior, and the rich, human complexity of the character's character stands revealed. As readers, we are then free to marvel at a great author's magnificent intuitions and, more importantly, to assimilate the character's humanity to our own, to participate most fully in that enhanced vicarious experience of life that great literature offers us.

Having gone out of my way to point out the limitations of the "clinical psychiatry" approach to *Don Quixote*, I want to close this chapter by calling attention to an isolated observation by

Carlos Gutiérrez Noriega which, had it been followed up by other investigators, or had he lived to follow it up himself, might have been the basis for a real elucidation of Don Quixote's character from a psychodynamic point of view.

> Cervantes related the transformation of personality to the human ages of greatest vital tension, adolescence and climacteric, when real psychological mutations, sometimes of pathological dimensions, frequently occur. Only recently have psychiatric and psychological studies recognized that these critical times of life are replete with dangerous proclivities, and that the personality changes which occur on these occasions can develop in the direction of psychosis.

As examples of personality transformation in the climacteric he offers Felipe Carrizales of *El celoso extremeño* [The jealous extremaduran] and Don Quixote himself. Of Don Quixote he says, "He is a sedentary man, a great reader, who suddenly becomes an adventurer." In both characters, he avers, "the entire tragedy and the principal novelesque motivation derive from an internal incident, a secret experience of transformation of the self, which suddenly impels them on a new course, a new form of adaptation to life."[26]

The present study is in a sense an exploration of the Peruvian psychiatrist's rather offhand observation. The idea that the characters' bizarre behavior at a particular point in the life cycle is "a new form of adaptation to life" is particularly rewarding, as we shall see. Gutiérrez Noriega himself, however, associates the climacteric or "presenile" period with a withdrawal from active life, a coming to terms with being passive and sedentary for one's remaining years, and thus the opposite of adolescence—and of Don Quixote. Knowledge of the psychodynamics of mid-life and aging has evolved considerably since 1944. It provides an excellent point of departure for the study of Don Quixote as a verisimilar literary character who acts like a real person, and I shall consider it systematically in chapter 2.

2
"NEL MEZZO DEL CAMMIN":
Men in Mid-life

The idea of a life cycle is of course not the invention of modern clinical psychiatry. Rather, it has been a constant theme in man's speculations on himself and on his life, its meaning and value, ever since he has indulged in such speculation.

Daniel Levinson, a Yale sociologist whose recent book on the subject, *The Seasons of a Man's Life*, betrays by the metaphor of its title the traditionality of the concept, offers examples from three different cultures of antiquity which attest to the universality of man's fascination with each individual's journey through time. According to Levinson, the Talmud, the *Analects* of Confucius, and the writings of Solon all have in common the following gross divisions of life into its "seasons." There is a preadult era that occupies roughly the first fifteen to twenty years. Early adulthood extends from the end of preadulthood to approximately age forty. It contains an initial formative period of some fifteen years in which a young man enters the adult world, gets married, and pursues an occupation. Only at about age thirty does he attain full strength. From thirty to forty a man's strength and energy are at their peak, but he has not yet attained his most mature capabilities. Middle adulthood lasts roughly from age forty to sixty. From forty-two to fifty-six, says Solon, "the tongue and the mind are now at their best." "Fifty is the time for giving counsel," says the Talmud. In the next stage, from fifty-three to sixty-three, man "is able, but never so nimble in speech or in wit as he was in the days of his prime." All three documents agree that the years from about forty to sixty permit the greatest realization of one's capabilities and virtues and the greatest contribution to society, despite some decline in youthful strength and energy. All agree that late adulthood begins around age sixty. The Talmud adds a final phase, beginning about age eighty, when a man attains a new strength of advanced age.[1]

Among Cervantes's contemporaries, both Sabuco and Huarte deal with the life cycle. Contrary to what we might expect, Huarte's comments are the least interesting, being derived in the main from antiquity and from Aristotle in particular. He divides human life into five stages: from birth to fourteen, childhood; from fourteen to twenty-five, adolescence; from twenty-five to thirty-five, youth; from thirty-five to forty or so, perfect age or age of consistency; from forty-five onward, old age. Old age—Don Quixote's group according to this scheme—is characterized as cold and dry. The body has gone to seed, but

> if the rational soul is the same as it was in childhood, adolescence, and consistency, without having suffered any alteration which might debilitate its faculties, it reaches this last age with a cold and dry temperament, and is most prudent and just, strong and temperate. At no time is the body more wasted than in old age, nor the soul more free and unencumbered in the use of its rational faculties. But even so, Aristotle notes six vices of the old, which they suffer because of the coldness characteristic of this age. They are cowards, they are greedy, they are suspicious, they lose hope, they are shameless, they are incredulous.[2]

The qualities Aristotle considers typical of old age, brought on by cold, are the exact opposites of Don Quixote's, which might therefore reasonably be attributed to his heat. But Huarte's characteristics—prudent, just, and so forth—coincide with those observed by Solon and in the Talmud, and it is Aristotle who is out of step. This is an example of the difficulties and dangers inherent in any attempt to establish a strict correspondence between a literary character and a particular contemporary medical (or political or economic) doctrine.

Another example is offered by Miguel Sabuco, whose ideas are in themselves, perhaps, more provocative than Huarte's. Sabuco saw the life cycle as ascensional and characterized by good health for the first half, until somewhere around age thirty to forty, and descending for the remainder. This apparently primitive concept prefigures Jung insofar as it suggests that something profound happens around age forty, and that the last half of life is different from the first. With respect to the characteristics of the second half, alas, Sabuco is even more pessimistic than Aristotle.

> In the decrement, flux or diminution, a man is timid. He lacks confidence and strength. Everything upsets him; he is frequently sad. He loses his memory; he is no longer wise, nor does he judge truly nor is he prudent. He errs in all things, from misconceptions of detail to full-blown madness. His temperament changes, he becomes angry more easily. His will becomes inconstant and his appetite no longer desires union. He no longer engenders his kind, he no longer plays, nor converses. He neither sings nor laughs. Rather, he groans, sighs and weeps.[3]

The pertinent sentence for Don Quixote in this passage is the one about error and its relation to madness. The idea that madness is an extreme form of error in judgment, a more or less natural concomitant of old age, is suggestive. Sabuco develops it further in his next chapter, and although he attributes the propensity toward error to a loss of cerebral fluid characteristic of the second half of life, his comments on the resultant change in behavior and its relation to free will are interesting indeed. In fact, the Inquisition was moved to expunge Sabuco's explicit reference to that sacred philosophical-theological concept from his text.

> The fluid falls from the brain and is no longer clear, but murky, and thus a change in temperament is effected. A man seems to have been emended by another author. His will becomes inconstant. All

men dance to this tune of rising and falling cerebral fluid, but they do not hear it and remain unaware of it. They are like someone who observes people dancing from a distance, too far away to hear the music. The dancers appear to move spontaneously, [according to each one's will] because the music which dictates all their movements in concert remains unheard. Thus do we all dance to the music of cerebral ebb and flow, and because we do not hear the sound, it seems to us that our actions are truly ours [and a manifestation of our will], and not the effect of that hidden cause.[4]

Sabuco appears to have observed, or intuited, two important phenomena that are now an accepted part of our knowledge about ourselves: first, as we have seen, the notion of a radical change, often accompanied by bizarre behavior, around the beginning of the second half of life; and second, the notion, basic to psychoanalysis, that we only think we dictate our actions through conscious exercise of our volitive faculty, that in fact a good many of our actions are the result of inner motivations that never become conscious. Phrased another way, Sabuco appears to have adumbrated the concepts of mid-life crisis and psychic determinism.

Among the moderns, C. G. Jung was the first to suggest that psychic life continues past infancy, early childhood, the latency period, and adolescence, and that, indeed, the second half of life, from approximately age forty onward, offers the possibility of a resurgence of individuation. According to Jungian thought, individuation is a developmental process through which a person becomes more uniquely individual. Acquiring a clearer and fuller identity of his own, he becomes better able to utilize his inner resources and pursue his own aims. Individuation is known to be a crucial aspect of development in childhood and adolescence, as we shall see when we review the ideas of Erik Erikson. Jung was the first to recognize that individuation occurs, and is sorely needed, in mid-life and beyond.[5] This important fact of life has been obscured until recently by the general preeminence in clinical circles of Freudian psychology, with its virtually exclusive emphasis on the preadult phase of the life cycle, during which all the rest is thought to be determined.

One Freudian who has considered the developmental phases of life from birth to death is Erik H. Erikson, who divides our psychic lives into eight stages, demarcated by what he calls the "nuclear conflicts." The first four of these occur during childhood, and it is the second group which concerns us here. During adolescence and the transition to early adulthood, roughly from age thirteen to age twenty-two, we wrestle with the issue of identity versus identity confusion. During our twenties, in early adulthood, we face and resolve in one way or another the question of intimacy and the ability to love versus isolation. Around age forty, at the beginning of mid-life, we are confronted with a new conflict, that of generativity versus stagnation. This is the characteristic conflict of the middle years, from forty to sixty, and is certainly pertinent for Don Quixote, as we shall see. Late adulthood, from about age sixty onward, brings with it the struggle between a final, dignified integrity and despair. Besides the obvious and immediate applicability of Erikson's ideas to the case of Don Quixote, it is important to consider that Erikson was the first of the moderns, and perhaps the first ever, to define the developmental phases of adult life in terms not of a set of behaviors appropriate to each age but rather of a specific psychic conflict that presents itself and must be resolved at each stage of life. Applying Américo Castro's precise characterization of the sixteenth and seventeenth centuries in Spain to psychology, we might conclude, with Erikson, that in life, every age is conflictive.

This is the underlying thesis of three recent books that together have produced a quantum leap in our knowledge of middle adulthood and aging. I have already referred to the work of the Yale sociologist Daniel Levinson and his associates. There is also the work of a Los Angeles psychoanalyst affiliated with UCLA, Roger Gould, *Transformations: Growth and Change in Adult*

Life,[6] and that of a Boston psychoanalyst affiliated with Harvard, George Vaillant, *Adaptation to Life*.[7] All three of these books have in common, first, that they are not theories but rather the results of extensive, empirical, longitudinal studies, and second, that together with Erikson, they conceptualize their findings in terms of a well-defined series of specific sets of issues to be resolved (Levinson), or (Gould) an entire complex of childish protective devices to be sequentially dismantled. Vaillant's work is concerned more with the various adaptive styles, ranging from "mature" to "psychotic," that various individuals develop in order to confront the sequential issues or nuclear conflicts as they present themselves. These new studies represent a radical reordering of our general concept of adult life. The traditional view is perhaps best, and certainly most familiarly, resumed in the "All the world's a stage" speech from *As You Like It* (act 2, scene 7):

> *They have their exits and their entrances,*
> *and one man in his time plays many parts,*
> *his acts being seven ages*

—infant, schoolboy, lover, soldier, justice, "pantaloon," and finally, the senile child. The new work, it cannot be emphasized enough, shows life not as a series of roles to be temporarily taken up and then discarded when one has grown too old to play them but as a series of crises, of intrapsychic conflicts to be dealt with and resolved, more or less dramatic and more or less conscious from individual to individual, but common to us all. We shall have repeated recourse to this body of knowledge.

The phenomenon of mid-life crisis had been the object of study for some time prior to the appearance of the books I have just mentioned. Most notable, from the clinical and behavioral standpoints, is the work of Bernice Neugarten and her associates, and the New York psychoanalyst Edmund Bergler has also made interesting contributions. Much of this research was cogently summarized in 1967 by Barbara Fried. The phenomenon known as mid-life crisis consists in its most extreme form in such wild shifts of direction and bizarre behavior as I noted in the general introduction—Gauguin leaving his job and running off to Tahiti to paint bare-breasted women, and the like. Bergler describes it as "an emotional second adolescence," a rebellion that all men go through in their mid-to-late forties and that affects all aspects of their lives, including their marriages, jobs, friendships, and social commitments.[8] Theories to account for this phenomenon may be classified as sociological, physiological, and psychological. We shall consider the case of Don Quixote in relation to his society in chapter 3, in terms of the particular time and place inhabited by him—and by Cervantes. For now let us turn our attention to the physical and the psychic possibilities.

Physicians speak of endocrine imbalances that occur in adolescence and mid-life. The teenager's hormonal system has not yet become completely stabilized, while the adult's established pattern is being upset by the advent of climacteric. The result is a set of "hormonally induced" physical symptoms. More specifically, the anterior pituitary, which is situated at the base of the brain, stimulates the other endocrine glands into action. It also functions as a bridge between the external environment—sense perceptions—and the internal environment of the body. It reacts to stimuli from the other endocrines and also to messages from the brain, and on the basis of either or both of these kinds of information, it initiates appropriate hormonal responses. Part of the reason a young man's fancy turns to thoughts of love in the springtime is that the anterior pituitary, aided by the pineal gland, obligingly mediates his exterior sensory awareness of higher temperatures and longer days into an increased production of gonadal hormones, thus "breeding desire out of the spring rain."[9] The idea that mid-life crisis might also be related to hormonal imbalance is supported by the fact that its outward psychological manifestations closely resemble those characteristically present during adolescence and in the later phases of the climacteric, both times when endocrine functioning is known to be unstable.

The idea of hormonal imbalance immediately brings to mind the old theory of humoral imbalance, and it suggests that, although the particular fluids and the particular mechanisms are not those envisioned by the ancients, their intuitions, on the basis of exterior observation, were powerful indeed. There is more specifically literary material for rumination here as well. Luis Andrés Murillo has observed that in Arthurian romance in general and in *Amadís de Gaula* in particular, the season is always a springlike summer, "a perpetual Spring, the mythical season, the dawn of the year, the vernal sunrise of any solar year, an enactment of the golden age of myth, when the first races of men lived in a climate and landscape of unending Spring."[10] This is the eternal spring of (literary) romance, an artistic re-creation of that time of year when as teenagers and middle-aged men our anterior pituitary is likely to go haywire and make us fall in love. Murillo has also pointed out, however, that Cervantes's treatment of the seasons in *Don Quixote* is a parody of the eternal spring of romance. In *Don Quixote*, springlike *verano*—defined by Cervantes's contemporary, the lexicographer Sebastián de Covarrubias, as the period 21 March, when the sun enters Aries, to 21 June, when it enters Cancer—becomes *estío* or high summer. Don Quixote sallies forth on one of the hottest days of July, with its attendant enhancement of his own bodily heat, his dryness, and his choleric temperament. Cervantes calls attention to this discrepancy by having his narrator refer to the season as *verano*—in accord with literary tradition—when *estío*—a reflection of real seasons and their characteristics—would clearly be more appropriate.

For Cervantes, then, there is an element of parody. Don Quixote is not twenty years old and the season is not spring. But from Don Quixote's perspective, it feels like spring and he feels like twenty. Don Quixote is consistent, and our enjoyment of the temporal dimension of his first sally is made possible by the contrast between his perception of reality (the eternal spring of literary romance and a knight-errant eternally in his youthful prime) and that offered by the narrator (the hottest days of July and a fiftyish madman who goes off acting like an adolescent). Renaissance humoral medicine and modern physiology, adolescence and mid-life, literary tradition and parody all converge here in strange and suggestive ways.

In addition to the "physical" hypothesis described above, we must consider the various versions of the psychological explanation for the often unconventional behavior of men in mid-life. Two psychoanalysts, Elliott Jaques and Roger Gould, have each related the emergence of this behavior to our realization, as we enter mid-life, of our own mortality, a fact we have never really had to confront—even if we inhabit a society like Don Quixote's suffocated with institutionalized reminders of death and admonitions to prepare for it. We become aware that we have stopped growing up and have begun to grow old. The first phase of adult life has been lived. Family and occupation have become established, or as Jaques points out, in a phrase pregnant with meaning for Don Quixote, ought to have become established, unless the individual's "adjustment has gone seriously awry."[11] Childhood and youth are gone and demand to be mourned. Death lies beyond. This realization, it is argued, can provoke different behavioral manifestations. One possible reaction, certainly neurotic, is an attempt to deny death altogether by sudden and passionate involvement in manic activity. Roger Gould writes: "When we feel the cold breath of death on our own neck . . . some of us redouble our efforts at work and reinvest in its illusions with a passion. The relentless pressure to make a quantum leap into the world of fantastic success, to end death with one master stroke

of achievement, increases."[12] We are all familiar with other manifestations of denial—the compulsive attempts to remain young,
the hypochondriacal concern for health and appearance, sexual
promiscuity in order to prove youth and potency—either
through our own experiences, through those of our friends, or, at
the very least, through the films of Claude Sautet and Paul
Mazursky.

A healthier reaction, suggested by both authors, is the
beginning of a search for authenticity. That is, we come to perceive our established niche, as defined by work and marriage, as
alienating. We can no longer work for the same reasons (necessity, the desire for promotion) that gave meaning to our work
before. Similarly, the earlier satisfactions of married life (physical
attraction, making a home for a growing family) either have
ceased to exist or now exist in some attenuated form. We come to
feel that persisting in our routine has become a pretense, an act of
bad faith, and that life is now too short to allow us to indulge in
this sort of estrangement from ourselves any longer. The "mid-
life career change"—the stockbroker becoming a cabinetmaker
or, more probably, a financial consultant to a nonprofit corporation—is frequently a response to this realization, as is the destruction of marriage or redefinition of it in a way that endows it
anew with authenticity and allows it to continue in an enriched
form. It may be objected that Don Quixote has no job—his status
as hidalgo prohibits it—and no marriage, and that therefore
considerations such as the awareness of personal mortality and
resultant career change and redefinition of relationship to the
love-object are simply irrelevant. I would argue that the reverse is
true, that Don Quixote's emergence as Don Quixote is precisely a
dramatic change in his relationship to both work and love and
that it certainly represents a quest for personal authenticity.

Psychoanalysis has also related the mid-life crisis, especially
in its aspect of heightened sexual awareness, promiscuity, and the

like, to a kind of replay of the oedipal drama acted out in infancy, early childhood, and adolescence. This intrapsychic conflict is characterized as the struggle to keep suddenly strong, unacceptable sexual and aggressive impulses—the same ones we feel originally toward the parent of the opposite and the same sex respectively—from becoming too openly and directly expressed. Normally, these impulses are kept under control and/or channeled into socially acceptable and presumably unrelated activities by a combination of ego defenses. They are banished from consciousness by *repression*, turned into something less violent by *displacement*, transformed into something socially acceptable and even useful by *sublimation*, changed into their opposite by *reaction formation*, or denied altogether by a process known, appropriately, as *denial*. In this way "psychic homeostasis" is maintained. At certain times of life there is an upsurge so strong that, in spite of our best efforts, our "forbidden" sexual impulses rise to the surface of consciousness and sexual activity—overt or fantasized—results. The teenage boy who suddenly discovers girls is in part pulled toward them by the girls themselves and in part pushed toward them by his intolerable attraction for his mother.

There is some evidence that suggests that the resurgence of instinctual drives in mid-life may be linked to a reactivation of oedipal feelings. Edmund Bergler, for example, reports that the inner conflicts that drove his patients to rebel and that made their revolt an "emotional second adolescence" were in part the result of revived oedipal fantasies in which they unconsciously confused their wives with their mothers. Even more suggestive is this passage from an autobiographical novel of mid-life written by a psychoanalyst, Allen Wheelis's *The Seeker*:

> A second change, beginning only in recent months, had been an upsurge in lecherous preoccupations. Desire for my wife had decreased, and drive for other women increased. There was nothing carefree about this. I had been beset with an intense and indiscriminate lust, a hunger for variety and possession and

penetration that would gather up and devour all the women in the world. I had not acted on these impulses, but they had transformed my inner life into a venereal phantasmagoria.[13]

In the less colorful language of the clinician, David L. Gutmann describes the progressive intensity of the inner life that accompanies aging and the consequent increased demands on the processes of defense to keep unacceptable impulses at bay. "Increased impulse life is likely to pose new threats to the aging personality as the struggle against aggressive, sexual and regressive impulses, viewed as ego-alien, must be refought by the ego."[14]

Once again, combining modern scientific knowledge with literary tradition yields what we might describe as the beginning of an insight for *Don Quixote*. The older man who is smitten by intense amorous feelings, and especially sexual desire, has been a stock figure of ridicule since Greek comedy. The late fifteenth-century antifeminist *Repetición de amores* of Luis de Lucena observes that "this ailment [love] is the more dangerous and deserving of mockery the older and wiser is the person who succumbs to it." Lucena's contemporary, Rodrigo Cota, dramatized the inappropriateness of an old man's desire for love in the *Diálogo entre el Amor y un viejo*, when Cupid appears initially to be disposed to honor the old man's request and then turns violently on him, reminding him of his age, his decrepit body, his inability to love. In the last stanza the old man "recovers his sanity" and confesses that his good sense had been put to sleep by a siren's song. He awakes to unpleasant reality as delineated by a long literary tradition. Closer in time to Cervantes, and in a position to capitalize on the fame of the *Quixote*, an obscure writer named Matías de los Reyes published a play with the title *Dar al tiempo lo que es suyo* [Render unto time that which is time's], whose plot concerns the unwitting rivalry of a father with his own son for the hand of a girl who, by her age, is clearly better suited to the latter. At one point, in her frustration at the unequal but profitable marriage her family has arranged for her, she exclaims, "And is that reason enough to give me over to some Don Quixote?"[15]

Which brings us to Cervantes. Don Quixote is a Cervantine extension of the traditional theme of the old man in love. He has, of course, no wife to confuse with his mother and hence make him attracted to some younger, clearly unmotherly woman. Nevertheless, he obviously feels a powerful upsurge of libido, which he has in common with the literary tradition exemplified by Cota's *viejo* as well as with the psychic reality documented by Bergler, Wheelis, and Gutmann. Instead of a more or less intellectual confrontation with Cupid (à la Cota), or a farcical pursuit (à la Reyes) of the youthful hand of Aldonza Lorenzo—who we are told is the object of his middle-aged affections—Don Quixote metamorphoses her into Dulcinea del Toboso and rides off in the opposite direction. That is, he sublimates his intolerable and socially unacceptable desire into something noble and unimpeachably worthwhile, as Unamuno observed long ago.

I shall have occasion to discuss Unamuno's ideas and the resultant critical tradition in some detail in chapter 3. For the present I should like to return to the relation between literary tradition and the psychoanalytical theory of reenergized oedipal conflicts. If it is true that the middle-aged man's pursuit of younger women is not an action but a reaction to his reenergized oedipal desire for his mother (now personified in his wife), it becomes clear that in Don Quixote's case something very basic is lacking: the stimulus that provokes the response, the action that determines the reaction. He has no wife. This fact, placed in the context of psychoanalytical theory, is what leads us to the brink of an insight.

Taking a wife is the normal denouement of the oedipal drama played out in adolescence, the transference of at least most of one's unacceptable desire for one's mother to an appropriate woman of one's own age, recognizing and channeling one's sexuality into the socially acceptable activity of procreating and raising a family. This is what Don Quixote, for whatever reason, has been unable to do, and this is why, as the work begins, we come upon him in every sense *in medias res*, a fifty-year-old bachelor whose closest friends are a celibate priest and a barber whose family, if he has one, is never mentioned. In other words, the oedipal conflict that Don Quixote reexperiences is one which was not resolved, at least in the usual way, in adolescence. It is possible, then, that the libidinous feelings he must discharge at age fifty are colored and indeed characterized by a lifelong conflict between sexual energy and a chronic inability to find sexual outlets for it. It is not merely desire that comes to the fore, but desire thwarted and ungratified, possibly from some deep-seated fear of women. But this is not an explanation, nor is it really literary criticism properly speaking. It is the beginning of an insight.

Erik Erikson, whose thought has by now influenced at least two generations of clinicians as well as countless undergraduates who have been exposed to his works as required texts in several different academic disciplines, considers that the mid-life period confronts men with what he calls a crisis of generativity. This occurs, he says, when a man reaches mid-life and looks at what he has generated, or helped to generate, and finds it either good or deficient—when his life's work as part of the productivity of his time either gives him some sense of being on the side of a few angels or makes him feel stagnant. The same thought is expressed by Philippe Aries in his classic treatise on western attitudes toward death. "Today the adult experiences sooner or later the feeling that he has failed, that his adult life has failed to achieve any of the promises of his adolescence. . . . This feeling was completely foreign to the mentalities of traditional societies, but it was no longer foreign to the rich, powerful or learned men of the late Middle Ages."[16] Elliott Jaques speaks of a middle-aged patient's "adjustment to the fact that he would not be able to accomplish in the span of a single lifetime everything he had desired to do."[17] Edmund Bergler observes: "The die is cast for him professionally; what the middle-aged man does not achieve in his forties he will not achieve later. What this 'later' means is not clear to him, and to avoid facing the question he lives timelessly; he acts as though daily routine could cancel the calendar."[18]

Erikson's concept of generativity provides a splendid link between the thought of the twentieth century and that of the sixteenth, for it immediately recalls Huarte's derivation of *ingenio* ('the ability to generate') from Latin *ingenerare* ('to engender') and Otis Green's systematic application of Huarte's thought to Cervantes's ingenioso hidalgo. Erikson's location of generativity in relation to its opposite, stagnation, as a crisis characteristic of a particular season of a man's life further strengthens both the web of associations and the verisimilitude of Don Quixote as a novelistic character. In Eriksonian and Huartean terms, an anonymous fiftyish hidalgo takes stock of his life and realizes he has generated nothing—not even a name. His life is rather a paradigmatic case of stagnation. This realization galvanizes him into action. His first attempt at generating involves the writing of a book of chivalry ("many a time he was tempted to take up his pen and literally finish the tale as had been promised"), but this soon yields to the more authentic project of becoming a knight-errant, with a name, and actually living a book of chivalry: generating himself instead of some literary work.

A most important aspect of Erikson's idea of the crisis of generativity versus stagnation in mid-life is that it reproduces in only slightly changed form the characteristic nuclear conflict of late adolescence, that of intimacy versus isolation. Barbara Fried employs the graphic term "middlescent" to suggest the similarities between the two developmental phases as she offers the following précis of Erikson's thought:

> Many a middlescent who for one reason or another was not able to solve conflicts about intimacy at the end of adolescence experiences a renewal of an earlier, grievous intuition of being unlovable—

different from all those other people who somehow seem to have grasped a secret about commitment in which he cannot or does not share. The negative counterpart of intimacy is isolation, and according to Erikson's developmental timetable, the conflict between these two ego qualities is resolved at some point near the end of adolescence. The correlations between this crisis and the middle-age crisis are especially evident: a capacity for intimacy is clearly a prerequisite for generativity, and an isolated maturity just as clearly prefigures a self-absorbed middle age. Furthermore, both these adjacent crises revolve around the establishment of relationships rather than around the development of internal, essentially subjective character traits—you can't, strictly speaking, achieve either intimacy or generativity all by yourself.[19]

To recapitulate: Eriksonian thought relates the mid-life conflict (generativity and stagnation) to the adolescent one (intimacy and isolation) and thereby suggests a close psychic bond between the two periods. The same bond is suggested by the psychoanalytical theory of a resurgence in mid-life of the oedipal conflict of adolescence, and by the physiological findings of analogous, though not identical, hormonal imbalance present in both developmental phases. This brings us back to the observation of the Peruvian psychiatrist Carlos Gutiérrez Noriega to the effect that Cervantes understood that adolescence (Tomás Rodaja) and middle age (Don Quixote) are the periods of maximum vital tension in our lives and created his characters accordingly. We are now in a position to add to this insight the strong possibility that Cervantes was aware, at some level of his psychic apparatus, that middle age shares certain crucial psychophysical characteristics with adolescence—that middle age brings with it a resurgence of the worst problems of adolescence—and that he created his most complete literary character accordingly. An assessment of Cervantes's genius may begin to arise from a cursory comparison of his willingness to explore these intuitions in a major work—innovative in many other aspects as well—whose hero is basically sympathetic, with the long-standing literary tradition (at least as old as Plautus's *Mercator*) of depicting the over-forty lover as an object of ridicule, too old to be doing (or even decently to be thinking about) what he is attempting to do. The high point of this tradition, unconscious denial of all the resurgences and similarities we have been discussing, is of course the conventional representation in Christian iconography of Saint Joseph as a bewildered, impotent old man.

As a society we are still collectively engaged in this massive denial of the analogies between adolescence and middle age, as the following anecdote will suggest. Some years ago in Madrid, on several different occasions and in several different theaters whose audiences varied widely in terms of socioeconomic class and cinematographic sophistication, I was fortunate enough to see a moving film, *Del rosa al amarillo*, by the brilliant Spanish director Manolo Summers. It is a film about love, divided into two segments whose only relation is thematic. The first concerns the hopeless love of a just prepubescent boy for a just postpubescent girl. Everyone in every theater seemed to enter into the spirit and identify with the male character. Although clearly foredoomed to failure, his adolescent and obviously oedipal infatuation for the girl with developing breasts and hair under her arms seemed a perfectly normal and acceptable part of life. The second half of the film deals with two people in an old-age home who fall in love and plot to run away together. Their courtship is carried out in what I can only describe as an adolescent fashion: love poems copied from Bécquer and surreptitiously passed from table to table at mealtime; chance meetings that have really been willed to happen and unconsciously engineered by both parties; extravagant melodramatic declarations of love; wistful, lingering glances after mealtime, as she prepares to go off and sew with the women and he to smoke and play dominoes with the men. In every theater the audience's reaction to this segment was laughter, from raucous guffaw to nervous titter. The director, it seemed, was considerably in advance of his audience, who experienced the idea of older people in love as shocking and somehow threatening and retreated into the safety of tradition by turning the two lovers into a pair of clowns. Intense love in adolescence is normal and natural. The same feelings in mid-life and beyond are some kind of perversion. If it is true that Summers was ahead of his audience in 1963, it is equally true that Cervantes was ahead of his in 1605 and, with no disrespect, ahead of Summers as well. Only now, thanks to a maturing tradition of theoretical speculation in concert with massive empirical investigation, are we in a position to overtake them.

I hope in the foregoing pages to have documented, from a variety of viewpoints and in a variety of styles, the fact of mid-life as a developmental phase in the adult life cycle which is characterized by a particular set of problems to be resolved. I hope further to have established a connection between mid-life and adolescence as developmental phases whose problems are strikingly similar and, finally, to have begun to explore some of the possible relations between these facts, the medical and literary traditions Cervantes had at his disposal, and the conception of the character Don Quixote. This has proved enlightening, but a major obstacle impedes the wholesale application of this knowledge to our novel. It may be true that we all experience some kind of crisis in mid-life, but most of us manage to get through it without dressing up in a suit of armor and tilting at windmills. The fact is that Don Quixote is crazy. Cervantes's narrator tells us so in the first chapter, and the clinical psychiatrists have supplied the name of his illness. We are still missing some knowledge that would allow us to locate Don Quixote's particular (psychotic) reaction to the stress of mid-life in the realm of the real world inhabited by real people and, on that basis, to elucidate the verisimilitude of his character. Before we can proceed to a detailed examination of the *Quixote*, therefore, we must arm ourselves with one additional conceptual weapon, one that will allow us to discuss him as a verisimilar novelistic character with much greater precision than would otherwise be possible.

In 1944 Carlos Gutiérrez Noriega referred to Don Quixote's madness as "a new form of adaptation to life." The real meaning of the phrase has only recently been elucidated by George E. Vaillant in an important work whose title is precisely *Adaptation to Life*.[20] This book is a kind of progress report, for the mid-1970s, of the lives of the 268 "Grant Study" men, who graduated in the classes of 1939–1944 from the most prestigious northeastern private colleges. Massive and detailed, the Grant Study has followed the lives of these men from college days to the present. For each man there are detailed reports of original and periodic examinations by physicians (including psychiatrists) and psychologists. There are records of interviews, and questionnaires answered by the men themselves. In the preparation of his book Vaillant correlated this preexisting body of data for each man still living with his own interviews (sometimes several) and resultant analysis. The outcome is an impressive array of fact which, along with the work of Levinson, Gould, and Gutmann, confirms Erikson's hypothesis of the relation between mid-life and adolescence. This is perhaps the least important aspect of Vaillant's work, however, since that relation had already been generally accepted. *Adaptation to Life* deals with men who are now in mid-life and are experiencing, or have recently experienced, its quasi-adolescent *Sturm und Drang*. Vaillant is concerned with uncovering the various adaptive styles the men developed over the course of their lives and through which they confronted the crisis of middle age. These adaptive styles involve the deployment, in crisis, of a group of ego defenses in a combination which forms a pattern and comes to be characteristic of the individual. This pattern constitutes his adaptive style, the techniques he has evolved for coping with reality, especially in its unpleasant aspects.

In order to delineate these styles Vaillant grouped eighteen discrete ego defense mechanisms into four levels: psychotic, immature, neurotic, and mature. This hierarchy of defenses can be used to predict adult growth and to define adult mental health. "Defenses," says Vaillant, "can become the critical variables that determine whether environmental stress produces madness or something analogous to the process through which an oyster, confronted with a grain of sand, creates a pearl."[21] If a man's characteristic coping style involves a preponderance of mature and neurotic defenses, we can make some reasonable and favorable inferences concerning the evolution of his mental health. If he typically has recourse to the immature and psychotic mechanisms, we have reason to be less optimistic. Because most of us are not familiar with this particular scheme, being more accustomed instead to Anna Freud's classic *The Ego and Mechanisms of Defense*, and because most of us literary critics have only a hazy idea of the difference between mental health, neurosis, and psychosis, I feel justified here in drawing extensively from Vaillant's writings on the hierarchy of defenses, the name and brief description of each mechanism, its distribution among the populace, and prognosis for modification. In this way we can equip ourselves with some fairly concrete notions of different human behaviors and what to think of them, and we can begin to apply the concept of adaptive style to Don Quixote, since we shall recognize him in a number of the descriptions below.

The mechanisms of *delusional projection* (frank delusions about external reality), *denial* (denial of external reality), and *distortion* (grossly reshaping external reality to suit inner needs) are all "psychotic." They are common in "healthy" individuals before age five and in adult dreams and fantasy. For the user, these mechanisms alter reality. To the beholder, they appear to be "crazy." They tend to be immune to change by conventional psychotherapeutic interpretation. Belief in evil giants, *malandrines*, despoilers of widows and maidens, and the consequent need to destroy them, is a form of delusional projection. Meta-morphosing a country inn into a castle and windmills into giants are examples of distortion.

The "immature" defenses are those of *projection* (attributing one's own unacknowledged feelings to others), *schizoid fantasy* (tendency to use fantasy and to indulge in autistic retreat into, first, self-reproach and then into complaints of pain, somatic illness, and neurasthenia, for the purpose of reproach toward others arising from bereavement, loneliness, or unacceptable aggressive impulses), *passive-aggressive behavior* (aggression toward others expressed indirectly and ineffectively through passivity or turned against the self), and *acting out* (direct expression of an unconscious wish or impulse in order to avoid being conscious of the affect that accompanies it). The immature defenses are common in "healthy" individuals aged three to fifteen, in character disorder, and in adults in psychotherapy. For the user these mechanisms most often alter distress engendered either by the threat of interpersonal intimacy or that of experiencing its loss. To the beholder they appear socially undesirable. Although refractory, they can change with improved interpersonal relationships, with repeated and forceful interpretation during prolonged psychotherapy, or with confrontation by peers. The entire enterprise of being Don Quixote is heavily dependent on the processes of schizoid fantasy and acting out.

The "neurotic" defenses are *intellectualization* (thinking about instinctual wishes in formal, affectively bland terms and not acting on them; the idea is in consciousness, but the feeling is missing), *repression* (apparently inexplicable naiveté, memory lapse, or failure to acknowledge input from a selected sense organ; the feeling is in consciousness, but the idea is missing), *displacement* (the redirection of feelings toward a relatively less cared-for object than the person or situation arousing them), *reaction formation* (behaving in a fashion diametrically opposed to an unacceptable instinctual impulse), and *dissociation* (temporary but drastic modification of one's character or of one's sense of personal identity to avoid emotional stress). These mechanisms are common in "healthy" individuals aged three to ninety, in neurotic disorder, and in mastering acute adult stress. For the user they alter private feelings or instinctual expression. To the beholder they appear as individual quirks or "neurotic hangups." They can often be dramatically changed by conventional, brief psychotherapeutic interpretation.

Finally, the defenses Vaillant classifies as "mature" are those of *altruism* (vicarious but constructive and instinctually gratifying service to others), *humor* (overt expression of ideas and feelings without individual discomfort and without unpleasant effects on others), *suppression* (the conscious or semiconscious decision to postpone paying attention to a conscious impulse or conflict), *anticipation* (realistic planning for or anticipation of future inner discomfort), and *sublimation* (indirect or attenuated expressions of instincts without either adverse consequences or marked loss of pleasure). These mechanisms are common in "healthy" individuals aged twelve to ninety. For the user, they integrate reality, interpersonal relationships, and private feelings. To the beholder they appear as convenient virtues. Under increased stress they may change to less mature mechanisms.[22]

Vaillant's hierarchy of defenses and its application to the study of men in mid-life confirms and supersedes the earlier work of David L. Gutmann, who has also studied comparative coping styles among aging men. Some of Gutmann's findings appear to have some relevance for *Don Quixote*, and for that reason I shall summarize them here. Gutmann used a sample of 145 men aged forty to seventy. He gave them the Thematic Apperception Test, in which the subject makes up stories to explain pictures, and on the basis of their responses classified their styles of coping, or "mastery." He distinguishes the following three categories: *active mastery* (making the environment conform to the individual), *passive mastery* (the individual adapts to the environment), and *magical mastery* (falling back on "extreme" ego defenses). The "magical" group is the one which interests us here.

> Their distinctive mastery mode is termed "magical" because, in time of trouble, these men operate on the principle of "wishing will make it so." At such times these respondents see in the world either what they want to see or what—for internal reasons—they must see. They alter the world by perceptual fiat, not by realistic, instrumental action. For example, when they can no longer assuage guilt and relieve anxiety through the conventional repertoire of ego defenses, these men fall back on more extreme forms, such as projection, and use minimal evidence to accuse others of harboring the sexual and aggressive motivations they fear and deny in themselves. . . . With increased age, there is an increased frequency of men in the magical mastery group, a finding which substantiates the general hypothesis of increased difficulty with inner life and changes in defensive structure in later life.[23]

Gutmann and Vaillant coincide in their insistence that the behavior associated with the defense is not a beginning but an end, not a cause but an effect, the response or adaptation to some inner, psychic disequilibrium that has become intolerable and must be reacted to. This is a fundamental concept for us as literary critics and readers in search of a vicarious experience of life in the pages of *Don Quixote*. If it is true that verisimilar literary characters act like real people, obey the same motivations, and exhibit the same behaviors, then our excursion into the only apparently unliterary terrain of scientific studies of men in mid-life has provided us with two basic principles by means of which we can begin the study of Don Quixote as a verisimilar character. The first of these is the fact that somewhere between ages forty and sixty we all experience what has come to be known as mid-life crisis, and that this crisis is, curiously, in many ways analogous to that of adolescence. The second principle, documented by Vaillant, is that how each of us confronts the crisis of mid-life—from graceful maturity to retreat into psychosis—is a function of the adaptive style each of us has developed over the course of our lives.

Now Cervantes obviously did not have the benefit of Erikson or Vaillant or any of the modern thinkers and clinicians whose work we have been reviewing in this chapter. Nor did he need them. It is only we moderns and scholars who must fall back on science to learn about life and its processes, about people and their ways. Cervantes was a genius who brought his powerful intuitions to bear on the materials he had at hand. When he sat down to write *Don Quixote*, Cervantes could draw on the long tradition of "the seasons of a man's life," on sixteenth-century theories of the life cycle, on literary tradition, on his observation of his fellows, and above all on his own experience as a man of fifty-some years of age. These are the raw materials he worked with, and in the succeeding chapters I shall attempt to ascertain what he did with them.

3
DON QUIXOTE'S HOUSEHOLD
AND THE ESCAPE
TO DULCINEA

"The mass of men lead lives of quiet desperation."
Thoreau

We first perceive our hero not as an individual but as a member of a class. He is "one of those hidalgos who always have a lance in the rack, an ancient buckler, a skinny nag and a greyhound for the chase" (I, 1). Spanish society in Cervantes's time was divided into nobles (hidalgos) and commoners (*pecheros*). Pecheros were expected to work and pay taxes; their name was in fact derived from a per capita tax they were all required to pay. Hidalgos were exempt from taxes, in lieu of which they were expected to serve the king in war. They did not work or engage in commerce but lived off the revenue from their lands. Now, this word *hidalgo* has two meanings: a general one that is "the opposite of *pechero*" (the king is an hidalgo in this sense) and a more restricted one that is "the lowest rung of the nobility" (the squire [*escudero*] in *Lazarillo de Tormes* and Don Quixote himself are hidalgos in this sense). Above the hidalgos were *caballeros*, *títulos* (marquises), *grandes* (counts and dukes), and finally royalty. These distinctions were basically a function of wealth, and in the traditional economy in which they came to exist, wealth was a function of landownership.

At the end of the sixteenth century, the class of hidalgos to which Don Quixote belongs was becoming extinct. Their normal function in times of war—to serve a higher ranking noble as escudero by carrying his shield (*escudo*) and weapons—was being eliminated as the nature of warfare changed. Traditionally a confrontation between two groups of individual knights, each supported by his own retinue, serving because to do so was the raison d'être of his class, and whose primary function was to engage in individual feats of heroism, combat had become a confrontation between two military units made up largely of professionals whose primary function was to obey orders.[1] When Don Quixote metamorphoses two flocks of sheep into two armies composed of individual champions (I, 18), or when he proposes as a defense against the Turkish threat that all the knights-errant in Spain be gathered together and turned loose on the enemy (II, 1), he is projecting himself imaginatively into a world that had disappeared forever and at the same time demonstrating his tenacious membership in that archaic class of hidalgos who were disappearing along with it.

If his military mission had disappeared, the hidalgo's peacetime situation was being rendered precarious by changes in the economic infrastructure. The traditional feudal agrarian system, in which wealth was a function of landownership, was evolving in the sixteenth century into the modern, capitalist system, in which wealth is based on the possession of money. This phenomenon, common to Western Europe, was aggravated in Spain by the massive influx of precious metals from America, which drove prices up and made life unbearable for the small landowners whose income was fixed and whose holdings were too small to permit them to absorb the increase in prices.[2]

In short, the class of small hidalgos to which Don Quixote belonged was being rendered irrelevant and incapable of sustaining itself by what we might summarize as the passage from medieval feudalism to modern capitalism, which destroyed its traditional economic bases. This, in combination with the survival of the archaic social structure, with its division into hidalgos and pecheros and its insistence on the maintenance of the distinction, caught Don Quixote's class in a vicious double bind. If these people, whose traditional economic base was crumbling away beneath them, attempted to move into other activities and seek other sources of support, they would lose their most precious possession, nobility itself. To work, to engage in commerce, or to pay the *pecho* was to jeopardize one's *hidalguía*.

Many hidalgos fled to the burgeoning cities to seek employment appropriate to their class as household servants to the higher nobility, the natural evolution of their traditional function in wartime. In spite of the growth of the urban nobility and its manpower requirements for purposes of ostentation, the market could not absorb all the poor hidalgos who attempted to enter it. The escudero in *Lazarillo de Tormes* is the best-developed fictional portrayal of this real situation.[3] A small landowner—an hidalgo—from Old Castile whose lands are no longer capable of supporting him, he moves to Toledo, the new imperial capital, but fails to find appropriate employment. When little Lazarillo meets him he is caught between his poverty and hunger, on the one hand, and the demands of his class—to maintain honor and with it hidalguía—on the other. His life has become a kind of institutionalized form of alienation, as it consists primarily in maintaining an inauthentic exterior facade quite at variance with the reality we know from our sojourn inside his house. Being-for-the-other and being-for-the-self are hopelessly out of kilter.

Other small hidalgos remained on their lands, eking out a living as best they could. Don Quixote is the best-developed fictional representation of this group. When we meet him our attention is directed, first, to his membership in a class whose characteristics we can now define with some precision and, second, to the utter monotony of his existence. His life is characterized by endless repetition of the same few elements. He has two suits of clothes, one for weekdays and one for Sundays. His menu is repeated virtually without variation every week of every year. The only "legal" activity in which he can engage is a vestigial simulacrum of warfare called hunting, which he does. Other than that, his poverty and the demands of his class—hidalguía must be maintained—reduce him to impotence and inactivity.

Don Quixote is a prisoner of his place within a socio-economic order whose dynamic side is ruining him financially and whose static side prevents him from doing anything about it. This conflict is shown most poignantly in the first pages of the novel when he sells off some land to raise capital—a tentative excursion into the new order—that he then uses to buy books of chivalry and retreat imaginatively into the old. That is, his first (and only) attempt to operate as a modern man in the modern world is immediately turned against itself and harnessed to the task of denying that world and defending Don Quixote from it.

Don Quixote is a country hidalgo, a member of a class. As we read the first pages, and indeed the entire first part of the novel, however, we form the impression that he is the only hidalgo in his anonymous little village. As we begin Part II, when he asks Sancho what people think of his exploits, we discover that our impression has been erroneous and that there are more hidalgos, and even some caballeros, in the place, for reaction to our hero's deeds seems to be a function of social position. Sancho informs his master that

> the hidalgos are saying that, not content with being a gentleman [hidalgo], you have put a "Don" in front of your name and at a bound have made yourself into a caballero. . . . The caballeros, on the other hand, do not relish having the hidalgos set up in opposition to them, especially those "squirely" ones [hidalgos escuderiles] who shine their own shoes and darn their black stockings with green silk. (II, 2)

Suddenly, the entire intranoble hierarchy stands revealed, complete with class distinctions and resentments. Don Quixote's village turns out to be well populated with his fellow noblemen. These people, our hero's peers and natural companions, never appear directly in the entire two volumes of the novel. Don

Quixote simply does not socialize with them. Either he shuns their company, or they his. Whatever the cause, the result is that Don Quixote is not only alienated by the demands of his class from participation in the real, modern world of 1600; he is also alienated within his class, estranged from that very corporation in which he is simultaneously imprisoned.

Don Quixote's double bind of class is repeated in his relationship to the members of his household. He is a fifty-year-old bachelor who is responsible for his niece, a girl approaching twenty. We are never told why the niece lives with her uncle instead of her mother, Don Quixote's sister. They are joined by a housekeeper, a woman more or less Don Quixote's age, and a *mozo*, a boy who saddles his master's horse and prunes the vines. I have chosen to enumerate the members of the household hierarchically in order to contrast this "official" arrangement with the real, human one that obtains. Officially, the household is composed of two aristocrats, Don Quixote and his niece, who are served by two commoners, the housekeeper and the boy. In fact, the boy disappears from the book as soon as he is introduced, and Don Quixote is left alone in a house full of women. The housekeeper and the niece form a unit defined by their sex, transcending the difference in their social classes, and both frequently oppose Don Quixote. Without exception, studies of "the women in *Don Quixote*" group the two together and tend to classify or dismiss them both as colorless, lacking in personality, and the like.[4] I shall have occasion to question this assertion presently. For now it is sufficient to note that Don Quixote's household is effectively divided into two women and one man and that each group has separate and frequently antagonistic interests.

Leaving aside this by no means uncommon arrangement—a staple of countless television "sitcoms," after all—we can discern further and graver problems in the personal relationships in this household, all of which stem from the fact that the man of the house is a bachelor. His niece can be seen as a kind of daughter once removed, but neither she nor the housekeeper is anything like a wife. Unamuno and, more recently, Arturo Serrano Plaja have noted this and remarked that had Don Quixote had a wife (and daughter), he would have had to assume responsibility for them, which would have tempered his desire to go off a-questing, and that, furthermore, a wife would have used every means at her disposal to restrain her husband from going off on his quixotic outings.[5] More important, I think, is the effect of the real arrangement on our hero. Don Quixote lives in a house full of women, but there is no woman in his life. His family life is as barren as his professional life. Whatever it was that in adolescence and young manhood inhibited him from embarking on normal relationships with girls, from falling in love and getting married, has ensured the absence from his life of any meaningful and satisfying relationship with the opposite sex, just as his status as hidalgo in 1600 had deprived him of the opportunity to engage in meaningful and productive activity.

Daniel Levinson observes that "in all societies, work is a major part of individual life and of the social structure. Every man is required to contribute his labor in some form of work deemed useful for the tribe. Universally, work is organized into a number of socially defined occupations that are taught, accorded differential value and reward, and integrated into simple or complex economic structures." He goes on to say that "in all societies, a man is expected to marry and to take certain responsibilities within a familial system," and he further observes that "a man usually wants to marry and to make his family a central component in his life structure."[6] Levinson's observations describe Don Quixote precisely, but in reverse, and identify him as a man in some respects out of tune with his own society and most certainly with what is generally considered normal and natural in the world at large. The two categories of activity he proposes have much in common with Freud's *lieben und arbeiten*, the capacity for which is generally considered to be the baseline criterion for mental health. Before Don Quixote "goes mad" in the sense of assuming his new identity as an anachronistic knight-errant and engaging in overtly psychotic behavior, before he stays up all night reading romances of chivalry and drying his brain out, before he loses the ability to discriminate between history (el Cid) and fantasy (Amadís), he is presented as lacking the capacity to work and to love. By the most generally accepted standard, Don Quixote is already estranged from mental health by the time the book begins.

Don Quixote has no meaningful occupation, he does not love a woman, he has no relationship with his peers, but he does have two friends, with whom he is united by at least one common interest and with whom he appears to spend a good deal of time. His friends are Pero Pérez, the priest, a graduate of one of the minor universities, and Maese Nicolás, the barber. Although, unlike their friend, both these men have professions, neither appears to be involved with women. The priest is of course celibate, and if the barber has a wife, she never appears in the story (in contrast, for example, to Sancho's Teresa). Don Quixote is what might be described as a loner, and his two friends and only associates seem to share this quality with him. The three especially enjoy discussions of the romances of chivalry; that is, they are fond of taking a small vacation from reality and retiring for a while into a make-believe world of knights and battles and ladies fair.

Besides his friends, Don Quixote's greatest outlet for the energies he might otherwise have expended on work and love is of course his own personal, intimate relationship with the books of chivalry. It is here that he parts company with his friends, for as everyone knows, his involvement with the books is so pervasive that it comes to fill up all his leisure time (most of the year, the text tells us) and all his waking hours (which he extends to twenty-four per day). It is so intense that he loses the ability to discriminate between historical fact and poetic fantasy. The Knight of the

Burning Sword becomes for him just as real as the Cid. Don Quixote transforms all of it—history and fantasy—into an intensely personal reality that comes to replace the objective reality of his situation as a member of an obsolete profession surrounded by women with whom he has only an institutional relationship.

Martine Bigeard has observed that the monotony of Don Quixote's home life, in concert with the repressive social system in which he is imprisoned, drives him to seek relief in the books of chivalry. The books are not the beginning but the end of a process, one that is both social and intrapsychic in nature.[7] Teresa Aveleyra also suggests that Don Quixote's reading is an escape, a response, and she proposes as its stimulus our hero's inability to put his desire for Aldonza Lorenzo out of his mind.[8] We shall examine this interesting hypothesis later in this chapter. For the present it is sufficient to note that, although the narration begins when Don Quixote is fifty, his life had begun fifty years before, that he was born into a certain situation of a certain social class at a certain time, that some forever-unexplained and still unresolved intrapsychic problems determined the course of his love life, that his life is useless, monotonous, and possibly weighted by practically uncontrollable erotic impulses, and, finally, that in order to deny these unpleasant realities, he mobilizes as a first line of defense an all-consuming passion for books of chivalry, which offer the possibility of a vicarious experience of a more fulfilling life. The intensity of his involvement with the books is a measure of the magnitude of the pressure and frustration he experiences.

As we know, this first line of defense proves inadequate, and Don Quixote next considers writing a book of chivalry, a project he rejects in favor of turning himself into a knight-errant and actually living a book of chivalry instead. In this way, with one stroke he denies the reality of his station by promoting himself from hidalgo to caballero. He denies the reality of the time he occupies by conducting himself as though the old feudal order were still in flower and the sixteenth century had never happened, and he denies the oppressive monotony of his home life by physically removing himself from it. It is at this point that Don Quixote becomes "certifiably mad," to use an only mildly misleading lay term. More properly, this massive denial of external reality, which will spawn all sorts of particular distortions and give rise to all manner of bizarre and antisocial behavior, marks the beginning of Don Quixote's definitive retreat into psychosis. What is important to understand is that psychosis is not a cause, but an effect, the last and most drastic weapon in the arsenal of defenses we humans can mobilize to cope with intolerable reality. In Don Quixote's case it has been preceded, as we have seen, by the obsessive reading of books of chivalry, a tactic that was ultimately unsuccessful. Contrary to a popular notion, Don Quixote does not go crazy because he reads the books too much. Rather— and paradoxically—he reads the books too much in an effort to keep himself from going crazy.

It is appropriate here to ask ourselves why the books were unsuccessful or, phrased another way, what it was in Don Quixote's relations to exterior reality that proved too powerful even for a semipsychotic withdrawal into a world of fantasy on the printed page. Before we can answer these questions we should arm ourselves with some idea of the concrete attributes of the chivalric life which seem particularly important or attractive to Don Quixote, for these may lead us back to the psychogenesis of his interest in them. I should begin by observing that Don Quixote is a knight-errant who comes to the profession of arms through the medium of letters. During his fifty years of life he has apparently never engaged in any of the warlike activities appropriate to his class and station. He has apparently never served the king in war, as his creator did at Lepanto, for example, nor has he soldiered in Italy or Flanders or America, as thousands of his fellow hidalgos did. Don Quixote is a man of arms who has never borne arms. In him the Renaissance duality of arms and letters—

one of his own favorite themes—exists in a strange kind of imbalance, an imbalance that gives rise to a series of correspondences we should explore.

The chivalric hero, from Arthur to Roland to the Cid to Amadís and company, is characterized by the possession of, among other things, a sword. In most cases the hero's sword is not just a sword, but it possesses some magical attribute as well. In every case the sword is the most basic and essential tool of the knight's trade. In every case but one, I should say, for Don Quixote does not have a sword, at least one that is ever mentioned prominently among the items of his equipment. He has instead a magic helmet. His concern for his helmet begins in I, 1, when he discovers that the one he has is incomplete and attempts to remedy it. After fashioning a visor of cardboard he puts it to the test and destroys it (with his sword, significantly). He rebuilds it, adds some reinforcement, and as every reader knows, refrains from subjecting it to a second empirical test. This is the beginning of quixotic wisdom, the imposition of inner necessity on exterior reality. Phrased another way, this is the first occurrence of a struggle between everything that is associated with mind and everything associated with body. It is along these lines that the correspondences to which I referred above will be developed.

Don Quixote's homemade helmet is destroyed in the combat with the Vizcaíno (I, 8–9), and its lack is mentioned in the following chapter, when Don Quixote swears vengeance on him. Sancho points out that further vengeance is inappropriate, since the fellow has already promised to appear before Dulcinea. At this point Don Quixote, who still needs a helmet, falls back on the Italian epic tradition and imaginatively resurrects the *yelmo de Mambrino*, which was supposed to render its wearer invulnerable. This magical-literary helmet appears in I, 21 in the guise of a barber's basin, and in I, 44 and 45 it becomes an object of metaphysical speculation. The point here is not to rehearse one of the best-known sequences of episodes in the novel but rather to call attention to Don Quixote's preoccupation with his helmet at the expense of his sword.

Edward Dudley has written in two places that Don Quixote seeks a magic helmet and not a sword because, in contrast to the other chivalresque heros, "his head, and not his arm, is the source of his power."[9] Luis Murillo observes that the helmet is a defensive weapon, which Don Quixote uses with some success, in contrast to the sword, an offensive weapon with which he fails. The sword comes to be a symbol of Don Quixote's failure at the knight-errant's task of righting wrong and slaying dragons.[10] Unamuno remarks, in regard to Don Quixote's defeat at the hands of the Knight of the White Moon, that "you were allowed to be vanquished in order that you might come to understand that you owe your eternal life not to the force of your arm, but to your love for Dulcinea."[11]

Let us return to I, 1. Don Quixote tests his helmet with his sword, then imposes his will onto it. The imposition of will is of course a function of the mind in opposition to the body. The helmet itself is an extension of the head, just as the sword is an extension of the arm. The head and the helmet are related to our hero's psychosis and to his intellect and imagination—to the creation of himself, of Dulcinea (whom he calls the "lady of his *thoughts*"), and to the general theme of "letters." The sword and arm are related to our hero's body, to the unrealized deeds of chivalry, and to the general theme of "arms." The "sword-body" group may also be associated with real sexual acts through the mediation of the aggression common to both, and the "helmet-mind" group may be related to the sublimation of real aggressive and sexual activities through feats of the imagination.[12] This is, I think, the first tentative conclusion to which our discussion of arms and letters has led us. Don Quixote is characterized by an overwhelming preponderance of imaginative sublimation over physical implementation of sexual and aggressive drives.

Within the sphere of chivalry the arms and letters dichotomy may be referred to the aggressive, militaristic aspects of the
profession as against those involving fealty and devotion to the
lady fair. This dichotomy is not exact, for under the loving aspect
of chivalry aggression is lurking just as surely as it is overtly
present in the militaristic aspect. Nevertheless, it will prove instructive to contrast Don Quixote's reaction to and interest in
these two great themes of the books that so inspired him.

Although his first acts are to see to his armor and then to
rename his horse, and although the idea of a lady fair seems to
occur to him only as an afterthought toward the end of I, 1, Don
Quixote is in fact much more concerned with the erotic-amatory
aspects of chivalry than with the aggressive ones. It has been said
that love in the books of chivalry is a fount of abnegation and
sacrifice and is the means to the hero's moral regeneration. Love
remakes the knight in the image of the beloved, and this, as
J. A. Maravall points out, is why Don Quixote can say that
Dulcinea "fights and conquers in my person, and I live and
breathe and have my being in her" (I, 30).[13] It has also been
argued that since Don Quixote imitates Amadís and since
Amadís practiced courtly love, with *Frauendienst* and all the rest of
it, Don Quixote must therefore also practice courtly love. Amadís
was in love with Oriana from the age of twelve. So pervasive is
courtly love in his life that it comes to define not only Amadís—*el
más leal amador* ("the most loyal lover")—but the very institution
of chivalry. To be a knight-errant is to be a man in love. Avalle-
Arce notes this and remarks that Don Quixote's profession of
knight-errant, which he chose freely, implies another, which he is
not free to choose or reject, that of courtly lover. Thus, his love is
directed toward Dulcinea, who is the *summum bonum*, the fount of
all perfections; and therefore, "knight-errant" being another
form of "knight in love," Don Quixote can recognize in I, 50 that

since he has been a knight-errant-lover, he has become brave, generous, and courteous. Love has taught him those virtues.[14]

Along with these ennobling visions of love in literary tradition, we may observe, on a more prosaic level, that Don Quixote is a man with love—often simply sex—on the brain. In I, 1 the narrator tells us that our hero is a great fan of a certain Feliciano de Silva and quotes a couple of passages Don Quixote particularly favors. Now this Feliciano de Silva was a writer of books of chivalry, perhaps the first author in Western literature to commercialize artistic creation by devising a formula and turning out the books he perceived the public wanted. The passages that strike Don Quixote's fancy, however, are not from any of Silva's books of chivalry but from his *Segunda Celestina*, a continuation of the famous tale of illicit love by Fernando de Rojas. In other words, in a situation where we might logically expect Don Quixote to wax enthusiastic over some description of knightly derring-do, he chooses instead to fall in love with some declarations of love out of a book whose subject is love.

John Weiger has recently pointed out that the name our hero chooses for himself—*quixote*—means a piece of armor that covers the thigh, and he remarks that "it is hardly necessary to turn to psychologists, symbolists or etymologists in order to associate the thigh with that portion of the anatomy surrounding the genital area and traditionally used in literature as a euphemism for the sexual center of the human body." He concludes that with the name he has chosen, Don Quixote wants to "cover and protect his sexuality."[15] The question, of course, is why Don Quixote would want to cover and protect his sexuality, unless he feared that it was protruding.

In I, 2 Don Quixote begins his chivalresque adventures at a country inn, where he transforms a pair of prostitutes who happen to be hanging around into high-born maidens and adapts an old chivalric ballad to his situation. In the ballad, Sir Lancelot arrives at a castle and he and his steed are attended by maidens and *dueñas*. By changing only a few words, Don Quixote presses the old verses into service in the new context. Says Don Quixote:

> *Never was there a knight*
> *by ladies so well served,*
> *as was Don Quixote,*
> *when from his village he came.*
> *For damsels waited on him,*
> *and princesses saw to his horse.*

The original from which our hero's adaptation is taken deserves to be rendered in extenso for the light it sheds both on Don Quixote's creative processes and on what was on his mind to begin with:

> *Never was there a knight*
> *by ladies so well served,*
> *as was Sir Lancelot,*
> *when from Britain he came.*
> *For dueñas waited on him,*
> *and damsels saw to his horse.*
> *That dueña Quintañona,*
> *that one poured him his wine.*
> *The beauteous Queen Guinevere*
> *took him to bed with her.*

The ballad, it turns out, is about the illicit sexual relationship between Lancelot and Guinevere, and the bedroom scene is interrupted by a violent and bloody murder as Lancelot is obliged to defend his new lady's honor by rising in the middle of the night to slay an anonymous "Proud One" who has threatened to kill the queen's husband and then lie with her.

What Don Quixote accommodates to his needs here is a story about illicit sex and violence and not merely a fanciful description of a knight's arrival at a castle. It has been argued that because our hero omits the sex and violence, he is only interested in the arrival scene.[16] This argument would be weighty indeed if Don Quixote's source had been some recondite story known only to a few bookish cognoscenti, but one of the properties of the

Spanish *romances*—the great corpus of popular ballads—is that everybody already knows all the stories. Indeed, because the outcome is a matter of common knowledge, a ballad may break off its narration of events at a particularly dramatic moment and allow each listener to supply the denouement from his own familiarity with the story. Don Quixote does not need to allude directly to the illicit sex or the violence; the opening lines of the ballad evoke the whole story for the reader of 1605, and certainly Don Quixote must have known the story he was abbreviating.

The fact that the innkeeper, an unlettered rogue, continues the ballad Don Quixote begins to recite when he first enters the place is eloquent testimony to the vitality and pervasiveness of the ballad tradition in their society. This ballad deals with the conditions of the knight-errant's life in general. The innkeeper informs our hero that, strangely enough, there are no real beds in his inn, to which Don Quixote responds that anything will do, for "my adornments are my weapons, / my rest is to be in battle." The innkeeper continues that, in that case, your "bed must be the hard rock, / and your sleep, constant vigil."

Besides demonstrating the vitality of the ballad tradition, this particular exchange introduces a thematically important physical object for Don Quixote: a bed. In literary tradition as well as in fact, bed is associated with comfort and the presence of the spouse or lover. Don Quixote's own fantasized narration of his departure from home that very morning evokes "Aurora, who, leaving the soft couch of her jealous spouse, now showed herself. . . . " The hard ground, in contrast, is associated with deprivation of both comfort and companionship. By choosing to become a knight-errant, Don Quixote has chosen to give up bed in favor of the hard ground. Metaphorically, he chooses to deprive himself of comfort and sex. But we know that he had no bed partner, so that he cannot be depriving himself of sex. We might conclude that he is merely depriving himself of comfort, were it not for his aggressively sexual association of the Lancelot-Guinevere ballad to his being attended by the two prostitutes. This clearly indicates that our hero is by no means unconcerned with sex and forces us to conclude, at least tentatively, that in giving up his bed for the hard ground, Don Quixote is attempting to distance himself from the idea, or perhaps even the threat, of sex— covering his own sexuality, as Weiger suggests. His inability to do so completely is signaled by the Lancelot ballad, in its attenuated form, with the sex and violence edited out.

Edited out, but clearly not forgotten, as we learn in I, 13, where Don Quixote discusses the institution of chivalry with a traveler named Vivaldo he meets on the way to Grisóstomo's funeral. In response to Vivaldo's questions, Don Quixote begins by identifying King Arthur, noting that he is thought to have been transformed into a crow (which explains why Englishmen do not eat that bird), and crediting him with having founded the order of the Table Round—the origin of chivalry. But instead of proceeding from there to a discussion of feats of arms and searches for the Grail, Don Quixote moves directly to the love affair of Lancelot and Guinevere, with appropriate attention to the role of Quintañona, and finishes his discussion with a reference to the Lancelot ballad.

> It was, moreover, in the time of that good king that the famous order of the Knights of the Round Table was instituted; and as for the love of Sir Lancelot of the Lake and Queen Guinevere, everything took place exactly as the story has it, their confidante and go-between being the honored dueña Quintañona, whence comes that well-known ballad that is such a favorite in our Spain, about
>
> > *"Never was there a knight*
> > *by ladies so well served,*
> > *as was Sir Lancelot,*
> > *when from Britain he came,"*
>
> with that progression, so sweet and gentle, of the course of their bold and amorous deeds.

This suggests that for Don Quixote, the Round Table has more to do with love than with arms, and that his casting of himself in the role of Lancelot in I, 2 is a fantasy reference to, and identification with, the famous knight's erotic exploits.

In response to Vivaldo's further questioning, Don Quixote insists that all knights-errant must be in love, for love is the essence of chivalry. He even goes beyond the texts of the books of chivalry, as we shall see, and imposes a love from his own fantasy where none existed in his presumed "source." "There cannot be," he begins,

> a knight-errant without a lady, for it is as natural and proper for them to be in love as it is for the heavens to have stars, and I am quite sure that no one ever read a story in which a loveless man of arms was to be found, for the simple reason that such a one would not be looked upon as a legitimate knight but as a bastard one who had entered the fortress of chivalry not by the main gate, but over the walls, like a robber and a thief.

Even Amadís's brother Galaor, who according to the books had no special lady fair, becomes for Don Quixote secretly in love:

> And in any event, I happen to know that this knight was secretly very much in love. As for his habit of paying court to all the ladies that caught his fancy, that was a natural propensity on his part and one that he was unable to resist. There was, however, one particular lady whom he made the mistress of his will, to whom he commended himself very frequently and very secretly, for he prided himself on being a knight capable of keeping a secret.

Throughout his encounter with Vivaldo, Don Quixote is much more vehement and passionate on the subject of love than on that of arms.

His involvement in the erotic side of chivalry to the detriment of the overtly aggressive side surfaces again, toward the end of Part I, in his confrontation with the Canon of Toledo over the books of chivalry, their necessity and their uses. In I, 49, when the Canon challenges Don Quixote's perception of the veracity of the chivalresque tradition, our man responds by dividing that tradition into its two components—love affairs and feats of arms—and begins by recalling a series of famous love affairs, all derived from fiction. Again, the Lancelot-Guinevere-Quintañona affair figures prominently: "The story of Princess Floripés and Guy of Burgundy. . . . the loves of Don Tristán and Queen Iseult, like those of Guinevere and Lancelot, and there are many people who almost remember having seen the dueña Quintañona. . . . and who can deny the truth of the story of Pierres and the beautiful Magalona?" Only after the series of love affairs does Don Quixote recall some famous feats of arms, these derived entirely from history.

There is a loose thread here we should catch up, for this episode contains two of the extremely rare references Don Quixote makes to his life before chivalry and before Don Quixote. The one is warlike—our hero claims to be descended from a real, historical knight named Gutierre de Quixada—and the other erotic—he recalls that his paternal grandmother used to tell him, whenever she saw a dueña dressed in the typical "venerable" hood, that the lady in question strongly resembled the dueña Quintañona. If we can believe what Don Quixote says about Gutierre de Quixada, a real knight who achieved considerable renown around the beginning of the fifteenth century, then he must indeed be descended from an important branch of real, historical, European chivalry, of which his own armor—that "rusty armor that had belonged to his great-grandfathers" (I, 1)—is a physical talisman.[17] We should recall Don Quixote's considerable efforts to clean it up and restore it to serviceable condition, and consider these efforts a measure of the distance, in both temperament and time, between our hero and his legitimate claim to the warlike aspect of his chivalresque heritage. The anecdote involving his grandmother, however, is much more immediate, and part of Don Quixote's experience of childhood: the relation between himself as a boy, his grandmother, and the dueña Quintañona is much more real to him than is the relation between himself and Gutierre de Quixada. Phrased another way, there appears to be some relation between Don Quixote's grandmother and our hero's fixation on the Lancelot-Guinevere story with emphasis on the role of the dueña Quintañona. I might suggest in passing that Don Quixote's grandmother and Quintañona were probably about the same age, that they were possibly of analogous social station, and that the boy could have easily identified one with the other. That is, it is not impossible that when Don Quixote mentions the dueña Quintañona, as he so often does, he is unconsciously evoking the memory of his grandmother and the impression she made upon him when he was a young boy.[18]

Let us continue our discussion of Don Quixote's response to the Canon's assertion of the falsity and nonvalue of the chivalresque tradition. After enumerating the famous love affairs and feats of arms, Don Quixote, in order to impress upon the Canon the powerful appeal of the books of chivalry, invents or fantasizes an episode that he considers might be typical of the genre. As we might expect, it is not warlike, but erotic. It is the story of a knight who casts himself into a boiling lake after hearing the mournful voice of a damsel in distress issue forth from it. Upon reaching the bottom he finds a bejeweled palace, and

> trooping out of the castle gate, a goodly number of damsels . . . and the one who appears to be their leader now extends her hand to the bold knight and . . . conducts him into the splendid palace, where she makes him strip until he is as bare as when his mother bore him, and then bathes him in lukewarm water, after which she anoints him all over with sweet-smelling unguents. . . . And after all this, we are told how they take him to another chamber . . . where he finds the tables all laid . . . and all those damsels serve him in deep and impressive silence. And then, when the repast is over, . . . there enters unexpectedly . . . a damsel far more beautiful than any of the others and, seating herself at his side, she begins telling him. . . . (I, 50)

This story of beautiful maidens undressing the knight, anointing him with perfume, serving him a sumptuous meal, and then retiring in favor of one even more beautiful than they is hardly the work of a man unconcerned with the erotic aspects of chivalry. In fact, since his narration never progresses beyond the palace and the maidens, we might reasonably conclude the reverse: that Don Quixote is a man obsessed by those aspects, and relatively unconcerned with the feats of arms.

Finally, when Don Quixote meets Don Diego de Miranda ("Knight of the Green Greatcoat") in II, 16, his reaction to questions concerning chivalry and his exercise of it again emphasizes the erotic over the warlike. As he introduces himself to Don Diego, Don Quixote remarks: "I have been able in good part to carry out my design by succoring widows, protecting damsels, favoring married women, orphans, and the young."[19] All these exploits are of course fantasies, unless we exempt our hero's intervention on behalf of little Andrés in I, 4, with its disastrous aftermath in I, 31. What is interesting here is that once again Don Quixote, who might have narrated his real single combat with the Vizcaíno (I, 8), or that with the Knight of the Mirrors (II, 14) only two chapters before—both of which he won—chooses instead to fantasize a series of involvements with women. In view of what we have already seen, it is not unreasonable to suggest that Don Quixote's fantasy of coming to all these women's aid is a reaction-formation dictated by his unconscious desire to do the opposite. At the very least, we cannot but be struck by the fact that although he has ample "warlike" material to share with Don Diego, he chooses to fantasize in the erotic sphere instead.

The foregoing has been an attempt to document—with suitable references to what the text tells us about Don Quixote in action—that of the two facets of chivalry, Venus and Mars, our hero is rather more intimately involved with the former than with the latter. He waxes ecstatic over passages in his books that depict the sweet torment of love. He greets the first innkeeper and the two women on the premises with a violent ballad of illicit sex. He defines chivalry itself in terms of the adulterous affair of Guinevere and Lancelot. He insists on that same affair as part of his defense of chivalry to the Canon, on which occasion he also tells a revealing anecdote concerning his own grandmother. He makes up an erotic fantasy in order to demonstrate the appeal of chivalresque literature. And finally, he chooses to fantasize about widows and maidens and married women instead of recounting his exploits in single combat with other men. Don Quixote is, I submit, a man with sex on the brain.

Having come to understand this essential aspect of our man's psyche, we can now return to I, 1 and attempt to answer the questions I raised a moment ago: Why is Don Quixote's first line of defense—shutting himself away from other members of his household and escaping imaginatively into chivalresque literature—inadequate, and why does he leave home altogether? Put another way, we might ask what it is in Don Quixote's humdrum existence that becomes so intolerable for him at this particular point in his life and determines his retreat into psychosis.

In a most pertinent and suggestive article cited earlier, Teresa Aveleyra posits Don Quixote's inability to free himself from his libidinous attraction to Aldonza Lorenzo—either by declaring himself to her and marrying her, or by sublimating the attraction into his reading—as the proximate cause of his madness. In this she is the most recent exponent of a theory proposed long ago by Unamuno and still to be taken very seriously. In 1905 Unamuno proposed that Don Quixote, unable to overcome his timidity and declare himself to Aldonza, metamorphoses her into Dulcinea (who comes herself to incarnate "Glory") and sallies forth to perform great deeds in her name. Our hero's insanity is determined, finally, by repressed impulses of love. "And now, my Don Quixote," writes Unamuno, let me be alone with you so we can speak heart to heart and say to each other what most people cannot say even to themselves. Was it really your love of Glory that led you to incarnate Aldonza Lorenzo, whom you had once loved, in the image of Dulcinea, or was it your ill-fated love for the good-looking farm girl that you transposed into a love of immortality? You fell in love when you were about forty . . . and your timidity, your insuperable timidity of a country hidalgo getting on in years. . . . And this love constrained, this love blocked in its path, for you could not find the force or the will to direct it along its natural course, this poor love formed your soul and was the fount of your heroic madness. Is that not true, my good knight? You probably didn't suspect it yourself. . . . There are loves that cannot break out of the vase that contains them, and so spill over inward. Their tremendous fatality sublimates and aggrandizes them. And, imprisoned there, ashamed and hiding from themselves, struggling to attain their own death, since they cannot flower in daylight and much less reach fruition, they become a passion for glory and immortality and heroism. Wouldn't you have given all the Glory in the world for a loving glance from your Aldonza Lorenzo?[20]

Unamuno is even more explicit, if possible, in a letter to Juan Zorrilla de San Martín, in which he relates the repressed love for Aldonza to the massive involvement in reading books of chivalry.

You do not know, my good friend, how much your letter did for me. Of everything that has been said to me concerning my *Vida de D. Quijote*, what you say is what excites me the most. You are the only one who has shown me the most painful personal discovery in my book, that Don Quixote's madness was a madness of love, a love both timid and ashamed, and that in order to silence it he gave himself over to reading books of chivalry.[21]

In 1905 Unamuno saw clearly the importance to the process of her sublimation into Dulcinea, and her ultimate metamorphosis into "La Gloria," of Don Quixote's having worshiped Aldonza from afar for twelve years. At about the same time, Freud was working out his theory of sublimation. Unamuno's ideas, with appropriate Freudian foundation, were reaffirmed in a well-known paper by Helene Deutsch in 1934,[22] and more recently by Donald Palmer in 1971.[23] We owe Unamuno a great debt of gratitude, for it was he who first began to place the behavior of a great literary character within the general context of possible, even plausible, human behavior. It appears in retrospect, however, that Unamuno did most of his thinking about this particular aspect of Don Quixote's personality and career in the early stages of the preparation of his book. He seems to have believed he had discovered a formula, which he states early on and then applies mechanically to his analysis of the remainder of the work. His Don Quixote is the same on page 200 as on page 2. Even when Don Quixote is on his deathbed Unamuno insists on Aldonza, when in fact Aldonza is not even a character in the second part of the novel. By the time Part II begins, she has been completely surpassed, in favor of Dulcinea. That is, Unamuno fails to take into account Don Quixote's history, the evolution, as a result of his contacts with the real world over a long period of time, of his behavior and of its unconscious motivation. The present work is an attempt to modify Unamuno's original hypothesis in the direction of increased psychic verisimilitude and to examine Don Quixote's interaction with the world, especially with women, throughout the two parts of the novel.

Unamuno's hypothesis, leaving aside its mechanical application, makes perfect sense until we ask ourselves why someone like Don Quixote should fall in love with someone like Aldonza Lorenzo, whom he does not know at all and who, as Sancho demonstrates so brutally in I, 25, is anything but his type. One does not normally fall in love with someone one sees a total of four times in twelve years, the frequency of Don Quixote's contact with Aldonza, as he tells Sancho in the same chapter. The fact is, as psychoanalysis has shown and everyone's personal experience corroborates, that we humans fall in love first with the immediate members of our families, and that the psychic energy (*libido*) invested (*cathected*) in these childhood relationships must be trans-

ferred during adolescence and early adulthood to members—
finally, to one member—of the opposite sex whose age is appropriate to our own if we are to reach maturity. The first woman in
every man's life is his mother, and the first man in every woman's
is her father. I mention these well-known facts of life here not to
suggest that Don Quixote suffers from some unresolved oedipal
conflicts, although that may very well be true, but rather in order
to insist on an obvious but frequently taken-for-granted corollary
of the family romance: the simple fact that our affects are most
forcibly engaged by those who are closest to us, with whom we
share the spaces (hearth, table, bed) and the times—in the sense
of both specific diurnal occasions and the accumulation of common experience, the growth of sensitivity to personality and
moods—of intimacy as well. This suggests that we should set
Aldonza aside for a moment and begin our search for Don
Quixote's unconfessed love object closer to home. We must consider the two real women with whom he shares the time and space
of intimacy: his housekeeper and his niece.

They are introduced in I, 1, first with reference to their ages
("Living with him were a housekeeper in her forties and a niece
who was not yet twenty"), and then specifically in relation to Don
Quixote's craving for chivalresque action, his desire to "real-ize"
the events described in his books ("And he would have liked very
well to have had his fill of kicking that traitor Galalón, a privilege
for which he would have given his housekeeper, with his niece
thrown into the bargain"). That is, at the very beginning a nexus
is established where Don Quixote's desire for action, his obsessive
reading of the books of chivalry (already defined as an attempt to
compensate for the monotony of his existence and to provide an
outlet for nearly intolerable erotic impulses), and the women in
his household all converge. Furthermore, the relation established
among these various elements is a precise one that may be para-
phrased thus: If Don Quixote could lose himself sufficiently in his
reading, he would then be free of the women. Phrased another

way, if he could only engage in a socially acceptable form of violence—all socially acceptable violence being a sublimation of unacceptable erotic impulses—he would be rid of the immediate object or objects of the erotic impulses and relief would be his.

These connections are admittedly tenuous at this point, but they are there, as the text shows, and they precede any mention of Aldonza Lorenzo. If it is true, as Unamuno, Bigeard, Aveleyra, and the others have demonstrated, that love precedes the obsessive reading and is not some kind of obligatory afterthought, then the fact that Aldonza is not mentioned until the end of the chapter suggests that it is she, Aldonza, who is the afterthought. The text confirms this hypothesis as well. After Don Quixote puts his arms in order, after he names his horse, and after he names himself, he casts about for someone with whom he can fall in love—in his new capacity of knight-errant. This last is an important qualification, for as we are seeing, the entire enterprise of being Don Quixote is at this point a function of his need to escape the existing situation: his status as hidalgo, his limited friendships, his ménage. In his new identity as knight-errant he needs a lady fair. Enter Aldonza.

The critics who have concerned themselves with the niece and the housekeeper have in the main dismissed them as drab and uninteresting, mandatory items of equipment in the household of a country hidalgo. Carmen Castro, however, has called attention to the radical difference in personality between the two women and Don Quixote. In her view, our hero needs them precisely because they are what she calls *inconvivibles* ('impossible to live with'). It is his need to free himself from them, she argues, that drives Don Quixote to the books of chivalry and then into an existence based on fantasy.[24] Castro's point is that these two women propel Don Quixote out of the house because they are so utterly devoid of interest for him. I agree—but for the opposite reason—that they are of crucial importance and that it is they who turn our hero inward, to the books of chivalry, and then propel him out of the house altogether. These women may be objectively dull, in terms of their ability to talk politics or literature, or to strum the guitar and sing, but they are by no means uninteresting, as I hope to show.

The time has come to return to the ideas I developed in chapter 2 and to recall here that not only is Don Quixote an hidalgo, a member of a redundant and useless social class condemned to an existence that is monotony itself, that not only is he the only man in a house populated by two women, with whom he shares the intimacy of time and space, and that not only does he have sex on the brain to the point of regularly conceiving the institution of chivalry entirely or predominantly in erotic terms with obsessive insistence on one particular adulterous affair, but he is also a fifty-year-old man with all that that implies. Avalle-Arce is one of a few recent critics who insist on this important fact. In two introductory pages of his provocative recent study the word *cincuentón* ('fifty-year-old-man') appears ten times to describe our hero as the novel begins.[25] Avalle-Arce further insists on the importance of Don Quixote's fifty-year prehistory, even though it is not narrated, to his history proper. Luis Murillo remarks on Don Quixote's age and status as mid-lifer in a more offhand but equally significant way. Regarding our hero as he sallies forth for the first time, Murillo comments, "the hidalgo evokes a mythical and youthful Apollo at the outset as if to signal a regeneration of his middle-aged powers, for the fictional cast he assumes for them, as an impassioned Roland or Amadís, are those of a youth's prowess."[26] Daniel Levinson observes that "there is an Age Fifty Transition, which normally lasts from about age fifty to fifty-five. The functions of this period of middle adulthood are similar to those of the Age Thirty Transition in early adulthood." He further notes that "it may be a time of crisis for the men who changed too little in their Mid Life Transition and then built an unsatisfactory life structure."[27] The last description applies to no one if not to Don Quixote.

Don Quixote acts like a real person, a real man of approximately fifty years of age in a not particularly uncommon situation, accompanied at home by his housekeeper and his young niece. It is precisely because the character of Don Quixote is so realistic, precisely because he acts the way real people act, that we must give up the idea of a long-standing secret love for Aldonza Lorenzo and turn instead to another hypothesis, one much more realistic in both literary and psychic terms. Because it is only just now ceasing to be a taboo subject, this hypothesis is bound to make us uncomfortable and uneasy and to elicit from us immediate and powerful reactions of denial. Nevertheless, I submit, it is the only one that offers a satisfactory explanation in human terms for Don Quixote's bizarre mid-life behavior. It is my belief that Don Quixote's retreat into psychosis at age fifty is his last, desperate defense against intolerable and forbidden libidinous urges— concretely, a powerful incestuous desire for his niece, who has matured from girlhood to young womanhood in his household, under his care, day by day, month by month, year by year, at the same time that he is experiencing the stress of mid-life, in its two aspects of the crisis of generativity versus stagnation and of the powerful resurgence of the *Sturm und Drang* of adolescence, in turn with its characteristic crisis of intimacy versus isolation.

This unfortunate temporal coincidence, by no means unique to Don Quixote, is summarized, first negatively and then in a positive way, by Vaillant:

> The adolescence of children and the second adolescence of their parents do not usually harmonize. Thirty-year-old men have fun bringing up their grade-school-age children . . . but at age forty fathers often acted as if there were no kinship to their adolescent children at all. *They were unaware that the heightened sexuality that so frightened them in their daughters was often a projection of their own forbidden wishes toward their suddenly attractive children* [emphasis added]. On the other hand, the importance of the interaction between teenage and middle-aged adolescents cannot be overemphasized. In his discovery of his adolescent children, the adult remembers, rediscovers and often defensively reworks parts

of himself. The adolescent has the capacity to get under our skin, rekindle old flames, and to stimulate parents in parts of their innermost selves, that they had forgotten existed.[28]

In the more colorful parlance of Los Angeles, Roger Gould avers, "As fathers, we do what we can to avoid staring at our daughters' curves or their friends who make a game out of seducing us; we do what we can to keep our wives from knowing."[29] Peck and Berkowitz make what they call "sexual integration" an important aspect of their study of healthy versus neurotic patterns of aging and observe that

> at the high end of the scale, these elements [various manifestations of the capacity to mesh one's sexual desires with other aspects of life] are integrated into a harmonious pattern. At the low end there may be either free indulgence of sexual impulse without regard for other aspects of the relationship or, on the other hand, intense repression. In the latter case, sexuality may become either unacceptable or so guilt-ridden that sexual behavior is emotionally dissociated from the self-concept as well as from the affectional aspects of human relationships.[30]

It cannot be emphasized enough that Peck and Berkowitz, along with Vaillant, are referring to mainly normal individuals who have at least had a sex life. In this sense Don Quixote is below the low end of the scale. As I observed in chapter 2, his particular resurgence at fifty of the crisis of adolescence is the resurgence of a crisis unresolved. Whatever it was that stunted our hero's psychic growth in his youth and caused him to evolve into a reclusive old bachelor with a hyperactive, compensatory fantasy life, whatever prevented him as a young man from displacing his normal oedipal desires onto some appropriate woman, courting, marrying, and having a family, is what now reemerges as his niece grows into young womanhood before his eyes.

The forbidden desire for his niece being of course intolerable, he defends against it first by throwing himself into his reading, hoping a vicarious experience of sex and violence will compensate for the realities of his situation. This first defense proves inadequate, as we have seen, and Don Quixote falls back to the extreme of denying his present existence, creating himself anew as a knight-errant, and leaving home altogether. At this point an erotic interest—a lady fair—becomes not only acceptable but obligatory, and he is able to begin to displace the unacceptable desire for his niece onto another, more appropriate woman. Enter Aldonza, a high-spirited farm girl from nearby El Toboso. This girl, as Sancho tells us in I, 25, is "a sturdy wench, fit as a fiddle and right in the middle of everything that's doing," capable of "tossing a bar with the lustiest lad in the village." "There is nothing prudish about her; she's very friendly with everybody and always laughing and joking."

Sancho's description of Aldonza begins to explain a curious phenomenon, namely, that Don Quixote's displacement of his forbidden desire for his niece onto her is not successful. Perhaps Aldonza is simply not a credible substitute for the niece. She is, according to Sancho's description, nothing if not gross, extroverted, and physical, whereas it is reasonable to conjecture that the niece, like her uncle, is slight of figure and spiritual of mien. Carlos Varo has remarked that Aldonza is clearly from a family of pecheros and presumably disqualified by that fact from involvement with a member of the hidalgo class.[31] It has also been suggested that Aldonza, like most residents of El Toboso, was of Moorish ancestry and presumably disqualified on those grounds from a relationship with Don Quixote, who has been variously described as both an Old and a New Christian. Perhaps Don Quixote is not ready for a real relationship with any woman, and in that sense, since he cannot bring himself to approach her, Aldonza becomes even more threatening than his niece. Whatever the reasons, the fact is that Aldonza Lorenzo is not an appropriate substitute for the niece, and she herself is immediately metamorphosed or sublimated into Dulcinea del Toboso.

Now, finally, Don Quixote has an outlet for his libido that is both acceptable (not his niece) and nonthreatening (not the jovially physical Aldonza). His libido itself can now suffer a transformation from sexual into aggressive energy that is ready to be employed in feats of arms undertaken in the service of justice and the ideals of chivalry. Furthermore, this new situation will take our hero both out of his house, with its oppressive atmosphere, and away from El Toboso, since the rules of chivalry that Don Quixote chooses to remember involve sending some vanquished malefactor to grovel at the lady's feet but do not require the knight's own presence there.

The "Unamuno hypothesis," to the effect that Don Quixote was secretly and hopelessly in love with Aldonza from about the age of forty, lacks psychic verisimilitude for the reasons we have seen. Don Quixote hardly knows Aldonza, he has seen her four times in twelve years, he has never spoken to her, and she is his polar opposite in both physical characteristics and personality. It is simply against logic and nature that he should love her. It is much more probable that he should be attracted to at least one of the women in his own household, either the housekeeper of approximately his own age or the niece who has matured physically while her uncle was experiencing the uncomfortable resurgence of his unresolved adolescent intrapsychic conflicts. Those interested in Cervantine irony may be amused to note that Cervantes has equipped his hero, a paradigmatic case of repressed sexuality never able to find its proper object, with two female companions whose respective stations—niece and housekeeper—identify them as the paradigmatic cases of illicit sexual companionship for presumably celibate men.[32] Of the two, the niece seems much the more logical choice, by reason both of the blood relationship she has with her uncle and of her age, as it is normal for men in mid-life to turn away from women their own age and seek out younger ones as they attempt to deny their own advancing years. Aldonza Lorenzo comes forward not as the original (impossible) object of Don Quixote's affections but in a much more realistic way as his first, failed attempt to find an acceptable substitute for his niece, who is the real original (impossible and unacceptable) love object. Aldonza presents her own problems, however, and must herself be rendered neutral by promotion to the rank of imaginary princess, unattainable by definition.

All this makes perfect sense, and an unconscious mechanism for controlling the psychic conflicts that Don Quixote has been experiencing as he progresses through mid-life appears to have been found. Yet as every reader knows, this is not the end but the beginning of our man's adventures. Two crucial problems are now created, and Don Quixote will have to deal with them as he makes his way in the world through the two parts of the novel. First, if she is to be viable even as a symbol, Dulcinea must have more to her than simply a name. Furthermore, in the course of his travels Don Quixote will be requested to describe her to those whose fealty to her he would command, and if he merely offers a description of Aldonza, Dulcinea will collapse. Aldonza will emerge in her place, and Don Quixote will have re-created the difficulties he thought he had solved at the end of I, 1. If Don Quixote is to survive as Don Quixote, he must succeed in making Dulcinea independent of Aldonza. Second, as Serrano Plaja has pointed out, for all his erotic problems Don Quixote is still a man who can be and is attracted to women.[33] In fact, as we have seen, his active but misdirected libido has determined his entire predicament. And since approximately half the people in the world are women, Don Quixote is bound to meet some to whom he is attracted in the course of his travels. As we know, however, Don Quixote is historically incapable of normal relationships with women. He is attracted to, but terrified by, them. His attraction to various of the women he meets will be a source not of satisfaction but of its opposite: an intense experience of anxiety and a threat which must be neutralized. That is, his original and still unresolved problems with his own sexuality are bound to resurface in some form in his encounters with women on the road. Don

Quixote's unswerving devotion to Dulcinea must be mobilized to help our hero keep these threats at bay.

Phrased another way, beginning with I, 2 the novel will have as one of its major themes the relation between Dulcinea (with all that lies behind her) and the real women Don Quixote meets in his travels. This will involve, on the one hand, her use as a buffer between the knight and the women he experiences as threatening and dangerous and, on the other, his progressive creation of her as an independent reality, distinct from Aldonza Lorenzo and, of course, from his niece. It is extraordinarily difficult to separate these aspects and deal with them individually without doing violence to the novel's almost miraculously seamless structure. There is a constant dialectic of memory, based on both reading and experience, with the situation of the moment which renders such analysis practically impossible. The reader will therefore have to bear with my predominantly chronological presentation of Dulcinea and the women, which at least offers the possibility of underscoring the historical evolution of the hero and of his unconscious motivations. We must keep in mind that we are dealing here with a life in a great work of art, which is furthermore the story of a life created, both consciously and unconsciously, as though it were a work of art. I will strive to do it as little violence as possible.

4
DULCINEA AND
THE REAL WOMEN:
Part I

Don Quixote's first recorded erotic adventure occurs in I, 2 as he rides forth for the first time, having slipped out of his house early on a hot July morning. It is a fantasy, part of a larger fantasy in which our hero conjures up his own historian and attributes to him (creates for him) a mythological dawn description, featuring the "rosy Dawn, arising from the soft couch of her jealous husband." At this point he addresses himself imaginatively to "Princess Dulcinea, mistress of this captive heart," and accuses her of having ordered him out of her presence. "Great wrong have you done me in sending me away and reproaching me with the rigorous mandate that I not appear in your beauteous presence. May it please you, my lady, to remember this subject heart of yours, that suffers such pangs for your love."

This is one of the clearest examples in the entire text of the unconscious relationship between Dulcinea and Don Quixote's niece. Aldonza Lorenzo could not possibly be responsible for the enforced exile of which Don Quixote speaks, for as he tells us later, he has been in her presence a grand total of four times in his life. Assuming, though, that she had banished him, he would merely be required to stay at home in order to comply, since the two of them live in different towns. Our hero's exile, however, is an exile from his own home and from the woman in whose presence he experiences intolerable discomfort: his niece, or as I shall call her (using the Spanish term), Sobrina. She has not actively ordered her uncle out of her sight, of course, but in a very real sense he is responding to the pressure she has unwittingly been exerting on him. If we ascribe Don Quixote's furtive departure from his home to the rigor of Aldonza Lorenzo, or to the force of literary tradition, we rob it of any possible verisimilar motivation and do violence to both our knowledge of human life and any serious artistic re-creation of it.

In the same chapter our hero begins actively to interact with real women, in an atmosphere charged with eroticism. He arrives at a country inn, which, through the mechanism of delusional projection of his own inner needs, he transforms into a castle. At the door are two youngish prostitutes, whom by the same mechanism he transforms into *doncellas* (noble maidens who serve in a great household). He adapts the erotic ballad of Lancelot—attended, as he says, by doncellas and princesses, then bedded by Queen Guinevere—to his own situation and allows the two women to remove his armor but not his helmet as he sits down to eat.[1] This last is an important detail and invites reflection. The situation is ambiguous, because Don Quixote is willing to be undressed, but not entirely. This less-than-total willingness to submit to the procedure is probably a manifestation of his underlying ambivalence in erotic matters generally. Quite simply put, Don Quixote wants to, but he doesn't want to. Given his preoccupation with his head (intellect and fantasy) as opposed to his arms, it is logical that he should be most anxious that that part of him remain protected. It is also possible that he insists on keeping himself covered because he is in the presence of two young women whose existence is defined by erotic activity, whom he also finds attractive, and to whom he is reluctant to reveal his grizzled, fifty-year-old face lest they find it unattractive and prosaic—a poor country hidalgo instead of a knight in shining armor. Don Quixote projects his needs onto these two prostitutes by promoting them to chivalric rank, but by no means does he desexualize them, as his every action in their presence dramatizes.

In I, 4 Don Quixote is forced to begin seriously the arduous task of creating a Dulcinea independent of both Aldonza and Sobrina, as a result of his chance encounter with a party of Toledan merchants. These gentlemen are proceeding down the road when our hero places himself in their path, stops them, and demands that they confess Dulcinea the most beautiful woman in the world. The merchants are reluctant to make such an affirmation sight unseen, and Don Quixote insists that they accept his premise on faith. In fact, he invokes a sequence of mental processes appropriate to the willful acquisition and defense of a militant religious faith and totally irrelevant to any question of physical beauty. "What is important," he says, "is that without seeing her, you must believe, confess, affirm, swear and defend. . . ." Don Quixote's analogy, between belief in Dulcinea's beauty and belief in an unseen, invisible, incorporeal God, has the effect of presenting Dulcinea herself as invisible and incorporeal. This is the first step in the process of separating her from Aldonza and Sobrina: total abstraction. The solution is of course untenable, and the merchants are in any event not disposed to let Don Quixote off so easily. They suggest that a representation, a portrait—a kind of analogue of Platonized Christianity—will do, and then take the final, irrevocable step. "And I believe that we are already so much on your side that even if her portrait should show her to be blind in one eye and with red and yellow discharge in the other one, in order to please you we'll say anything you want us to in her favor."

Don Quixote's incorporeal Dulcinea has suddenly been replaced by a physical vision of her that is of course unacceptable to him and that must be neutralized and then itself replaced. "There is no discharge," he retorts, "but amber and civet wrapped in cotton; and she is not one-eyed or hunchbacked, but straighter than a spindle from Guadarrama." Don Quixote's description of concrete, visualizable attributes is of capital importance, for it represents the first step away from the bloodless abstraction he had initially attempted to substitute for any real woman in his life. Dulcinea begins quite literally to take form, and she does so thanks to a dialectical process in which an unacceptable vision imposed from without must be countered by a creative effort generated from within.[2]

The real women who inhabit Don Quixote's household and whose uncomfortable propinquity drove him from home make their first appearance as speaking characters in the interim between his first sally, which ends in I, 4, and his second, which begins in I, 7. Ama (housekeeper) and Sobrina function as a kind of chorus, commenting on Don Quixote's flight into madness and the books that appear to have been responsible. In paired speeches with the priest and the barber each offers her own interpretation. A difference in their respective orientations is worth noting. Ama, a woman of Don Quixote's age, although his social inferior, identifies with her master, cursing those books that have "overturned the most subtle and delicate mind in all La Mancha." Sobrina, by contrast, identifies with the forces of social conformity and berates herself for not having denounced her uncle's strange behavior to the authorities so that appropriate corrective action could have been taken. In addition, she actually confronts Don Quixote and attempts to dissuade him from any further exercise of folly. In her speech she suggests a comparison between her uncle's sallying forth and the proverbial characters who "go for wool and come back shorn." Don Quixote reacts, not to the general spirit of his niece's remarks, but specifically and angrily to the cliché about getting shorn. "Oh niece of mine, how little you understand of these matters! Before they shear me, I will have plucked and stripped the beards of any who dare to touch the tip of a single hair of mine." By focusing on the sanctity of his beard, Don Quixote has turned Sobrina's remark about fools rushing in into some kind of attack on his manhood. The beard is a symbol of masculinity, an upwardly displaced analogue of the virile member. The medieval insult consisting in pulling some hairs out of another man's beard, most familiar in Spanish literature through the story of the Cid ("he of the great beard") and his enemy Count Garci Ordóñez, is thus an upwardly displaced symbolic attack on his genitals. This is the unconscious chain of associations that leads Don Quixote to react so vehemently to Sobrina's offhand remark.

By the middle of I, 7 both Ama and Sobrina have again been left behind and Don Quixote is once again on the road. This time, however, he is not alone, but accompanied by his squire, Sancho Panza. The relationship between these two men has already been the subject of considerable discussion, so I shall limit myself to remarking that, like Don Quixote, Sancho is leaving behind a household dominated by women, and that these women—Sancho's wife Teresa and his daughter Sanchica—are analogous by their ages to Ama and Sobrina. Sancho and Don Quixote seem to be approximately the same age. It is possible, then, that their analogous behavior—mid-life career change consisting in abandonment of a household filled with women and striking out in search of adventure in the company of another man—might be the result of analogous motivation. That is, rather than considering Don Quixote and Sancho, respectively, as the incarnations of idealism and materialism or of the New and Old Christian segments of society, it may be more instructive from the point of view of verisimilar fiction to consider them simply as two men in mid-life who respond each in his own way to the pressures of that season. It is more than likely, for example, that Sancho has been affected by Sanchica's passage through puberty into young womanhood as Don Quixote has been affected by Sobrina's. In Sancho's case the superego pressure to remove himself from that intolerable situation is probably complemented by another kind of desire, to get away from a wife he experiences as shrewish and nagging. His first name for her is "mi oíslo" ("my 'Are you listening to me?' ").[3]

We should not push these analogies too far, however, especially now. We must not, for example, lose sight of the fact that
Sancho is not a reclusive, celibate bachelor like his master but has
had some experience with women, experience that has led in the
normal way to marriage and fatherhood. Sancho never believes
himself to be anyone other than Sancho Panza; his association
with Don Quixote does not involve the assumption of a new
being, as it does for his master. Like Don Quixote, Sancho is
escaping from his ménage, but unlike him, he is not escaping into
psychosis. For the present it is enough to note the similarities and
differences between the two men and between the situations from
which their relationship arises. I shall have occasion to chart the
course of that relationship as it evolves.

Their first adventure together is of course that of the windmills in I, 8. As Don Quixote rides to the attack he "commends
himself with all his heart to his lady Dulcinea, beseeching her to
come to his aid in this peril," an imitation of knightly behavior
derived from the books of chivalry. That night, again in imitation
of his bookish models, Don Quixote remains awake "thinking of
his lady Dulcinea, in order to accommodate himself to what he
had read, when the knights spent many nights kept awake by
memories of their ladies." By morning, however, something
interesting has happened. "Don Quixote refused breakfast
because, as we have noted, he sustained himself on savory
memories." The memories of the preceding night belonged to
the knights in the books. Those of the morning are Don Quixote's
own. Clearly, he cannot be remembering any encounter with
Dulcinea, whom he has yet to met, and it is extremely unlikely that
Aldonza Lorenzo's four flashes across our hero's consciousness
could have been the source of those "savory memories." They
should rather be ascribed to their most verisimilar source; the girl
he left behind him. Only Sobrina has spent enough time imping-
ing on both Don Quixote's consciousness and his unconscious to
provide the kind of psychic sustenance to which he refers.

Until now our hero's efforts to block Sobrina out of his mind and replace her with a mental image of a Dulcinea who is neither she nor Aldonza have been severely hampered by his limited exposure to other women. He did his best with the two prostitutes in I, 2, and he conjured up a vision both clear of eye and straight of spine in I, 4, but the uncomfortable fact is that he really has nowhere to turn for inspiration except to the ladies of his books, who kept him awake at night, and to Sobrina, who nourished him the following morning. Don Quixote's frustration is present below the surface of the oft-quoted Discourse on the Golden Age with which he regales the goatherds in I, 11. Louis Combet has observed that the knight's speech is "saturated with sexuality," that approximately half of it is devoted to erotic themes, and that these themes are entirely absent from the source material (Ovid and Vergil) Don Quixote follows practically word for word on the subjects of nature's abundance, the absence of greed and fraud, and the like. Combet concludes that Don Quixote's nostalgia for the Golden Age is a nostalgia for the undifferentiated primitive eroticism of the breast, a desire to return to a time when sexual differences—the division of the race into men and women, and consequent necessity to interact with the opposite sex—were irrelevant.[4] Combet's provocative analysis suggests the pervasiveness of Don Quixote's obsession with sex, in uneasy coexistence with the absence from his life of any real women except the one whose presence is intolerable. This lack will begin to be remedied in the same chapter, when Don Quixote and Sancho are drawn into the orbit of the beautiful Marcela and the men who pursue her.

A kind of thematic introduction to the story of Marcela and her suitors is provided by a love song sung by a certain Antonio to his beloved Olalla and overheard by Don Quixote and Sancho. Antonio sings about normal physical attraction, which he hopes will lead to marriage. If Olalla is unwilling to "yoke herself to him in Christian matrimony," he threatens to remain in the mountains forever or become a Capuchin monk. Antonio's situation is never resolved, for his recital is interrupted by news of the death of Grisóstomo from his unrequited love for Marcela. The Grisóstomo-Marcela situation is analogous to that of Antonio and Olalla, although the former story is fleshed out and extended through a wonderfully Cervantine demonstration of the technical possibilities of multiple narrative points of view in relation to the creation of character.

The analysis of this literary practice will be the subject of another study. For the present it is important to summarize what we know about Marcela from secondhand sources—the goatherds, Grisóstomo's suicide note in verse, Ambrosio—and compare that with her own presentation of herself, her values and her motivations. Marcela is a girl who has blossomed into a strikingly beautiful young woman. She has attracted virtually all the local lads as well as those from the nearby villages as her swains. Her beauty is accompanied by the possesion of wealth, inherited from her parents, who have left her an orphan. She lives with her celibate priest uncle—a fact that suggests an analogy with Don Quixote and Sobrina—who administers her estate and takes responsibility for her person. Offers of marriage have been made, which she has declined. Her uncle is not displeased by her decision to postpone marriage, and Pedro the goatherd, our source for this information, obliquely suggests why when he observes that Uncle "took no notice of the profit that would accrue to him as long as his niece remained unmarried." In the next sentence he remarks that malicious small-town gossip had accused the good gentleman of precisely the opposite. The relationship between Marcela and her uncle, of which we are offered an ambiguous, partial, and finally unsatisfactory glimpse through Pedro's narration, is obviously a complex one, and Marcela's subsequent behavior is clearly motivated to some degree by it. But it is useless for us to speculate. What we know for certain is that Marcela rejects marriage, at least for the time being: "She did not care to marry and, because she was still so young, did not feel herself capable of bearing the burden of matrimony." She also rejects her uncle's company, for after he has accepted her decision and called off the suitors, she suddenly abandons his household, transforms herself into a shepherdess, and goes about the countryside with her flock. She has chosen for herself an existence based on a literary model—the shepherdesses of *La Diana* and *La Galatea* in general—just as Don Quixote has based his on Amadís, Orlando, and company. Even before they meet their choice of a literary lifestyle may be considered a common bond between them. I would prefer, however, to call attention to the fact that both Marcela and Don Quixote have chosen such a life-style as their response to an intolerable domestic situation and that this may constitute a still greater bond between them.

In choosing her new life as shepherdess, Marcela has rejected marriage—the expected behavior for a young woman her age—rejected her uncle and a domestic situation we can only guess at, and simultaneously put herself on view not just to the rustic swains who had previously heard of her beauty but to every man of every station in the surrounding area. As Pedro observes: "And as soon as she went out in public and her beauty was discovered, I can't tell you how many wealthy young men, both nobles and farmers, have put on shepherd's clothing and are out courting her in the countryside." Pedro is quick to point out, however, that although she has put herself on view, and although she engages freely in conversation with the men who pursue her, she has never done anything that might redound to the discredit of her honor, and "as soon as one of them declares his intentions, even if they are the most holy and just, leading to marriage, she flings him away from her like a catapult." From the point of view of the men involved, who judge her conduct only insofar as it relates to them, Marcela is a bitch, a tease who raises their hopes only to dash them cruelly. As more detached observers, we are in a position to remark that Marcela's behavior is motivated by ambivalent attitudes. Like Don Quixote, she wants to but she doesn't want to. She is obviously attracted to men—otherwise there would be no point in her putting herself on display as she has done—but she is terrified by the possibility of real physical intimacy. Not only does she reject marriage as an institution but she "flings from her like a catapult" any man who begins to encroach on her private space.[5]

"Freedom," preservation of some territorial integrity, fear of intimacy, terror of the vulnerability necessary to any serious relationship with a man, rejection of marriage as an institution—all these intellectual and psychic concepts crystallize for Marcela in their physical analogue: the preservation of virginity. And in fact the entire episode featuring herself, Grisóstomo, and the latter's friend Ambrosio is an examination of the human consequences of the psychic attitudes that lead to the rejection of marriage and glorification of virginity as a theological posture. The names of the players reveal Cervantes's game.

Grisóstomo is the Spanish version of Greek Chrysostom, a name whose only resonance is through the writings of Saint John Chrysostom, one of the post-Nicene Greek fathers of the church. Saint John lived a mildly ascetic life at Antioch in the fourth century, studying while living with his devoted mother. Upon her death in 373 or 374 he moved into the country to practice asceticism in earnest. For four years, under the direction of an old Syrian monk, he lived the life of a zenobite. Then in 378 he retired alone to a cave in Mount Sylpios, devoting himself to reading the Old and New Testaments and in the process ruining his already fragile health. He returned to Antioch in 380 and was ordained deacon in 381. He composed most of his ascetic treatises during his tenure as deacon. Representative titles include: *Against the Detractors of the Monastic Life*, *To the Young Widow*, and *On Virginity*. This last offers a comparison of the relative advantages and disadvantages of marriage. Marriage has in its favor, first, that it saves those who enter into it from fornication, and second, that it serves to glorify virginity by contrast. Its disadvantages are manifold: incompatibility between the spouses, jealousy that can lead to violence, conflicts created by unions unequal in terms of wealth, anxiety brought on by fear of illness and death, anxiety of the bride about to be married to a man she hardly knows, frictions with the in-laws over matters relating to the dowry, and finally, the care and education of children.[6] To say the least, Chrysostom goes well beyond Saint Paul in recommending celibacy over marriage. His work enjoyed great influence, and *On Virginity* is one of the standard sources of support for the dogma of the virginity of Mary. The name of Marcela's ill-fated lover, in other words, leads the reader, through an ironical Cervantine about-face, to an unimpeachable source of justification for the life-style that Marcela herself has adopted.

The name of Grisóstomo's friend Ambrosio has practically identical resonances, in this case to Saint Ambrose, Bishop of Milan, a scholar, father of the church, and staunch defender of virginity. In 367 Ambrose translated Flavius Josephus's *De bello judaico* from Greek into Latin. In 374 he was named bishop and was baptized. There followed a number of treatises on the subject of chastity, for example, *De viduis, De virginitate, De institutione virginis et de S. Mariae virginitate perpetua,* and *Exhortatio virginitatis.* This last was the title of a sermon he delivered in 394 at the dedication of a basilica financed by a wealthy widow. Of all these works, the one that most interests us is one, written in 377, whose complete title is *De Virginibus, ad Marcellinam sororem libri tres*: It seems that Ambrose had an older sister named Marcellina, who took vows of chastity and received the veil of the Consecrated Virgins from the hand of Pope Liberius in the Vatican Basilica in 353.[7]

The three principals in Cervantes's story of the unfortunate consequences of insistence on the preservation of virginity (Marcela, Grisóstomo, and Ambrosio) all have names prominently associated in the Christian tradition precisely with the rejection of marriage and the glorification of virginity. This cannot be due merely to coincidence. Nor is it coincidental that Erasmus translated the sermons and homilies of both Ambrose and Chrysostom, so that Cervantes might have had access to them directly or through his first mentor, the Erasmian Juan López de Hoyos. It is the nexus of Erasmus and his ideas concerning the relative merits of the monastic versus the active life, virginity versus marriage, which enables Cervantes to ironize on the names of three professional virgins. But Cervantes goes beyond Erasmus by creating a fiction involving a verisimilar character, Marcela, who like Don Quixote cannot mesh her own psychic life with the normal expectations of her society and who takes refuge in a syndrome of bizarre, antisocial behavior.[8] Her defense of this behavior, structured around the sacred notion of "freedom" in her speech to the assembled company at Grisóstomo's funeral, is both self-serving and self-deceiving, the former because it allows her to disclaim any responsibility for the young man's death, and the latter because it allows her to conceal from herself the real motivation for her flight into the freedom and purity of nature.

Don Quixote's positive reaction to Marcela is too well known to bear repetition here as a general phenomenon. I should like to point out, however, that before he even meets her his imagination has been fired by what he has heard about her, and he identifies with her many suitors. After hearing Pedro's narration he "passed most of the night in memories of his lady Dulcinea, in imitation of Marcela's lovers" (I, 12). Don Quixote assimilates Marcela to Dulcinea, and himself to her other lovers. That is, he first perceives her as an ambiguously charged erotic object, at once the object of his desires and by definition safely unattainable. This apparently insignificant throwaway phrase also suggests how Don Quixote might incorporate new experience into the unconscious substructure of his thought, with consequent evolution of the thought itself. What he has heard about Marcela could serve as new raw material for the further creation of

Dulcinea and her hoped-for final independence from Sobrina. Conversely, it is easy for Don Quixote to fall in love with Marcela because he projects onto her the image of Sobrina.

When he finally meets Marcela at Grisóstomo's funeral and listens to her impassioned rhetoric of existential freedom, Don Quixote is even more taken with her. The term "soul mate" comes readily to mind to describe his perception of her. Everyone has noted that she, like he, has adopted a life-style derived from imaginative literature and that this fact constitutes a strong bond between them. Yet Grisóstomo and Ambrosio have adopted the same literary life-style, and Don Quixote is not overwhelmed with sympathy for either of them. Don Quixote and Marcela are joined in a more important and fundamental way, which springs from their motivations for having adopted their analogous life-styles. They are both attempting to deny part of their own erotic impulses—hers of adolescence, his of middlescence—that exert intolerable pressure on them and force their escape into a new environment. Don Quixote really springs to Marcela's defense only when he perceives that her desire to preserve her virginity is under attack. When some of the men present at her speech "who had felt the powerful dart of her glances and bore the wounds inflicted by her beautiful eyes showed signs of wanting to follow her, in spite of the plainly worded warning she had just given them," Don Quixote goes into action, offering himself as her champion and commending again and again her virtuous intention. After the threat has passed and the funeral ended, Don Quixote "determined to go and seek Marcela himself, to offer her everything of which he was capable in her service."

Even while Marcela is haranguing the assembled men on the subject of chastity, she is making eyes at them, and her behavior has created in Don Quixote the same desire it had stirred in the other men: to follow her into the forest and offer his services. These two characters are certainly not lacking in libido. Fortunately, their respective identities as literary shepherdess—by definition chaste—and knight-errant—by definition a defender of chastity—restrain them from the necessity of having to act on their impulses. Marcela has metamorphosed herself into an unattainable literary shepherdess, in whom Don Quixote sees Sobrina, whom he has already metamorphosed into an unattainable princess. His defense of her chastity can be seen, finally, as an only partially successful reaction formation mobilized and displaced onto her in order to defend against his own unacceptable desire for Sobrina, also transferred to her.[9]

Now, between the time Don Quixote first hears about Marcela and falls to imitating her lovers (I, 12) and when he actually meets her at Grisóstomo's funeral (I, 14), he falls in with a traveler named Vivaldo and is forced to continue the process of creation and definition of Dulcinea, as he was forced to do by the Toledan merchants in I, 4. I have already observed how on this occasion our hero defines the institution of chivalry totally in erotic terms, and how he quotes some lines from his favorite ballad, the one about Lancelot and Guinevere, with attention to the role of the dueña Quintañona as intermediary. After ascertaining that because all knights-errant have ladies fair, Don Quixote must also have one, Vivaldo invites him to reveal "the name, native land, lineage and beauty of your lady" (I, 13). Don Quixote is fleeing from Sobrina, and his imagination has been fired by descriptions of Marcela, to whom he has already begun to assimilate Sobrina. Instead of describing a Dulcinea who might embody some or all of the features of Sobrina, Don Quixote does the opposite and makes a brave attempt to create a Dulcinea on the basis of a combination of the clichés of Petrarchan love poetry and a rejection of all or most of the real noble family names around the Iberian Peninsula.

"Her name," he tells Vivaldo, "is Dulcinea. She is a native of El Toboso. In rank she must be a princess, at least, for she is my queen and lady. Her beauty, superhuman, for in her are realized and made true all the impossible and chimerical attributes of beauty the poets bestow on their ladies: that their hair is gold, their forehead Elysian Fields. . . ." Dulcinea is, quite literally (and somewhat disconcertingly) the Word made Flesh, recalling again our hero's instructions to the Toledan merchants: "Believe, confess, affirm, swear and defend." Her lineage is a rejection of the real, existing, entrenched nobility. Don Quixote takes us on a whirlwind tour of the peninsula, citing the noblest families of each region in turn, and concludes that Dulcinea is none of these, "but she is of those of El Toboso of La Mancha, a lineage which, although modern, can provide a generous beginning for the most illustrious families of the future."[10] In short, the interlude with Vivaldo affords Don Quixote the opportunity to distance Dulcinea from Sobrina and Marcela, who are obviously having an effect on him at this moment, in an attempt to insulate himself from the too-real women. His reaction to Marcela in the next chapter demonstrates the near futility of his efforts.

Two chapters later our hero is plunged into close physical proximity with three women at Juan Palomeque's inn, where he and Sancho take refuge after the drubbing administered by the Yanguesans. The three are presented immediately: the innkeeper's wife, who was "naturally charitable and pained by the ill-fortune of her fellow man"; her daughter, "a maiden, a very nice looking girl"; and the Asturian maid Maritornes, whose chubby, ugly little person is described in some detail. Like the women of Don Quixote's household, the innkeeper's wife ("Ventera") and maiden daughter ("Hija Doncella") have no names and are only identified by their roles. Mother and daughter undress Don Quixote and when he is in bed apply plasters to his wounds. Maritornes holds the lamp for them.

An important aspect of the maiden daughter's character is at least hinted at at the very beginning, when she recounts to Sancho a recurring dream in which she is falling from a tower but awakens before she reaches the ground. Upon awakening, however, she finds her body bruised as though she had actually fallen

to the ground. Arturo Serrano Plaja offers a suggestive interpretation of the maiden's dream according to which the dream
expresses in the disguised form of falling from a tower the girl's
repressed desire for forbidden sexual experience. The metaphor
of falling and the presence of the phallic tower lend credence to
this interpretation. The bruises she feels on awakening are the
result of her internal censorship, self-inflicted punishment for
her unacceptable desires.[11] The maiden daughter, it seems, is
wrestling with the same sort of psychic dilemma that we have
uncovered in our hero and, not incidentally, just observed in
Marcela: powerful erotic impulses experienced as unacceptable
and held in check. The means by which this last is accomplished
varies, of course. Marcela and Don Quixote retreat into a fantasy
existence borrowed from literature, whereas the maiden
daughter banishes her impulses from consciousness. With unerr-
ing psychic verisimilitude, the repressed material surfaces in disguised form in her dream.

Don Quixote is anything but unaware of this attractive girl's
presence around his bedside. In fact, the first words he utters in
the inn are a declaration of his desire for her. He takes her
mother's hand in his and remarks, "I would to Heaven that love
held me not captive and subject to its laws, and to the eyes of that
beautiful ingrate whose name I cannot speak aloud, for those of
this beautiful maiden would then be the masters of my freedom"
(I, 16). Mother and daughter are unable to grasp the details of a
message couched in Don Quixote's flowery and anachronistic
prose, but they "understand very well that it was all compliments
and sweet talk."

It is important to observe in this passage the presence of
three—or perhaps four—women. Don Quixote casts the innkeeper's wife in the role of intermediary, thus suggesting that the
Lancelot-Guinevere-Quintañona story is lurking somewhere in
his mind and that the older woman is identified with the dueña of
romance. The maiden daughter is of course the object of our

hero's attraction. She is identified with Sobrina as Sobrina (we have observed similarities both exterior and interior) and opposed to Sobrina as Dulcinea, through the conceit of the eyes. As in the case of Marcela, the innkeeper's daughter is a young woman who reminds Don Quixote of his niece and is attractive for that reason. Her eyes in particular are singled out as the agents of transference. In addition, she is attractive in her own right, and furthermore she has awakened physically and psychically to adult eroticism. She is, then, very easy for our hero to fall in love with. It is precisely because Don Quixote's attraction for her is determined in part by his projection onto her of the memory of his niece that he must interpose Dulcinea as a barrier between his unacceptable desire and its transferred object. This is why he invokes "the eyes of that beautiful ingrate whose name I cannot speak aloud," meaning Dulcinea, and this is why, incidentally, he cannot speak her name aloud. Dulcinea, Sobrina, and maiden daughter are all in perilous proximity in our hero's mind as he attempts to settle down for the night.

His nocturnal fantasy and its burlesque denouement with Maritornes afford Don Quixote the opportunity to sort these women out and differentiate clearly between Dulcinea on the one hand and Sobrina-maiden daughter on the other. His thoughts reveal the painful ambiguity of his erotic life in general—desire *cum* terror—and in addition offer a splendid example of the fusion he effects of stimuli derived from his immediate situation (in love with maiden daughter), from the more remote situation from which he is fleeing but which keeps overtaking him (in love with Sobrina), and from his vast knowledge of chivalric literature. "He imagined that the innkeeper's daughter was the daughter of the lord of the castle and that she, smitten by his charms, had fallen in love with him and promised that she would come and lie with him a goodly while. . . ." Here is desire, stimulated by Don Quixote's highly developed imagination. But in the very same sentence desire is opposed by our hero's equally strong terror of physical intimacy: ". . . and he commenced to feel great anguish and to consider the danger to his chastity, and he proposed in his heart to commit no treachery toward his lady Dulcinea del Toboso. . . ." Here is the fear for his virginity, followed by the mobilization of Dulcinea as a defense. To accede to his own desires would not be an act that terrifies our hero and for that reason impossible; it would instead be an act of treason against his sworn commitment. By invoking Dulcinea Don Quixote legitimizes—to himself, of course—his general and historic inability to engage in normal relationships with women, now compounded by and entangled with his unacceptable incestuous desire for his niece. But this privileged overview of our hero's psychic battleground is not yet complete, for in the same sentence the immediate situation is associated to a literary analogue: ". . . even though Queen Guinevere herself and her dueña Quintañona should appear before him."

This last clause is interesting for two reasons. First, as soon as Don Quixote is able to displace the real (Sobrina-daughter) into the imaginary (Dulcinea, Guinevere, Quintañona), he has begun to resolve the immediate crisis—in his typical, psychotic way it is true, but the crisis will be surmounted nevertheless. Second, the fact that he recalls the dueña Quintañona in addition to the beautiful Guinevere, and not specifically in the role of intermediary, suggests that his imagination is crossed by not one but two images of forbidden desire, the one young and beautiful (a combination of Sobrina, Marcela, maiden daughter, and Guinevere) and the other a woman Don Quixote's age or even older (perhaps a combination of the innkeeper's wife and Quintañona). We shall be interested to see if this possibility is developed further. For the moment it is sufficient to call attention to the seamless joining in one sentence of Don Quixote's background readings, his "base" situation at home, and the immediate situation at the inn.

Critical and reader response to the episode at the inn has centered on the farcical encounter between Don Quixote and

Maritornes which occurs immediately following our hero's anguished meditation and in which he gives a splendid demonstration of his ability to impose his inner needs, by the mechanism of delusional projection, on the most prosaic reality, to create by an (unconscious) act of will the environment he needs in order to live out his chivalric existence. Here Don Quixote overrides all the data provided by his senses and concludes that Maritornes is beautiful, that her attire is the finest, that her foul breath is perfumed, and the like, in order to act out his fantasy about the maiden daughter with all its attendant implications. Don Quixote sincerely believes the woman he is holding and to whom he is explaining why he cannot gratify their mutual desires is not Maritornes at all, but maiden daughter. Hence, everything he says to her must be taken seriously. He believes she is in love with him, we know he is in love with her, and we also know that for that very reason she must be kept at bay. Don Quixote seeks to accomplish this by informing her, first, that he is physically incapacitated and, second, that his heart is already pledged to Dulcinea. Again Dulcinea is mobilized as a defense against unacceptable erotic impulses, and this aspect of her at least has become clearly differentiated from her original "source." Don Quixote is still having difficulty creating and differentiating her physically, as we have seen.

The following day Don Quixote discusses his adventures with Sancho, insisting that the woman in his arms was "the daughter of the lord of this castle" and implying that they had been intimate. "What can I tell you about the adornment of her person, about her splendid intelligence? What can I say about other, hidden things that I shall leave intact and in silence in order to keep faith with my lady Dulcinea?" (I, 17). Don Quixote, a fifty-year-old virgin, brags to Sancho like an adolescent boy who in fact did not have the sexual experience he ardently desired but secretly feared and who brags to his friends the next day. Anyone who has ever been an adolescent boy will understand.

When he and Sancho leave the inn our hero exchanges a long look with the maiden daughter, accompanied from time to time by a soulful sigh. "The innkeeper's daughter was also watching him, and he did not take his eyes off her, and from time to time he sighed a sigh that seemed to come from deep inside him, and everyone thought that he was sighing that way from the pain in his ribs." As Serrano Plaja observes, surely the girl who has the recurring dream of falling from a tower knows what to make of Don Quixote's staring and sighing, and she apparently returns his soulful gaze. This encounter with the innkeeper's maiden daughter has certainly constituted Don Quixote's most intense recorded erotic experience to date. Teresa Aveleyra suggests perceptively that this "woman who is still almost a child" exerts a strange fascination on the "fifty-year-old bachelor," that she is the "only woman he allows himself to desire," and that he "transforms her into a princess without dehumanizing her," and she concludes that the innkeeper's daughter is "perhaps the only feminine figure treated in a truly, although incompletely novelistic fashion, who could have become the feminine protagonist of the novel."[12] These are important intuitions, for they insist on the age difference between the two and document from another perspective the intensity of the forever embryonic relationship; but Professor Aveleyra is concerned with the observable phenomena—the effects—to the exclusion of their causes. The present study seeks to uncover the unconscious motivation for Don Quixote's attraction to the innkeeper's maiden daughter. It should be noted, finally, that she appears again, along with her mother and Maritornes, in I, 32, where she offers her reaction to the amorous aspects of the chivalric romances, and once more with Maritornes in I, 43, where the two "semivirgins" play a trick on Don Quixote, leaving him all night with his arm extended and tied to a window grating. The trick depends, as Serrano Plaja has observed, on our hero's libidinous response to the daughter's whispers in the night.

Before moving on to Don Quixote's next erotic adventure, a fantasy princess in I, 21, I should pause to summarize his success to this point in creating a Dulcinea strong enough to meet his psychic needs, independent of both Aldonza and Sobrina, and capable of filling his thoughts and allowing him to fend off his very real attraction toward the women he meets. In this regard, Aldonza can be fairly dismissed. Not only has she not appeared overtly—neither has Sobrina except for the interlude between Don Quixote's first and second sally—but none of the women with whom our hero has come into contact seem to bear any resemblance to her. Sobrina, however, and his massive and uncomfortable experience with her, is always present just below the level of consciousness, and he has assimilated both Marcela and maiden daughter to her as only semifantasy erotic objects. As we have seen, Dulcinea is also confused with Sobrina-daughter. In this respect, then, our hero's efforts have not been crowned with success. On every woman he meets he projects the imago of his niece and thereby renders any real relationship hopelessly complex and finally impossible. His efforts to create a concrete, visualizable Dulcinea who is not Sobrina have been limited first to his response to the Toledan merchants (a straight back and no ocular discharge) and then to his reply to Vivaldo (the incarnation of all the clichés of feminine beauty from the Petrarchan tradition, all this within a context analogous to that surrounding the acquisition and propagation of a militant religious faith). When the chips are down, though, and there is a real woman present, Don Quixote assimilates her to his niece. Nonetheless, we should not conclude from this that his efforts are entirely in vain, for we have seen our hero interpose Dulcinea rather effectively between his attraction to Sobrina-daughter and his terror of intimacy. The Dulcinea thus interposed, however, remains basically an abstraction, a name for Don Quixote's mechanism of internal prohibition.

In chapter 21 we become aware of another facet of our hero's inability to confront the challenges of courtship and marriage. In an extended fantasy, verbalized to Sancho, he creates a king in distress, whose kingdom he saves and for which action he is about to be rewarded with the hand in marriage of the monarch's beautiful daughter. Suddenly things begin to go awry. Don Quixote's lineage is found wanting. The king cancels the wedding plans. Don Quixote vows to elope with the princess or, should she fail to agree to elopement, to carry her off by force. In short, Don Quixote is afraid that he will prove unacceptable to the girl's father. In I, 37 the same fear surfaces again, this time in connection with Dorotea-Princess Micomicona. Sancho has observed that the princess has been transformed into a woman named Dorotea who is engaged to a certain Don Fernando. Don Quixote immediately concludes that the transformation has been effected because Princess Micomicona's father had decided that our hero was not capable of killing the giant and restoring his kingdom to him. This is an interesting variation on the theme of Don Quixote's difficulties in love. It recalls most immediately the presence of an angry father—the innkeeper Juan Palomeque—as a character in the recent encounter with the woman known only as "maiden daughter." It is pointless, no doubt, to speculate on Don Quixote's relationship with his own father, who, unlike Sobrina, is not even a character in the book. The fact remains, however, that one of our hero's problems as an adult takes the form of feelings of inadequacy in the presence of the father.

After the liberation of the galley slaves and its unfortunate aftermath in I, 22, Don Quixote and Sancho take refuge in the rugged terrain of the Sierra Morena, where they stay until the end of I, 31. Women, cowardice, love, and insanity are important themes in this segment. Here Don Quixote meets Cardenio and hears about his romance with Luscinda, which is complicated by the machinations of Don Fernando. Here he deliberately goes mad himself, imitating the actions of Amadís and Orlando—and more importantly, of Cardenio. Here he reveals to Sancho the relation between Dulcinea and Aldonza and sends Sancho on a potentially disastrous mission to El Toboso. And here, finally, Don Quixote meets the next real woman in his life: the beautiful, strong-willed, sexy Dorotea. These ten chapters command our careful attention.

Don Quixote and Sancho find Cardenio's suitcase, along with his amatory sonnet and "sour grapes" love letter. Between the reading of each of the latter, Don Quixote announces to Sancho his intention of writing a letter in verse to Dulcinea. That is, the stimulus for the letter he finally writes is not his reading of *Amadís* or *Orlando furioso* but the unexpected discovery of Cardenio's work. Similarly, the idea of doing penance in the Sierra is suggested to our hero by the shepherd's account of his recent encounters with Cardenio. "He [Cardenio] told us not to wonder at his running around the mountains that way, because he was doing it to perform a certain penitence that had been assigned to him for his many sins" (I, 23). Two of the central elements of Don Quixote's own actions in the Sierra—the letter to Dulcinea and the penance—have been suggested to him by the experience of Cardenio at one remove, before he ever meets Cardenio. When this meeting finally takes place an instantaneous bond is established between the two men. Cardenio himself now tells Don Quixote the story of his love for Luscinda, from his own point of view, and Don Quixote offers to "help him weep for his unhappiness." Unamuno observes that implicit in our hero's offer is the projection onto the Cardenio-Luscinda story of Don Quixote's own frustrated desire, which Unamuno mistakenly identifies as directed toward Aldonza Lorenzo.[13]

The most important aspect of the encounter between the two lovesick madmen, from my point of view, is not Cardenio's story but Don Quixote's interruption of it, which results in a violent altercation between the two. When our hero discovers that

Luscinda is a great reader of chivalric romances, he takes it as a sign of "the nobility of her intellect," and suggests she could have enjoyed certain erotic episodes from them, for example, the adventures of "Doraida and Garaya, and the discreet remarks of the shepherd Darinel, and his admirable bucolic verses." Where does Don Quixote get these associations? Doraida and Garaya are characters in Feliciano de Silva's *Rogel de Grecia*. It will be recalled that Don Quixote is a great fan of Silva and quotes from the convoluted prose of his *Segunda Celestina* in I, 1. It should also be noted that the "shepherdesses" Doraida and Garaya are really two men. They have disguised themselves as women and gone off to Greece to pursue certain amorous interests there.[14] Don Quixote and Cardenio fall out over the proper interpretation of a nonexistent love episode from *Amadís de Gaula*, the relationship between Queen Madásima and Master Elisabet. Cardenio, imposing his own amorous situation and his intense feelings regarding Luscinda and Don Fernando onto literature, makes Queen Madásima a cheap sexpot—as he would like to be able to consider Luscinda—and affirms that "that sonofabitch Master Elisabet was shacked up with her." At this point Don Quixote unconsciously identifies the good queen with the object of his own affections, whose purity must be maintained at all costs and who must not be permitted to give herself to anyone, and springs violently to her defense. "Queen Madásima was a most noble lady, and it is unthinkable that she could be carrying on with a cancre cutter!" The narrator is impressed enough with our hero's fervor to comment: "A strange case! He took up for her as though she really were his true and natural liege lady!"

It should be remarked at this point that although Queen Madásima and Master Elisabet are characters in *Amadís*, they are not a couple. Elisabet was a surgeon, priest, and language teacher. Don Quixote's characterization of him as "cancre cutter" (*sacapotras*) is obviously derived from his function as surgeon. It is of course significant that from all the surgeon's functions, with which Don Quixote surely must be familiar, he chooses the one that is simultaneously the most erotic and the most repellent: a remover of venereal tumors.[15] Later, when Sancho asks him why he flew into such a rage and truncated Cardenio's story, Don Quixote replies that it is "a great blasphemy to suppose that a queen could be involved with a surgeon" (I, 25). The use of the generic *queen* and *surgeon* instead of the personal names suggests a wider application. In Don Quixote's time a surgeon was normally a barber; or, rather, it was the barber who performed many surgical procedures. One of Don Quixote's two close friends is Master Nicolás the barber. The other of course is Pero Pérez the priest. Elisabet resumes both functions, suggesting the possibility of some unconscious fear on Don Quixote's part that his two friends are ignoble, unworthy, and sexual predators, perhaps even rivals. Dulcinea is after all a princess.

Don Quixote's encounter with Cardenio produces both identification and violent disagreement between them. We have just had occasion to observe the disagreement, and we should turn now to the positive identification. I should begin by remarking that the violence we have just seen springs finally from what is common to both men: fear of intimacy with a woman, fear of inadequacy as a man, and recourse to extreme, even psychotic defenses in an effort to deny these fears. Coexisting with these fears are powerful erotic urges, as we have already observed, and therein lies the problem. Furthermore, both Don Quixote and Cardenio have fixed their terrified attraction on very specific objects. Because the relationship between Cardenio and Luscinda is socially acceptable and even desirable, Cardenio can be "saved" from his fears by a series of public confrontations at Juan Palomeque's inn. This possibility does not exist in the case of Don Quixote and his niece. But that lies in the future. For the present Don Quixote and Cardenio are united by their common fear of both intimacy and their own possible inadequacy. This bond is of course much stronger than their common interest in romances of chivalry.

Now Cardenio has defended against his fears by a straight-forward retreat into psychosis, accompanied by physical flight from the scene of his unpleasant experience with Luscinda and Don Fernando. Michèle Gendreau-Massaloux has recently called attention to the clinical accuracy of Cervantes's depiction of the love-maddened young man and how closely it conforms to the description of erotomania offered by Jacques Ferrand in 1610.[16] When Don Quixote decides to take advantage of his mountain environment to imitate the penitence of Amadís along with the violence of Orlando, he is in fact unconsciously responding to his recent encounter with Cardenio, whose impotence and inability to declare himself have obviously made a powerful impression on him for the reasons I have noted. Critics are generally agreed that lurking under the conscious imitation of Amadís or Orlando or both is the unconscious imitation of Cardenio, resulting in the spectacle of a madman (Don Quixote) who decides more or less deliberately to convert himself into a pretend madman, in imita-tion of a real madman (Cardenio).[17] Among the concrete aspects of this imitation are the verses Don Quixote composes that are quoted in I, 26, inspired by Cardenio's sonnet in which Luscinda is metamorphosed into "Fili" (I, 23), and, most importantly, Don Quixote's letters to Dulcinea and Sobrina, inspired by Cardenio's undelivered letter to Luscinda. Once again, an episode in our hero's life takes shape as the result of a seamless joining of his unconscious and unconfessed needs, his vast reading, and his recent experience, catalyzed by his immediate situation. As I have already noted, Don Quixote creates his life as a work of art in exactly the same way that real artists create art.

I remarked that Don Quixote consciously decides to imitate furious Orlando and melancholy Amadís, to convert himself into a "pretend madman." This quality of willful pretense is important, and our hero's remarks to Sancho at the outset include a number of terms that refer specifically to playacting: "playing the part of the suicidal melancholic, of the fool and of the madman";[18] "I shall make a resumé of those feats of madness that seem most important to me" (I, 25). We should not conclude, however, that Don Quixote is being frivolous. In the first place, as I have just remarked, he is creating an episode in his life, which means simply that he is creating himself. In the second place he is groping for the means to deal with the sentiment that he feels toward Sobrina and that has been brought close to the level of consciousness by his encounter with Cardenio. This will involve, on the one hand, a disguised form of communication with her and, on the other, a truly masterful misdirection of attention—Sancho's and ours—away from her. Let us pursue this second aspect first.

As every reader knows, Don Quixote in I, 25 takes Sancho into his confidence and describes for him the progress of his love for Dulcinea. It is here that Sancho (and we) learn that he has seen her a maximum of four times in twelve years, and it is here that Don Quixote inadvertently lets slip her parents' names, allowing Sancho to identify her as Aldonza Lorenzo. Sancho then proceeds to describe Aldonza, whom he has obviously known for years, and we learn that she is large, loud, coarse, vulgar—the very opposite of the model of maidenly modesty Don Quixote has depicted. Like Sancho, Unamuno takes Don Quixote's slip at face value, identifies Dulcinea with Aldonza, falls to lamenting, and finally asks our hero: "Tell me, wouldn't you have loved the daughter of Lorenzo Corchuelo and Aldonza Nogales? And would you not have given up for her all the glory that you were attempting to win through her?"[19] Unamuno's Don Quixote would have exchanged his identity for the pleasures of rural married life had he only the courage to declare himself to Aldonza. Unamuno apparently missed Sancho's description of her, or did not stop to ponder how a man like our hero could be attracted to such a girl. Much more recently, addressing himself to precisely that question, Louis Combet concluded that Don Quixote is generally attracted to what he called "venal or facile women"—for example, the two prostitutes at the first inn (I, 2) and Maritornes (I, 16)—and found it perfectly natural for our hero to fabricate from Aldonza a "Dulcinée, putain villegeoise."[20] Neither of these extreme interpretations deals adequately with the events of I, 25, because both assume that Aldonza is in fact the real object of Don Quixote's affections and ignore the discrepancy between Aldonza as described by Don Quixote and as described by Sancho.

Let me begin by insisting on this discrepancy. The girl Don Quixote describes has no physical features. She is distinguished by her modesty and inaccessibility—he has seen her perhaps four times, and in all probability she noticed only once that he was looking at her—and by her lineage. Don Quixote names both her father and her mother (first and last names), so Sancho has no trouble identifying her. Indeed, until our hero lets slip the parents' names it is impossible to ascertain whom he is describing. To say the least, Don Quixote is not interested in the physical reality of Aldonza. This is in violent contrast to Sancho, who describes the girl he has obviously known for years in unpleasant detail. Aldonza turns out to be physically strong—able to compete in athletic events with the strongest young men—possessed of a great booming voice, and "a girl with hair on her chest," in Sancho's words. Furthermore, she is anything but modest and retiring. "And the best thing about her is that she's not at all prudish. Instead, she's very sociable, friendly with everyone, always laughing and joking." Don Quixote's evocation of disembodied modesty is thus rudely replaced by Sancho's vision of a coarse, loud, fun-loving village girl who gets in and mixes with everybody. It is difficult to believe that the the two men can be referring to the same person.

Yet they must be, for Don Quixote never questions Sancho's

description of her. He objects only to the implication that Aldonza is not suitable raw material for the fabrication of Dulcinea. This brings us to a provisional conclusion that in turn points us back in the direction of my original hypothesis. Don Quixote is simply not interested in the concrete reality of Aldonza, only in the fact of her existence. As we have seen in I, 4 and I, 13, when Don Quixote is called upon to describe Dulcinea he does not begin with Aldonza Lorenzo and alter her attributes to fit some ideal. Don Quixote's descriptions of Dulcinea begin either from the immediate stimulus—the unacceptable vision proffered by the Toledan mechants—or from some verbal source transformed by a psychic analogue of religious faith—the Word (the clichés of Petrarchan love poetry) made Flesh in I, 13 and the progression from acceptance to militant defense of a quasi-religious belief outlined in I, 4. If there are memories, they are memories of Sobrina; when Don Quixote is attracted, it is to women who remind him of her. Throughout, Aldonza's physical attributes have been conspicuous by their absence, as they are here in Don Quixote's sudden and unexpected revelation to Sancho of what is presumably the true identity of Dulcinea.[21]

If Aldonza has not hitherto been present at Don Quixote's attempts to create Dulcinea, there is no reason to suppose that she should be present here in I, 25, either. Yet she is present, and by name. The conventional wisdom has assumed that Don Quixote makes a nearly disastrous unconscious slip when he allows her parents' names to pass his lips in this conversation with Sancho. There is no textual basis for this supposition, as we have seen. It is not Aldonza but Sobrina who lurks just below the surface of our hero's consciousness. How is it possible, then, that Aldonza should suddenly erupt into consciousness—and speech—at this particularly awkward moment? Phrased another way, the question is whether Don Quixote's revelation of her name to Sancho is in fact an unconscious slip or whether some other motivation is at work in him.

I propose that Don Quixote's "unintentional" revelation of
Aldonza's presence in Dulcinea is at once a sincere attempt to
dissociate Dulcinea from Sobrina and a kind of ruse to misdirect
Sancho's attention away from Sobrina even as our hero begins to
speak openly about her and actually prepares to make contact
with her. These complementary unconscious motivations explain
in a verisimilar fashion Don Quixote's otherwise nonsensical invocation of Aldonza at a time when she could only do him harm.
It is we—Sancho and Unamuno and Combet and all the rest of
us—who believe that harm has been done. Don Quixote, in the
depths of his unconscious, knows better. For him, the invocation
of Aldonza is an effort to help himself, to allow him to simultaneously approach Sobrina and keep his distance from her.

This is accomplished by the two letters that our hero writes
and that Sancho is charged with delivering: the one a love letter to
Dulcinea, which the poet Pedro Salinas has called "the best love
letter ever written in the Spanish language," and the other a
prosaic missive addressed to Sobrina and ordering her to release
three ass colts to Sancho in payment for his services. Stylistically as
well as thematically the two letters could not be less similar. The
first is addressed only to "High and Sovereign Lady." It is
couched in the archaic language of the chivalric romances, complains of enforced absence (a throwback to the fantasy of I, 2
when Don Quixote has just left home for the first time), and
suggests death as the only possible remedy for his amorous ills. It
is signed: "Yours unto death, the Knight of the Sad Countenance." The other letter is couched in the redundant prose of late
sixteenth-century legal documents and instructs Sobrina to transfer certain property to Sancho. The first letter carries no notation
of date or place. The second is dated "22 August, in the depths of
the Sierra Morena," and is signed not with a name but with a
rubric—a special individual flourish—that Don Quixote knows
Sobrina will recognize. That is to say, the first letter exists outside
of time and space, involves only a "sovereign lady" and a "Knight

of the Sad Countenance," and is concerned exclusively with the presentation of emotions. All that is real, concrete, and identifiable in this letter is the emotion it expresses: the enforced absence and the anticipation of death. The second letter complements the first. It exists within time and space, it is addressed from one real, legally recognizable individual to another, and its subject matter is trivially banal. In the one intense emotion is ascribed to fantasy people, and in the other real people are concerned with insignificant issues.

This complementarity is too neat, too rigorous to be the result of chance. In order to understand the real thrust and the real intended recipient of these two letters it is necessary to telescope them into one, whereupon it becomes apparent that Don Quixote identifies the object of his affections in his second letter, and only in the first does he refer to the complex emotions—desire and despair—she arouses in him. In this way, by unconsciously bifurcating his approach to Sobrina, Don Quixote is able to gratify his contradictory impulses toward her. On the one hand he invokes the legalistic language and institutionalized relationships of the second letter to keep his distance from her, while on the other he simultaneously confesses his feeling for her in the first letter, addressed only to "Sovereign Lady." This dangerous game is rendered less dangerous by the fact that Sancho sincerely believes that the object of the knight's affections is a loud and lusty farm girl named Aldonza Lorenzo. But even this safeguard is not enough, for the approach is still experienced by Don Quixote as too daring, and furthermore, as we have seen, he has no real interest in establishing contact with Aldonza anyway. This is why he suggests Sancho wait three days before setting out and then deliberately fails to give him the letters to deliver ("because Don Quixote had kept [the notebook] and had not given it to him, and Sancho did not remember to ask him for it" [I, 26]).

In I, 28 the beautiful, strong-willed, sexy Dorotea makes her appearance. Our first view of her, which we share with three

other voyeurs (Cardenio and Don Quixote's friends the priest
and the barber) is just that—a view of certain parts of her body
normally kept under cover. It is essential to bear in mind that at
first we all assume she is a boy and that what we are offered is a
kind of "male impersonator" striptease. We are treated first to her
feet, "which seemed two pieces of crystalline whiteness born
among the others in the stream bed." The three men are "aston-
ished by the whiteness and beauty of her feet." Next we learn that
"she had her trousers rolled half way up her leg, which shone like
white alabaster." After drying her beautiful feet, she raises her
face, and "those who were watching her had occasion to see an
incomparable beauty." She removes her cap and her long hair
reveals that she is "a woman, and delicate." Her hair is then
described for its own value, "long and blonde, not only did it
cover her back, but all the rest of her as well." She combs it with
her hands, and "if her feet in the water bed seemed pieces of
crystal, her hands in her hair seemed pieces of molded snow."
When she becomes aware she is being spied upon she attempts to
flee, "but she had not taken six steps when she fell to the ground.
Her delicate feet could not resist the harshness of the stones."
The gradual metamorphosis of an attractive boy into a beautiful
woman ends in a graphic demonstration of her feminine vulnerability as she attempts to escape from the men who have observed
her toilette from their hiding places. After contact has been
made, her fears have been allayed, and her narration is about to
begin, Dorotea "covered her hair and put on her shoes *most
chastely* [emphasis added]." Even as they disappear from view the
reader is reminded of the erotic charge contained in these parts
of her body. No other woman in this novel is introduced and
described in such overtly erotic terms. It would be fair to conclude
simply that Dorotea is presented as a sex object.[22]

   She sees herself the same way, as an object of men's desire.
In the course of her narration she observes that for her parents
she is the receptacle of the family honor, that she is the object of

Don Fernando's desire, that her family had assumed that she had run off with her own servant to engage in an illicit (and socially demeaning) sexual relationship, and that she became the object of the servant's lust, murdered him, and went to work for a master who himself attempted to seduce her when he discovered she was a woman. She begins her narration with a reference to the fact that she is a vulnerable woman alone in the wilderness. Her detailed account of her seduction by Don Fernando was considered steamy enough to have been eliminated in its entirety by the Portuguese Inquisition in 1624. When Sancho first lays eyes on her in I, 29, after she changes out of her masculine disguise and into womanly finery, he considers her the most gorgeous creature he has ever seen. Can we wonder at the effect this woman will have on Don Quixote?

When she enters our hero's presence Dorotea dismounts "with great *desenvoltura*," a word which is variously translated as "grace" or "lewdness (chiefly in women)." Opting for some kind of just mean, we may conclude that Dorotea dismounts showing perhaps a bit of leg or thigh. She then kneels facing Don Quixote and gives a brief synopsis of her story. At the conclusion she attempts to kiss his hand, but he "raised her up and embraced her, with great courtesy and restraint." The embrace functions on two levels. First, it signifies that Don Quixote and "Princess Micomicona" are equals, she by virtue of her rank, he by his status as her champion. Second, it is always pleasurable to embrace a beautiful woman, however courteously. The first encounter between Dorotea and Don Quixote is charged with erotic overtones.

At the conclusion of her narration, Dorotea offers to marry Don Quixote after he kills Pandafilando de la Fosca Vista and restores her kingdom to her. He is at first grateful and excited, among the reasons because her offer corroborates what he has been telling Sancho all along about how these things work. "What do you think, Sancho my friend? What did I tell you? Look at us here with a kingdom to rule and a queen to marry!" (I, 30).

Almost immediately, however, his fear of intimacy reasserts itself and he "comes to his senses," invoking first his unshakable loyalty to Dulcinea and then, in a moment of rare candor, his total unsuitability for marriage. "You are free to dispose of your person as you like," he tells Dorotea, "because as long as I have my memory occupied, my will captivated and my intellect abandoned to that woman . . . I say no more. And it is not possible for me to face the thought of marriage, even to the Phoenix herself."

Here the terror of marriage seems stronger than the attachment to Dulcinea, who remains unnamed. For this reason it is possible to read this passage as a straightforward, although unconscious, statement of Don Quixote's real desires and his predicament. He does not name Dulcinea because he is not thinking of her but of Sobrina. In this context the remarks concerning the impossibility of marriage are self-explanatory. At the same time, Dorotea is beautiful and Don Quixote is attracted to her and simultaneously terrified of her. His strategy for keeping her at bay has raised the specter of Sobrina, this time not as an imago imposed on Dorotea but as a competitor. Our hero's predicament has only worsened. Here is a perfect opportunity, indeed an imperious necessity, to invoke Dulcinea as a buffer between himself and both Sobrina and Dorotea. Sancho throws him the life preserver he needs, by objecting to his master's refusal to marry Dorotea and suggesting an unflattering comparison of Dulcinea's beauty—which he naturally associates with Aldonza Lorenzo—to hers. At this Don Quixote flies into a rage, strikes Sancho, and proceeds to the creation of Dulcinea. Once again he follows the religious model. Sancho's remarks about his lady are called "blasphemies." Don Quixote calls Sancho, among other harsh names, "excommunicated rogue." He ascribes to Dulcinea all his valor, his victory over Dorotea's tormentor, and Sancho's elevation to the nobility, and he concludes with "the valor of Dulcinea, taking my arm as the instrument of her works. She fights in me, and conquers in me, and I live and breathe in her, and have my life and being." Unamuno identifies the last phrase as a version of Saint Paul's Letter to the Galatians 2:20. Again Don Quixote invokes an unseen, incorporeal deity, a spirit who comes to inhabit the body of the believer.

In the midst of the Dorotea-Micomicona affair and the "Pauline" creation of Dulcinea, Don Quixote suddenly turns his attention to Sancho's mission to El Toboso and his delivery of the letter to Dulcinea. It is difficult to assess our hero's unconscious motivation here. It would appear that between Sobrina and Dorotea he already has enough women on his mind and that to invoke the boisterous Aldonza would only add to his troubles. At the same time he continues his efforts to create Dulcinea as some kind of analogue of Christ, calling Sancho a blasphemer when the squire clumsily reveals he has never seen the lady. Sancho takes advantage of his master's request for the story of his trip in order to attempt to wring a concession from him. If Don Quixote will stop punishing him for what he said in I, 25—the reduction of Dulcinea to Aldonza—he will tell the story. Besides, he says, he has repented of those evil ways and now "loves and venerates Dulcinea like a relic." Don Quixote remarks that he is bothered by memories of the conversation in I, 25 and then informs Sancho that he was not punishing him for that but for what he had just said about never having seen Dulcinea, "and you know what they say: 'A new sin demands a new penance.'!" (I, 30).

Don Quixote continues to invoke the rhetoric of Christianity in his dealings with Sancho, at the same time beginning to invoke the presence of Aldonza by asking Sancho for an account of his mission to El Toboso. It seems to me that this apparent paradox—the disembodied spirit coexisting with a coarse physical presence—can be resolved if we consider that Don Quixote's attempts to create Dulcinea by some analogy with religious faith have not been particularly successful. The present situation, with two women on his mind, is especially stressful. The "spiritual"

Dulcinea is not enough to tear his thoughts loose from Sobrina and Dorotea.

Sancho's narration begins with a discussion of the letter Don Quixote failed to give him in the first place. Since he did not have the text, he says, he was forced to re-create it from memory. Don Quixote asks for a sample, which Sancho then provides. Of course it is a grotesque deformation. *Soberana* ("Sovereign") *señora*, for example, is transformed into *sobajada* ("soiled from handling") *señora*. Instead of upbraiding Sancho as we might expect, Don Quixote reacts to his destruction of the letter with: "All of this does not displease me. Proceed with the story" (I, 31). How could this latest Sanchesque blasphemy fail to displease Don Quixote? And yet he professes to be quite unruffled by it. Don Quixote maintains this curiously uncritical posture throughout Sancho's narration of his meeting with "Dulcinea" in El Toboso. This narration is entirely imaginary, for as we know, Sancho never went near El Toboso. In answer to a series of leading questions supplied by Don Quixote, he invents his story by imagining what Aldonza Lorenzo would have been doing had he gone there and seen her. She would have been winnowing wheat and loading heavy sacks of grain onto a mule, for example. She would naturally have been perspiring and exuding a strong odor. She would not have stopped to read Don Quixote's letter because she cannot read. In a word, Sancho destroys Dulcinea by imposing Aldonza on her, just as he did in I, 25.

Don Quixote is in turn forced to rectify each feature of his squire's narration, to replace the unacceptable vision of Dulcinea offered by Sancho and based on Aldonza with one more in keeping with his own ideas. This is very hard work. Dulcinea appears to hang in the balance, now reduced to a sweating farm girl, now heroically reconstructed by Don Quixote as a serene princess. Incredibly, as this dangerous and psychically draining game nears its end, as Sancho is about to narrate how he took his leave, Don Quixote remarks, "Everything is going well so far." Going well? How can he possibly believe that everything is going well? It seems to me that everything is going well in two senses. First, accompanying Sancho on his imaginary journey to El Toboso and reliving his fabricated encounter with Aldonza has the immediate effect of taking Don Quixote's mind off Dorotea by forcing him to confront another set of problems. Second, and to my mind more important, Sancho's creation of a grotesquely inadequate Dulcinea on the model of Aldonza provides our hero with precisely the kind of stimulus he needs in order to create a viable Dulcinea in dialectical opposition to her. Sancho's narration allows Don Quixote to continue the nonspiritual aspect of the process he began in I, 4 in response to the physically unacceptable Dulcinea suggested by the Toledan merchants. It is this physical aspect that our hero has been missing on those occasions when he has needed an idea of Dulcinea to counter the threat posed by the presence of real women. It is in this sense that Don Quixote can truthfully say that everything is going well when Sancho tells him Dulcinea is a coarse, mannish farm girl.

Now, although all may be going well for the moment, Sancho's imaginary trip and the subsequent conversation about it will have unsettling consequences later on. Dulcinea has been immensely strengthened in Don Quixote's mind, in the sense we have just seen. She has also been located in El Toboso. Furthermore, in the course of his narration Sancho has told his master that Dulcinea had "requested and commanded that he come out of the wilderness, cease his silly penance, and get on the road directly for El Toboso, if no other commitment precluded it, for she had a great desire to see Your Grace" (I, 31). Of course this mobilizes our hero's defenses against the threat of intimacy, and fortunately for both of them Sancho reminds him of his preexisting commitment to Dorotea-Micomicona. From Don Quixote's point of view, he is relieved of the necessity of going to El Toboso to confront we are not exactly sure whom. From Sancho's perspective his lie remains undiscovered and his expectation of some material recompense from the Micomicona adventure remains intact. Two immediate crises have been resolved. First, Don Quixote has strengthened Dulcinea in order to ward off Dorotea. Second, the newly strengthened Dulcinea now becoming the threat, Dorotea, in the form of the knight's commitment to Princess Micomicona, is mobilized to ward her off. For the moment everything is resolved, and indeed, the entire question of the existence and viability of Dulcinea is left at precisely this point, in this state, for the rest of Part I. By the time Part II begins, however, the strengthened Dulcinea in El Toboso, together with the summons she has transmitted through Sancho, has become so real in our hero's mind that the third sally begins precisely with a journey to El Toboso to see her. The crisis so neatly avoided here is re-created in a more intense form and becomes the basis for the entire action of Part II.

In addition, Don Quixote has more women to face here in Part I. The atmosphere at Juan Palomeque's inn, where all repair after leaving the mountains, is physically populated by a veritable army of loving couples and psychically charged with eroticism. It is in this environment that Don Quixote is brought into contact again with the innkeeper's maiden daughter, who made such a powerful impression on him—and he, apparently, on her—in I, 16–17. Here Don Quixote is surrounded, inundated, by the presence of women, all or most of whom are in love.

The atmosphere at Palomeque's inn fairly drips with love, surreptitious kisses, and sighs and other forms of secret communication. It is here that Dorotea finds and recovers Don Fernando and that Luscinda is restored to Cardenio. These two happy couples are joined shortly by the captive Captain Ruy Pérez de Viedma and the beauteous Zoraida whom he has brought from Algeria. Almost immediately thereafter come the Captain's brother Juan, a circuit judge, accompanied by his daughter Clara, a girl of sixteen, with a certain young Don Luis in hot pursuit. All the women present are attached save Maritornes the maid and Palomeque's maiden daughter. The erotic implications of the presence of so many men and women under the same roof are accentuated by the narrator's description of the sleeping arrangements. "It was decided . . . that all the women should sleep in the aforementioned room together, and that the men should remain outside, on guard" (I, 42). This description recalls a similar arrangement in Cervantes's pastoral *La Galatea* (1585), a work by definition devoted to love and relations between the sexes. "All the men slept outside on the fresh grass, except for a few who ranged themselves as sentinels around the sleeping shepherdesses."[23] In both cases the men are protecting the women from the other men, which is to say, from themselves.

Don Quixote is of course not immune to this atmosphere, especially in combination with the renewed presence of the maiden daughter, who had been the subject of an intense erotic fantasy in I, 16 and with whom he had exchanged lingering, soulful glances in I, 17. Indeed, our hero rises magnificently to the occasion, as we shall see. When he is questioned by members of the Holy Brotherhood (a kind of rural police) and they are attempting to arrest him for having freed the galley slaves in I, 22, Don Quixote flies into a rage and vents his spleen in a series of rhetorical questions. These questions move implacably from matters purely legal to matters entirely erotic. Who was the idiot, he asks, who signed the warrant for his arrest, who forgot that knights-errant are exempt from normal laws? What knight, he asks, ever paid taxes, or ever paid a tailor for making him a garment? At this point the thrust of his questions abruptly changes, incorporating his previous experiences at Palomeque's. "What castellan received a knight into his castle and then charged him for his lodging? What maiden did not fall in love with him and surrender herself entirely to his pleasure?" (I, 45). Don Quixote has clearly not lost his interest in sex or in the innkeeper's maiden daughter.

She is not idle herself. In I, 32 there is a round-table discussion of chivalric romance which includes many of those present. Each discussant in turn speaks of his or her own unique relationship with the books. The servant Maritornes prefers "when they tell about the other lady embracing her knight under the orange trees, and a dueña is standing guard over them, dying of fright and envy." Her attitudes seem to be a function of her personality—she likes sex, as we know—and of her status as servant. She imaginatively escapes the role of the dueña dying of envy and attempts to identify with "the other lady." The maiden daughter prefers the more sentimental aspects of the sexual relations depicted in the books. She feels sorry for those knights whose ladies do not yield to their amorous advances. Dorotea, who as we know is something of a sexpot herself, asks roguishly if the daughter would "help" the lovesick knights if she could. She replies that she does not know for sure but cannot understand why the ladies are so cruel, and she adds that if they are concerned for their honor, they should marry their knights. At this point the girl's mother intervenes and reprimands her daughter for knowing and talking more about these matters than befits her maidenly status.

Mother is right, of course. The girl's comments here are simply a more discreet, socially acceptable version of the sentiments her contemporary Maritornes has voiced openly. Maritornes's desires are normal and her behavior overt; she makes a late date with the muleteer in I, 16 and prefers the openly erotic episodes in the books. For that reason she is a relatively uninteresting literary character. The daughter's desires are equally normal, but because of her social status and the presence of her parents she cannot gratify them as Maritornes does. They are instead diverted into dreams about falling, imaginary succor rendered to imaginary knights whose imaginary ladies treat them cruelly, and a combination of soulful glances and sighs together with some cruel pranks whose object is a strange old bachelor who shows up one day. For this reason she is a much more interesting character than Maritornes. The relation between the two is relatively simple. Maritornes actually does what the daughter can only dream about doing, and this, incidentally, explains the narrator's reference to both of them as "the two semi-doncellas" in I, 43. Cervantes is playing with two meanings of the word *doncella*: 'maid' (a servant) and 'maiden' (a virgin). Dorotea has already exploited this ambiguity in the story of her seduction by Don Fernando ("and when my doncella left the room, I stopped being one"). Maritornes is a servant but not a virgin; the daughter is a virgin but not a servant. Like Don Quixote's two letters to Dulcinea and Sobrina, Maritornes and maiden daughter exist in a relation of complementarity.

There are two encounters between our hero and Palomeque's daughter which we must consider here. The first is rather positive and sentimental in nature and occurs following Don Quixote's epic battle with the wineskins. He is dressed for the occasion only in his shirt, which does not cover his thighs in front and is six fingers shorter in back. Dorotea, whose reaction is described first, "when she saw how briefly and how breezily he was dressed, refrained from entering the room where he was doing battle on her behalf" (I, 35). After Don Quixote is put to bed, the innkeeper's wife flies into a rage and recounts all her encounters with our hero and his friends in some detail, always considering how much money his presence at her inn has cost her, and vows that he'll not get away this time without paying. Maritornes joins in her mistress's expressions of anger. Among all these more or less hysterical reactions, the maiden daughter "remained silent, and from time to time she smiled." This enigmatic smile has made of the daughter a kind of Spanish Mona Lisa in prose, attracting the attention of, among others, Unamuno ("a halo of pity in a storm of laughter"), the poet Manuel Machado ("divine silence, precious smile"), and Carmen Castro ("her adolescent smile, the smile of a woman who knows").[24]

The smile is enigmatic indeed, for whereas it clearly indicates some interest in and sympathy for our hero, it does not
result in any sincere attempt at intimacy but leads instead to the
practical joke at Don Quixote's expense recounted in I, 43. Now,
it may be that simple social pressure prevents Miss Palomeque
from approaching Don Quixote and that she is an unwilling
participant in a game organized by Maritornes. It is perhaps more
likely that her cruel treatment of our hero is unconsciously willed
and constitutes a reaction-formation, a defense she mobilizes in
order to avoid having to recognize and acknowledge her own
erotic impulses by transforming them into their polar opposite.
In any case, she and Maritornes attract Don Quixote to a window,
convince him to raise his hand above his head, and then tie it there
and leave him for the night.

As Serrano Plaja has observed, the prank would have been
impossible had Don Quixote not responded so readily to the
daughter's whispered summons, had he not become intoxicated
by the atmosphere at Palomeque's and filled his mind with
thoughts of erotic adventure. As we know, when our hero finds
himself in this predicament he reacts by interposing Dulcinea as a
barrier between himself and the real women who have stimulated
his desire. It is not surprising, therefore, to find him at the
beginning of this episode engaged in a soliloquy directed to his
lady, nor is it surprising to observe that he is trying to create her as
an abstraction: "the extreme of all beauty, acme of discretion,
repository of grace and chastity, and finally the idea of everything
profitable, chaste and delightful in the world!" (I, 43). The fact
that our hero has fallen back on his old disembodied Dulcinea is, I
think, a measure of the powerful effect lately wrought on him by
the presence of so many real, attractive, flesh-and-blood women,
among them the maiden daughter so easily assimilable to Sobrina. His soliloquy may be viewed as a deliberate flight from the
threatening reality of too many real women into the secure realm

of idealized abstractions that demand no response. Alas, Dulcinea in the abstract proves no match for the maiden daughter's whispered invitation, and our hero's attempts to ward off his impulses end in humiliating failure.

It is important to note that when Don Quixote has approached the window, Maritornes informs him that Palomeque's daughter had come to the rendezvous at the risk of her honor and of her father's wrath, for if he found out where she was he would slice off her ear at the very least. Don Quixote vows horrible vengeance on him, but the text of his speech broadens the issue from the father who punishes his daughter's erotic behavior to the father who lays hands on his daughter's delicate body. "But he [the father] will be well advised to refrain from that, if he wishes to avoid the most disastrous end a father ever had in this world, in recompense for having laid hands on his enamored daughter's delicate limbs." That is, the focus of Don Quixote's anger shifts quickly from punishing the father for his anger to punishing him for his assaults on his daughter's body: for his incest. Now, while Palomeque might well be lusting after his daughter in his heart, the text gives no indication of it and Don Quixote certainly cannot be aware of it. The incestuous desires that arouse his indignation are of course not Palomeque's but his own, directed toward Sobrina. Don Quixote's attraction to Palomeque's daughter is in part at least a transference from Sobrina, resulting in a simultaneous projection of his own unacceptable desires onto Palomeque, who is to his maiden daughter as Don Quixote is to his niece. Having exteriorized the "bad" desires in this way, our hero is free to punish them (or threaten to) in a way he never could if they were still lodged in himself.

Perhaps this projection of his own desire onto Palomeque is what accounts for the difference between the leave-taking in I, 46 and that in I, 17. Here there is no exchange of soulful glances but rather a properly chivalric offer of the strength of our hero's arm in defense of all the ladies present. The daughter has changed as well. Instead of reacting differently from the rest, she joins them and all pretend to cry as Don Quixote takes his leave. Her attitude toward him has changed, possibly before but more probably as a result of her mastery of him through the prank of I, 43.

Although she disappears from the book here, Palomeque's maiden daughter is more than a circumstantial character. I have already pointed out Aveleyra's characterization of her as the only possible feminine protagonist of the novel, the only woman Don Quixote allows himself to desire. Serrano Plaja too has called attention to the daughter's repeated appearances in connection with our hero's libido, her own flash of preadult sexuality, and the mutual attraction between the two characters. I can only offer a psychologically verisimilar cause for the effect observed by both critics: the transference effected by Don Quixote of his unacceptable desire for Sobrina.

Don Quixote leaves Palomeque's inn under the spell of a bogus enchantment practiced by his friends the priest and barber and assisted by Don Fernando and the rest. They have placed him in a cage, have set the cage in an ox-drawn cart, and are transporting him in this way back to his home and the possibility of a cure. Before he reaches home, which incidentally is the worst possible location for the proposed therapeutic effort, Don Quixote elaborates for the Canon of Toledo his chivalric-erotic fantasy of the knight who, plunging into the boiling lake, is taken into a crystalline palace and undressed and regaled by a bevy of beautiful damsels. In addition, Don Quixote comes into contact with two more ladies in distress, and his reactions to them are strongly charged with erotic undertones. The point of all this is simply to suggest that although sexual excitement as an overt theme has reached its climax in the events at Palomeque's, our hero has by no means abandoned his own obsession with sex and women. Indeed, the fact that he is physically restrained—in a cage—and under the interdiction of the "enchantment" allows him to fantasize more freely than he could otherwise. The buffer he has

attempted to create (with the success we have observed) by interposing the idea of Dulcinea between his desire and its object is
here provided by his physical situation.

Don Quixote and the rest fall in with Eugenio the shepherd,
who recounts to them the story of the beautiful Leandra and how
he and his friend Anselmo were rivals for her, how she was
seduced—only mentally, it turns out—by the dashing soldier
Vicente de la Roca, and how she ran away with the soldier, was
robbed of her possessions, and retired to a convent. Eugenio's
story is a wonderful recapitulation of several major themes and
episodes—the pastoral myth (Marcela, Grisóstomo, Ambrosio)
invaded by reality, the friendly rivalry (Camila, Lotario, Anselmo) that ends in disaster, virginity and its preservation, the
transmutation of painful experience into art—but I shall be concerned here only with the effect of its denouement on Don
Quixote. Her virginity intact but her honor destroyed, Leandra
retired to a convent, where she has remained ever since. Don
Quixote, who has imaginatively transformed her into a typical
chivalresque heroine, assumes she is being held there against her
will and swears to Eugenio that, were he at liberty to do so, he
would go there and free her, "in spite of the Abbess and anyone
else who would stand in my way, and deliver her into your hands"
(I, 52). At this point our hero's mini-fantasy takes an unexpected
turn. He would deliver Leandra into Eugenio's hands, he says, "so
that you could use her according to your entire will and pleasure."
The rescue of the damsel in distress degenerates into procuring a
woman for immoral purposes. This sudden emphasis on sex is
swiftly brought under control: "Observing, however, the laws of
chivalry, which command that no damsel be treated ill by force."

The threat to Leandra's chastity comes from Don Quixote's
imagination, not from Eugenio. The story of her flight with
Vicente de la Roca and the near loss of her virginity has excited
our hero and caused him to fantasize her at the mercy of a man.
At this juncture his censorship mechanism intervenes to "make

right" the erotic part of the fantasy by bringing it back from unacceptable sexual aggression to its polar opposite: liberation, justice, and safety. This is the same pattern we observed when Don Quixote swore to punish Juan Palomeque's presumed incestuous attack on his daughter. Don Quixote's own sexual aggression rises to the surface, is expressed as projected onto another man, and then is quashed by a powerful intervention of his superego.

The second lady in distress our hero encounters on his way home is the Virgin Mary herself, or rather an image of her being paraded through parched fields by pious farmers imploring rain. Don Quixote identifies her as "some noble lady whom those disrespectful rascals and evildoers are carrying away by force" (I, 52). This distortion of reality is induced, at least in part, by our hero's generally agitated mental state, which has been the effect on him of Eugenio's story and of his subsequent fantasy of Leandra being held in the convent against her will. Like the one immediately preceding, this episode recapitulates a number of themes from earlier in the novel. We see here an Erasmian attack on the worst kind of empty formalism in unholy alliance with the worst kind of ignorant superstition—the procession mounted in order to induce rain—culminating in the physical confrontation between Don Quixote and the religious establishment. Or again, this episode constitutes a reprise of the adventure of the nocturnal religious procession in I, 19, but here the irony is anything but subtle, so that the dullest reader can be made to perceive that religious processions and apparitions from hell are easily confused. But the religious satire does not exist in a fictional vacuum, for its own sake alone. The confrontation is provoked by our hero's all-too-human imposition of a recent erotic fantasy on a new situation that is at least superficially analogous. And at the end, when Don Quixote lies beaten on the ground, he locates the entire episode within the series of adventures in which the presence of a real erotic stimulus is opposed by the invocation of

Dulcinea. "Who lives apart from you, sweetest Dulcinea, must endure worse even than this."

Finally, the oxcart carrying Don Quixote in his cage reaches the village. It is Sunday and everyone is out. Our hero and his entourage are forced to cross the plaza and be seen by all before arriving at his house. Figuratively, our hero's entrance recalls one aspect of the standard punishment for criminal offenses in his society, exposure to public shame. More in keeping with the imaginative context, Don Quixote's return is a burlesque inversion of a stock episode from the chivalric romances, one that is particularly dear to him personally: the arrival of the famous knight at the castle amid attendant manifestations of general interest and special care. This has been a recurring fantasy for him, operative virtually from the first evening of the first day of the first sally, and with it Cervantes brings his narrative full circle to its ironic conclusion.

The personnel of Don Quixote's house, the people who actually receive and attend him, are of course Ama and Sobrina. They "received him, undressed him and laid him in his bed. He regarded them with sidelong glances, and could not ascertain where he was" (I, 52). There are two important aspects to this brief quotation. First, Don Quixote is not aware that he is home, nor does he appear to recognize Ama and Sobrina. For him, apparently, this is some new "castle" and the women who attend him are part of the household. Second, the scene described here is the classic one: the knight arrives and his needs are attended to by ladies of the castle. The three of them are acting out the same scene Don Quixote played with the two prostitutes in I, 2 and with Maritornes and Palomeque's daughter in I, 16. It is the scene captured in the Ballad of Lancelot which Don Quixote is so fond of quoting and which is so deeply internalized in his psyche.

Never was there a knight
by ladies so well served,
as was Sir Lancelot

when from Britain he came.
For maidens waited on him,
and dueñas saw to his horse.

We know that the section of the ballad quoted is the prelude to a narration of illicit sex. We can also see, here at the end of Cervantes's narration, that a clear correspondence has been established between Don Quixote and Lancelot as well as between Ama and Sobrina on the one hand and, on the other, the two prostitutes, Maritornes and Palomeque's daughter, the dueñas and doncellas of the ballad, and Quintañona and Guinevere. For our hero, a most unfortunate combination.

Don Quixote left home fifty-two chapters earlier because he could not master his middle-age upsurge of sexuality, which was directed toward a forbidden object, his own niece. He tried first to lose himself in the vicarious experience of life offered by the romances of chivalry. In the process he incorporated and internalized a number of stereotypical erotic situations, but the experience was not powerful enough to sublimate his libidinous energy and he was forced to take flight, physically. Along the way he was attracted to several women, three in particular, two of whom were strongly reminiscent of Sobrina. He experienced his desire for them all as unacceptable and tried desperately to create Dulcinea del Toboso as a barrier between his desire and these women who were the objects of it. By and large his efforts failed, principally because he could only conceptualize Dulcinea as a series of abstractions and could not visualize her as a woman. Now, finally, he has been brought home again, with all his reading and its charge of erotic stimulation, with all his recent experience with real women, and delivered into the very situation from which he fled. The situation this time is incalculably worse, for now Don Quixote's readings and his experiences are part of him, and instead of relieving the pressure of his attraction to Sobrina, they can only serve to increase it. This incorporation of reading and experience is the meaning of this stereotypical final scene in

135

which Ama and Sobrina undress Don Quixote and put him to bed, recalling Quintañona and Guinevere as well as Maritornes and maiden daughter.

In this environment the cure desired by the priest and barber is doomed a thousand times over. Don Quixote will stay put only as long as he is physically unable to flee, as Ama and Sobrina seem to understand. "Finally, they remained confused, and fearful that they would find themselves without master and uncle as soon as he improved, and it happened just as they imagined."

5
DULCINEA AND THE REAL WOMEN:
Part II

Although Part II continues the story of Don Quixote's life and his evolution, both physical and psychic, in a perfectly logical way to his death, so that in a sense Part I remains incomplete and always in need of Part II, there are important differences between the two. Cervantes was supremely conscious in Part II of writing a new and different book, one that was definitely not a repetition of Part I and that was much more than a continuation of it. Before we begin our own consideration of Part II it might be well to review some of these differences.

The adventures in Part I are characterized by spontaneity. Don Quixote typically finds himself in a situation onto which he projects his inner needs. Windmills become giants, an inn becomes a castle, and events take their course. In Part II the adventures are the result of what might be termed a dialectic of nature and art. Since this is properly the subject of a separate monograph, suffice it to observe here that in Part II adventures typically begin when someone deliberately attempts to stage-manage reality, to create a contrived situation in which a predictable response from someone else will be elicited. In Part II people attempt to dominate nature, to turn it into art. Nature, however, has a way of asserting itself; human response, even to an artificial, contrived situation, cannot be controlled. Plans go awry.

The attempt at control—a thesis—encounters an antithesis in the form of an unplanned eruption of life in all its spontaneity, and the resulting new situation becomes a thesis to be opposed in turn by a new antithesis. We shall have occasion to observe this process, for example, in Sancho's enchantment of Dulcinea in II, 10. It is crucial to the structure of Part II, especially in opposition to Part I.

An important corollary to the process described above concerns Don Quixote's continuing ability to generate the kind of fantasies he requires to shape reality as he needs it in order to be Don Quixote. In Part I our hero's rich fantasy life is the product of the joining of his inner life—unconscious needs, reading consciously remembered, events of the recent past recalled—with his situation of the moment. Don Quixote imposes his inner needs, by the processes of distortion and delusional projection, on his immediate environment. A barber's basin becomes Mambrino's enchanted helmet because at that moment it is available and Don Quixote needs a helmet. The resultant episodes all follow naturally from Don Quixote's initiative. In Part II our hero is frequently forced to adapt his behavior to the situations deliberately prefabricated by others, to follow a script written by someone else. Two things happen as a result. First, the basic tool available to Don Quixote for the fabrication of his own existence, the ability to control his environment by projecting some fantasy onto it, passes to someone else. The second consequence of this new *modus operandi* is simply that our hero's imaginative faculty—in Huarte's terms, his ability to generate the kind of situations and sustain the beliefs he needs—grows rusty from lack of use. This inability any longer to come up with a life-sustaining fantasy is one of the proximate causes of Don Quixote's death in II, 74.

Although Don Quixote had a fifty-year history when we first met him in I, 1, it was not the history of Don Quixote but rather of an anonymous rural hidalgo. The history that determined his inability to relate to women, so crucially important to his middle-aged retreat into psychosis, is in fact a prehistory in the sense that it is not narrated, not available for our direct observation. The history of Don Quixote of La Mancha as a public person, however, begins in I, 1 and continues before our eyes for fifty-two chapters. We see him make certain choices instead of others, and we watch him react to situations in certain ways and not in others. By the time we reach the end of Part I, we have quite definite ideas about him. We can imagine him proclaiming his love for Dulcinea, but we cannot imagine him getting drunk, for example. All this is to say that during the course of Part I our hero has acquired a history, a history that in turn has given him a recognizable character that distinguishes him from other men. Ortega observed long ago that man has no essence, only a history. That observation is nowhere as true as it is with respect to Don Quixote. By the time Part II begins, our hero's possibilities for action, his choices, are circumscribed by his history. He cannot now act "out of character" without destroying his own integrity and changing the novel from a work of verisimilar fiction into something else.

A corollary to this observation relates to the presence and importance of literature in Cervantes's text. Part I is dominated by all sorts of preexisting genres and even specific texts: the chivalric tradition in prose romances, ballads, and epics; the picaresque tradition; the pastoral. Don Quixote quite consciously sets out to imitate Amadís de Gaula and mad Orlando. In Part II it is to Part I that characters turn for models to imitate and for inspiration. Don Quixote's own character continues in Part II what was established over the length of Part I. Other characters relate to our hero according to whether they have or have not read Part I. The duke and duchess derive many of the pranks to which they deliberately subject him from specific episodes in Part I. The "Countess Trifaldi" incident (II, 36–41), for example, is an expanded version of the "Princess Micomicona" episode from Part I.

I need to comment briefly on the evolution of Dulcinea and of Don Quixote's relationship with Sancho throughout Part I before beginning a chronological survey of Dulcinea and the real women in Part II. I concluded in the last chapter that Don Quixote has not been particularly successful in his efforts to create a concrete, visualizable—not merely conceptualizable—Dulcinea in opposition to Sobrina. He tried manfully in I, 25 and I, 31 by giving Sancho the opportunity in turn to offer him the physical reality of Aldonza Lorenzo to transform by a dialectical process into a "real" Dulcinea. But at the end of Part I there are still no permanent, physical characteristics we can associate with her. Is she tall? Short? Buxom? Slim? Blond? Brunette? Are her eyes green? Blue? Brown? When he is hard pressed, Don Quixote over and over falls back on some abstract, incorporeal Dulcinea related either to religious faith or to Platonic idealization: the Word made Flesh in I, 13; Christ as evoked by Paul in I, 29; the idea of all that's fair in I, 43. Dulcinea is literally not materializing, and our hero's inability to engender her is most probably a function of the presence of Sobrina as a physical image just below the level of consciousness.

Now, although he cannot get Sobrina out of his mind, and although his attempts to create a viable Dulcinea have not been entirely successful, Don Quixote has, beginning in I, 7, been involved in a constant, intimate, and evolving relationship with Sancho. He has in fact been living in greater proximity—physical and psychic—to his squire than to his niece virtually since the beginning of the narration. As I observed earlier, those human relationships most highly charged with psychic significance are the ones that combine intimacy—the sharing of certain times and spaces—with custom. This is why, for example, Don Quixote is in love with Sobrina and not with Aldonza. This fact in turn invites us to consider his relationship with Sancho as a kind of alternative to his relationship with Sobrina, from whom he is separated for precisely the time he spends with Sancho.

The relationship between the two men is emphatically not homosexual in nature. In fact it is not sexual. It does, however, partake of characteristics of what Leslie Fiedler has called a homoerotic relationship and which for Fiedler defines the great "couples" of American literature: Huck Finn and Jim; Natty Bumppo and Chingachgook; Ishmael and Queequeg.[1] The idea is that, a normal relationship with a woman being for one reason or another impossible, these men seek out each other's company and enjoy together a psychically intimate relationship whose physical-sexual side is sublimated into various manly out-of-doors pursuits: going off in search of adventure, sleeping out under the stars, fighting and engaging in feats of arms. We know that Don Quixote's retreat into psychosis has been motivated precisely by a powerful upsurge of libido cathected onto an impossible object in deadly combination with a long-standing inability to relate normally to women. He flees from his household, and his relationship with Sancho, who is likewise escaping from a house full of women, allows him to find an acceptable outlet for the psychic energy misdirected at Sobrina by sublimating his forbidden desire into socially useful activity and into a richly rewarding human relationship whose proper name is love. There is absolutely no question that the relationship between Sancho and Don Quixote is much deeper, more significant, more rewarding, in every way better than any other relationship either one of them enjoys with anyone else of either sex. I shall consider this relationship in passing in this chapter, in connection with certain episodes of particular significance, and I shall attempt to treat it more systematically in the conclusions.

Let us now turn to the first seven chapters of Part II and consider what is accomplished structurally and thematically before Don Quixote and Sancho set out on the knight's third sally. The fictional continuity with Part I is established as the narrator tells us that one month had elapsed since Don Quixote had come home in the cage when his friends the priest and barber went to call on him. They find him more dried out than ever, an indication according to the theories of Huarte that he is still unbalanced and therefore still subject to his insanity. Insanity itself is established as an important theme, first by the presence of two stories about madmen in the prologue and then by the barber's story of the monomaniac who had almost succeeded in getting himself discharged from the asylum when, by chance, another patient elicited from him a display of his particular delusionary behavior. This is precisely what his friends elicit from Don Quixote when their conversation turns to warfare and the threat of a Turkish invasion. After a month of rest and attempted cure, Don Quixote is still Don Quixote and still insane.

The bond between Don Quixote and Sancho is insisted upon, first, through conversations between the priest and the barber. The latter remarks, "I am not as struck by the madness of the knight as I am by the simplicity of the squire," to which the priest responds that "such a knight and such a squire must have been cast in the same mold" (II, 2). Later Don Quixote himself reminds Sancho that "we went out together, we traveled together, and the two of us have suffered the same good and ill fortune together." He further establishes an organic relation between them by analogy with the head and the body (*quando caput dolet, caetera membra dolent*) and insists that he participated spiritually in Sancho's physical mistreatment at the hands of Juan Palomeque and his friends.

It should be noted that Sancho is not entirely willing to accept his master's analysis of the situation—otherwise there would be no need for Don Quixote to insist as he does on the equality of their suffering. The fact of a close relationship does not imply complete unanimity of opinion or the absence of conflict. Indeed, real differences of opinion are worth expressing only in significant relationships. In II, 7 just such a difference of opinion is expressed. At his wife's urging, we learn later, Sancho attempts to establish a modern, capitalistic relationship between service and recompense and suggests that Don Quixote pay him a monthly wage. Don Quixote, who besides having no money to spare is still emotionally attached to feudalism, throws back to him the example of chivalresque literature, where salaried squires are unknown. Sancho persists and Don Quixote threatens to find another squire. At this point the personal relationship evolved over Part I asserts itself and proves to be more important to Sancho than a salary. The narrator reports that "the sky clouded over for Sancho and the wings fell from his heart." Just then Sansón Carrasco, a recent university graduate and something of a prankster, enters and offers to be Don Quixote's squire himself. Don Quixote, who really desires no other squire than Sancho, politely refuses Carrasco's offer and remarks that he will make do with anyone, "inasmuch as Sancho will not deign to join me." Sancho is undone: " 'Yes I will,' he responded with tears in his eyes . . . 'and I offer myself again, to serve you faithfully and truly, as well as or even better than any squire ever served a knight-errant' " (II, 7). Sancho's strong personal attachment to Don Quixote triumphs for the moment, but the question of a salary will become a persistent bone of contention between them as Part II progresses.

Chapters 5 and 6 show us the relationship in a different light, when the two men are apart from each other and each engages in a discussion with the women of his household. The conversations are strikingly similar. Both men affirm the values of chivalry and the necessity to set off again, and Sancho corrects Teresa's malapropisms in exactly the same way Don Quixote habitually corrects his. This is a most important detail, for it demonstrates that Sancho has evolved as a result of his close and extended relationship with Don Quixote. Salvador de Madariaga observed this evolution long ago and called it the "quixotification" of Sancho.[2] Madariaga's insight, however, should be tempered by attention to the crisis of the salary which we have just observed. If Sancho actually became like his master, and Don Quixote like his squire, they would both cease to be interesting characters. Fortunately their relationship, which evolves constantly, does not evolve in this direction. It will in fact be tested by several different crises in the course of Part II.

In II, 3 Don Quixote discovers the existence of Part I, and while he is waiting for Sansón Carrasco to come tell him about it, he falls to thinking how it might be. Prominent among his thoughts is a concern for the book's treatment of his love life. "He was afraid that his love had been treated indecently, so as to besmirch the chastity of his lady Dulcinea. He hoped the book declared the fidelity he had always shown her, rejecting queens, empresses, maidens of all stations, holding his own natural impulses at bay." In this combination of fact and fantasy, self-awareness and self-deception, Don Quixote demonstrates once more the presence within him of powerful erotic impulses—and his awareness of them. He has in fact been attracted to several different women, and as we have seen, he has had to work very hard to deny his impulses. This passage also reaffirms the function of Dulcinea as a buffer between his desires and their real-life objects. He does not, of course, understand this function himself.

The real, primordial object of Don Quixote's desire continues to be Sobrina, and as she and Ama come to realize that he is planning a third sally, they both attempt to dissuade him from it. In the process they establish potentially important distinctions between their respective personalities and between their respective attitudes toward our hero. Ama appears much the more sympathetic of the two, perhaps a function of her age and experience. She asks Don Quixote if he could be one of the knights who serve the king at court instead of sallying forth in search of danger. He makes the appropriate distinction between courtier and knight-errant and concludes with a warlike fantasy. He is cordial and patient with her and she is not insulting to him.

Sobrina, however, is different. She first shows her religious-conformist side by demanding that all the romances of chivalry be burned or, failing that, identified as heretics with a special covering, called a *sambenito*, worn by those individuals found guilty by the Inquisition. She recalls the inquisitorial parody of I, 6. Don Quixote labels her remarks "blasphemy," thus opposing his liberal, Erasmian religiosity to her Establishment variety. Then the exchange becomes more personal as Sobrina begins to attack her uncle on the grounds that his ideas and behavior are inappropriate to his advanced age and real social position. She observes in him "a blindness so great and a foolishness so notorious that he believes he is brave when in fact he is old, that he is strong when in fact he is sick, that he rights wrongs when in fact he is overcome by age, and above all, that he is a caballero when in fact he is not, for although some hidalgos are also caballeros, they are not the poor ones" (II, 6).

Sobrina's speech is motivated by the arrogance of youth, a fact that does not alter its vehemence. Of all the things that any woman has said to our hero in the two parts of the novel to this point, this is the only one that exemplifies the rigor and rejection that he typically associates with Dulcinea. It will be recalled that he complains at the beginning of the first sally that his lady has treated him harshly by ordering him out of her presence. This suggests another feature of the difficulty our hero encounters whenever he attempts to create Dulcinea. At the same time that she is supposed to be an alternative to Sobrina, Dulcinea at least in part *is* Sobrina. I have already postulated her physical image just below the level of Don Quixote's consciousness, and now we can observe her mental attitudes there as well.[3]

Don Quixote bears the attack graciously. He makes an enigmatic remark about lineage which appears to be in response to Sobrina's chatter about hidalgos and caballeros but could also refer to the bond of blood between them. "You are right in what you say, my niece, and I could tell you things about lineage that would amaze you. But to do so would be to mix the divine and the human." Instead, he launches into a most general discussion of the vicissitudes of lineage in the world at large. Two pages earlier he had identified Sobrina as the daughter of his sister, so their relation is clearly on his mind. In addition he calls her "a girl who still can't handle more than twelve bobbins [*palillos de randas*] at a time," a reference to the household fabrication of laces, typical women's work. It is Don Quixote's only real contribution to the controversy between age and youth, but it is an important remark for two reasons. First, the expression *hacer randas* had a sexual connotation in Don Quixote's time, and second (and more important), our hero uses the same phrase to characterize a girl named Altisidora, to whom he is powerfully attracted beginning in II, 44.[4] This Altisidora, as we shall see, has more than a little in common with Sobrina.

In the following chapter Ama again expresses her concern for Don Quixote's well-being and attempts to persuade Sansón Carrasco to intervene and stop the proposed third sally. She recalls how her master returned from the first one, beaten up and slung over a mule, and from the second, "thin, yellow, his eyes sunk into the furthest recesses of his head," and remarks how she fed him more than 600 eggs to enable him to recover his strength.[5] This expression of concern contrasts violently with Sobrina's gratuitous cruelty and demonstrates again the existence of an important difference between the two women in Don Quixote's household with respect to their attitudes toward him. Ama, a woman of approximately his age, shows real sympathy and compassion for him. Sobrina considers him an embarrassment, insists on the great difference in their respective ages, and harps on what she perceives as the degeneration of his physical powers.

There is one last event we should consider before Don Quixote and Sancho set out. In II, 4 our hero requests that Sansón Carrasco compose some acrostic verses of farewell to Dulcinea. A technical problem arises from the fact that no known strophic form in Spanish is composed of seventeen lines, the number required by the letters in Dulcinea's full name. Don Quixote insists on the acrostic, on the absolute identification of the woman, the name, and the poem. This is another manifestation of our hero's typical tendency to create his lady fair along abstract-verbal rather than concrete-physical lines. What is new here is his willingness to delegate the task to Sansón, or phrased another way, his willingness to relinquish control of the creative process to another. This is the beginning of a dangerous tendency whose result, at the end of Part II, will be Don Quixote's final inability to maintain the myth of Dulcinea at all, an inability to generate which literally proves fatal.

"Blessed be Allah!" we can say with Cide Hamete Benengeli, for Don Quixote and Sancho are finally on the road beginning in II, 8. Their destination is El Toboso, their goal to pay respects to Dulcinea. What happens in and around El Toboso during the next three chapters will chart the course of the action for the remainder of Part II. What Don Quixote and Sancho decide to do here will establish the basic conditions for our hero's erotic life in fact and fantasy and for the evolution of his relationship with Sancho. This will be modified and complemented by the machinations of the duke and duchess, but their intervention too will be based on what happens here at El Toboso.

My guess is that the trip to El Toboso, with all its attendant risks, has been motivated by our hero's imperious need to get away from Sobrina and to involve himself with some direct alternative to her—that is, with Dulcinea. The effect of Don Quixote's decision is to re-create the ambiguous and threatening situation of I, 31, when Sancho reported that Dulcinea had requested his presence. That crisis—the danger of Sancho's lie being exposed and of the nonexistence of Dulcinea becoming an inescapable fact—was mercifully averted by the priority of Don Quixote's commitment to Princess Micomicona. Here the crisis, which jeopardizes both the relationship between Sancho and Don Quixote and that between the latter and Dulcinea, becomes the point of departure.

As the two approach El Toboso it becomes clear to Sancho at the level of consciousness, and begins to dawn on Don Quixote at a deeper level, that this mission must be aborted. Some indications begin to appear before they reach El Toboso. Don Quixote insists, incredibly, that they wait until nightfall to enter the city. He begins to fill his discourse with religious references, a sure sign that he is laboring mightily to engender Dulcinea within himself. He thinks "that huge bulk" must be Dulcinea's palace; in fact it is the church. When Sancho suggests he must know where her palace is, since he must have seen it "thousands of times," our hero retorts: "You drive me to desperation, Sancho. Come here, you heretic" (II, 9). Again, belief in Dulcinea is like belief in the Divinity. Failing to accept this belief is heresy. "Haven't I told you a thousand times that in all the days of my life I have never seen the peerless Dulcinea, nor ever crossed the threshold of her palace, having fallen in love with her only by hearsay, because of the great fame of her beauty and discretion?"

This is important. Never having seen Dulcinea is clearly not the same as having seen Aldonza four times. Dulcinea is not Aldonza. Dulcinea ascends here to some superior plane of being, perhaps divorced from Sobrina, and certainly no longer referable to Aldonza. She begins to exist as an independent entity. We shall observe several instances in the next few chapters where a reference to Aldonza would seem obligatory, and where none is made. In fact, Aldonza Lorenzo is not a character in Part II at all, with the single exception of Sancho's identification of Dulcinea as Aldonza (II, 36) to his wife, Teresa, who would otherwise be totally disoriented.[6]

Dulcinea is not Aldonza, Dulcinea is incorporeal, and Dulcinea is not to be found in El Toboso: the mission must be aborted. Don Quixote proposes a solution that is an excellent example of the tendency (to which I have already referred) in

Part II to attempt to stage-manage reality. Sancho first suggests they hide outside the city until daylight, whereupon he, Sancho, will enter El Toboso and make every effort to locate Dulcinea. Don Quixote instantly agrees, praising Sancho for his discretion—a fact that indicates Don Quixote's own interest in never locating her: he is willing to eliminate 50 percent of the search force.[7] He then equips Sancho with a series of elements, some of extreme verisimilitude, which Sancho can use to fabricate his narration of an interview with Dulcinea, which of course can never take place. That is to say, Don Quixote proposes a return to I, 31. All Sancho has to do is to wait a decent interval and then return to his master and report something to the effect that Dulcinea did not wish to see him and instead commands him to take to the road in search of adventures. Don Quixote is perfectly prepared to receive this kind of message and would even be grateful for it, since it would call off the search for Dulcinea and get him and Sancho out of town. It is this sort of response that he attempts to engineer when he tells Sancho to notice Dulcinea's mannerisms, her unspoken reactions to Sancho's entreaties on his behalf. He is in effect instructing Sancho to do what he has done in I, 31, but to do it right this time, to make it verisimilar. That Don Quixote can do this at all is of course an indication of how sensitive he and Sancho have become to the communication that takes place below the cognitive level of the spoken word: in short, an indication of their intimacy.

Perhaps Sancho is in fact not as sensitive as Don Quixote believed, or perhaps he thinks he knows better, or perhaps he is just perverse. In any case, he rejects the script proposed by Don Quixote and decides to work out his own solution. He sits down under a tree in II, 10 and examines the situation. In his analysis he never once refers to Aldonza. This is a most significant advance over Part I, where he simply fantasized an encounter with Aldonza as the basis for his report of his interview with Dulcinea. Here in Part II that possibility appears not to occur to him at all.

He knows Aldonza well, as we have learned from I, 25, and presumably knows where she lives. He also knows, again from I, 25, that in some sense she is "really" Dulcinea, and he believes that Don Quixote is secretly in love with her. Nothing could be more logical than to seek her out, as he pretended to do earlier. The only explanation for his failure to do so is that for him as well as for Don Quixote, Dulcinea is not Aldonza but an incorporeal ideal whose existence must be accepted on faith, and it is on this basis that he constructs his plan to deceive his master and save his own "honor."

As every reader knows, Sancho decides to convince Don Quixote that Dulcinea has been enchanted, cast into the form of the first farm girl he happens to see. Communication will of course be precluded, and Sancho will have escaped El Toboso with his lie of I, 31 intact. In other words, Sancho changes the rules of the game that Don Quixote has just proposed. Phrased another way, Don Quixote has attempted to convert life, nature, into a work of art by a process of stage management, by contriving a situation and controlling Sancho's response to it. Sancho throws away the script. His plan—the enchantment of Dulcinea— represents an eruption of life in all its unplanned spontaneity, the antithesis that opposes Don Quixote's original thesis. This sequence of events is the first part of the first round of a continuing dialectic of nature and art.

When Sancho identifies one of the three farm girls coming down the road as Dulcinea, Don Quixote cannot accept this predicate without enormous difficulty. Try as he might, he sees only three coarse farm girls. Because too much is at stake, though, he cannot challenge Sancho's identification openly. Instead the controversy is displaced and focuses on the proper name for the animals the three girls are riding.[8] The reason our hero experiences such difficulty in accepting a work of the imagination which will end the search for Dulcinea and get him and Sancho out of El Toboso is simply that the Dulcinea he is being asked to accept is not his own creation, but Sancho's. Sancho has seized the initiative and offered the only Dulcinea now possible. Don Quixote finally believes the enchantment story because the only alternative would be to abandon belief in Dulcinea altogether.

In the short range, Sancho's solution to the immediate crisis provides an absolutely unassailable rationale for pursuing Dulcinea no further, which otherwise threatens to expose her non-existence. She is, in a word, safely on ice. Her enchantment here in II, 10 is analogous to the creation in I, 6 of the "enchanters" who pursue our hero so assiduously. Both incidents provide him with a publicly acceptable reason for not having to come to grips with reality—his failure to vanquish the giants in I, 8 or the need in II, 10 to admit that Dulcinea exists only in his mind. Sancho's enchantment of Dulcinea allows Part II to proceed. As Richard Predmore has remarked, however, "the enchantment perpetrated by Sancho will in the long run do his master more harm than good."[9] This is due quite simply to the fact that Dulcinea is no longer Don Quixote's creation as she was, however imperfectly and abstractly, in Part I. Our hero's difficulty is one of internalizing an intimate fantasy not of his own making. That he is willing even to try bears witness to the intensity of his need to preserve Dulcinea. In the end, however, so many diverse hands have meddled in her creation and preservation that the effort proves too much for him.

In the course of my elucidation of this important episode—the events in and around El Toboso culminating in the creation by Sancho of a new, enchanted Dulcinea and her acceptance by Don Quixote—it should have become apparent that the entire concept and function of Dulcinea have changed. In Part I she was an idealized displacement of Don Quixote's unacceptable incestuous desires for Sobrina, and she also functioned as a buffer between himself and the other women (Marcela, Palomeque's daughter, Dorotea) that he met and desired. In Part I, then, Dulcinea is a means to an end. Here in Part II she emerges as an end in herself. Independent of Aldonza, she comes forward as a myth, the belief in which must be maintained. Instead of attempting to endow her with concrete physical attributes, the goal now is to render her incorporeal and unattainable. Preservation of the myth of Dulcinea, as the key to the maintenance of the existence of Don Quixote himself, now becomes paramount. This change in her function is what explains Don Quixote's increasing reluctance to push the search for her as he and Sancho approach El Toboso, his grateful acceptance of Sancho's tacit offer to get them out of there, and his final acceptance, not without extreme difficulty, of the new, enchanted Dulcinea.

In II, 14 Sansón Carrasco, disguised as the Knight of the Mirrors, overtakes Don Quixote and introduces himself. In the course of their conversation he describes Don Quixote, whom he claims to have vanquished, to Don Quixote. One of the features he mentions is that Don Quixote "has for the lady of his will a certain Dulcinea del Toboso, formerly known as Aldonza Lorenzo, as my lady is called Casildea de Vandalia because her name is Casilda and her home is Andalucía" (II, 14). Sansón has dressed himself up as an imitation, or more precisely a mirror image, of Don Quixote in order to vanquish him and send him home to be cured. An aspect of his imitation of Don Quixote is the transformation of prosaic Casilda into Casildea de Vandalia. Sansón has imitated the Don Quixote of I, 1, who sprang from Sobrina to Aldonza to Dulcinea, but the Don Quixote who confronts him here in II, 14 has evolved considerably and is no longer concerned with Aldonza. He answers Sansón by reporting the latest news, which excludes Aldonza altogether, that Dulcinea has been enchanted and transformed into a coarse and vulgar farm girl. This girl is in fact quite similar to Aldonza as Sancho describes her, but no one—not Sancho, not Don Quixote, not Cide Hamete Benengeli—ever suggests the resemblance. Aldonza is simply not here, in any form.

Two chapters later, when Don Quixote has vanquished his antagonist on a fluke, he discovers that the latter looks exactly like Sansón Carrasco. He invokes the enchantment of Dulcinea to "prove" that it is not Sansón inside the armor but someone transformed into his likeness by enchantment. Sancho cannot afford to disagree, so he remains silent, with the result that Sansón's disguise strengthens Sancho and his deceit and helps Don Quixote to accept the new, enchanted Dulcinea invented by Sancho. This delicate play of counterbalanced vested interests, unacknowledged by the characters but present just below the surface, was begun in Part I but really comes into its own here in Part II. It is a most important aspect of the evolving relationship between Don Quixote and Sancho.

After the ugly, coarse farm girl and her friends, the next real woman of any consequence Don Quixote meets on this third outing is the beautiful Quiteria, betrothed to the wealthy Camacho but won ultimately by the man she really loves, the poor but clever Basilio. The episode has resonances of both the Marcela-Grisóstomo and the Cardenio-Luscinda-Don Fernando episodes of Part I, recast into the new conceptual framework of Part II, but this is not the place for such an analysis. It is Don Quixote's reaction to Quiteria as a woman that interests us here. Don Quixote comes into contact with Quiteria's beauty by hearsay. Everyone for miles around praises her beauty, and at the celebration someone calls her "the most beautiful woman in the world." Our hero reacts instantly: "It seems clear that these people have never seen my Dulcinea del Toboso, because if they had, they would not praise Quiteria's beauty so hastily" (II, 20). Here there is no evocation of particular features. Don Quixote cannot be comparing one woman with another, for he has seen neither. Dulcinea is rather invoked as an ideal of beauty to whom Quiteria, however beautiful she may turn out to be, cannot measure up. Phrased another way, the fact of Quiteria's presumed

beauty allows Don Quixote to deny the ugly farm girl, the en-
chanted Dulcinea of II, 10, and restore her to her incorporeal
Platonic eminence. This is an attempt to create, or re-create—or
better, to regain control of—the process of creating Dulcinea.
Quiteria's fabled beauty serves as the stimulus that makes Don
Quixote's effort possible.

The struggle over the control of Dulcinea's creation is the
central theme of Don Quixote's dream in the cave of Montesinos,
which he recounts to Sancho and a character known only as the
"cousin of the Licentiate," hereinafter the Primo, who has guided
them to the place. This episode (II, 23–24) is a most important
one in the evolution of our hero's relationship both to Sancho and
to Dulcinea, and its disquieting, almost surreal features have
made it one of the most studied sequences in the novel. It
deserves our careful attention.

I should first insist that Don Quixote's experience in the
cave of Montesinos is in fact a dream, a perfectly normal function
in a verisimilar literary character such as our hero, and not some
kind of allegorical nonsense referable only to some inverisimilar
literary tradition. I should also insist that Don Quixote's dream is
a plausible—that is, a verisimilar—one and that it responds to the
analysis of dreams as normally practiced in psychoanalysis. I
should like to preface my analysis of our hero's dream as he
narrates it to Sancho and the Primo with the following common-
sense observations by a competent professional, George Devereux, on the plausibility of literary dreams in general.

> The psychological plausibility of a literary dream, quite as much as
> the realism of Rembrandt's painting of a beef carcass, can be
> ascertained in terms of specifiable criteria. . . . The criteria . . . are
> those of psychoanalysis. . . . It is hardly necessary to add that this
> procedure no more turns the poet's Menelaos into a real person
> lying on an analytical couch, than finding that the texture of
> Rembrandt's beef carcass correctly represents the texture of high
> quality steak renders that painting edible. . . . The demonstration
> that Menelaos' dream is properly oneiric does not necessarily imply

that Aischylos carefully set out to contrive a psychologically plausible dream. . . . I assume only that he tried to write the best drama (and dream) he could devise. . . . I set myself the task of studying what he had done and of ascertaining whether that was "true to life" in terms of specifiable criteria and techniques of dream analysis. . . . Since all men dream, we need not suppose that Aischylos, Sophokles, Euripedes had to read Freud in order to devise plausible dreams. . . . But I had to read Freud in order to demonstrate their plausibility.[10]

Mere plausibility, however, does not guarantee any integration into the total personality of the literary character or into the total aesthetic system of the work. Norman N. Holland has provided both an excellent example and a splendid methodological caveat in his analysis and interpretation of Romeo's three-line dream about being awakened from death and then transformed into an emperor by his lover's kiss.[11] Holland considers it essential first to establish the context in which the dream was dreamed and the chronology of day residue that may appear in it. Second, although we lack the dreamer's associations to his dream—a powerful tool in real dream analysis in the clinical situation—we can still provide an interpretation of the symbols and the analyst's associations to them. Finally—and this is most important—we must ask, Of what use is the analysis of the dream to our comprehension of the work? In order to transform our observations from the status of psychological curios to valid critical insights, Holland proposes a simple test: "To see whether the psychological description of the character (or event) can be phrased in words that apply to the total work, be they ordinary critical language or the technical terms of psychoanalysis." The dream must be placed in the context of everything we know about the dreamer's life. Only in this way can a literary dream—or a real one, for that matter—yield any insights.

Let us turn to the dreamwork and consider those features of it which allow us to identify Don Quixote's experience in the cave as a dream. By the term *dreamwork* is meant the experience of the dream itself plus the secondary elaboration grafted onto it as it is recalled and narrated by the dreamer. The dreamwork is what Don Quixote tells Sancho and the Primo. First, we may observe that Montesinos as Don Quixote reports him is dressed not in the garb of chivalry but, incongruously, as a scholar. This is an example of what is termed the "day residue"—recollections left over from our experiences during the hours of wakefulness—and of their effect on the creation of the dream: Don Quixote dresses Montesinos like the Primo, with whom he has spent the day. In addition we can note the presence of a number of anomalies of the kind we can all agree are possible only in dreams. The controversy over whether a dagger or a dirk was the weapon used to remove Durandarte's heart, the fact that Montesinos had the heart salted down so it would not smell as he transported it, Durandarte's totally anachronistic and inappropriate expression, "Have patience and deal the cards again," and finally the mention of Belerma's lack of menstrual periods are all examples of the kind of incongruous details that populate our dreams.[12]

Don Quixote narrates a plausible dream, a message not from beyond but from within. Its theme, logically, is a matter with which our hero has been wrestling since II, 10: the fact that the Dulcinea now operative in his life (at least his conscious life) is the new, enchanted Dulcinea invented by Sancho and "transformed" into a coarse farm girl. At the time he could not afford to argue with Sancho because Sancho's Dulcinea was the only one available, and to destroy her would have been disastrous for Don Quixote. So she exists, precariously, in his consciousness, but if he is to regain some semblance of authenticity in his own existence he must internalize Sancho's Dulcinea—come really to believe in her—and he must regain control of her continued evolution. That part of the dreamwork in which he narrates her presence, along with her two companions, in the enchanted nether world of Montesinos's cave is therefore of paramount importance. It is a great victory in the sense that she is there, below the level of consciousness, in that preconscious zone where dreams are made. She has percolated down at least to this level of our hero's psyche, and he has assumed the task of her continued evolution. She is needy, she approaches him for a loan, she refuses to talk to him, and the like. Sancho is dismayed by what to him is proof of his master's accelerating flight into more aberrant forms of madness, since he knows that this new Dulcinea was in fact his creation. Sancho does not yet grasp the full significance of the fact that the new Dulcinea now exists independently of her original creator. The duke and duchess will make it painfully clear to him beginning in II, 33.

For now it is sufficient to note and rejoice in her presence below the level of Don Quixote's consciousness, in his dream, and simultaneously to observe the absence of Sobrina from that level. This too is cause for some optimism, for although it does not mean necessarily that the unacceptable desire for her which drove our hero from his house in the first place has simply ceased to exist, it does indicate that it is not as close to the surface of consciousness as it once was. Contrary to a belief widespread among laymen and us literary critics, a dream is not simply the expression of thoughts and attitudes buried in the unconscious which come bubbling up to the surface when the repressive mechanisms of consciousness are relaxed during sleep. Rather, the manifest content of a dream—that is, what the dreamer reports, the dreamwork—is itself a disguised form of some unacceptable unconscious thought that if allowed to surface would wake us up and cause unpleasure. The function of dreams is to allow us to remain asleep. This is accomplished by a kind of censorship mechanism that operates, even in sleep, below the level of consciousness at what has been termed the preconscious level. It is here that the dream is fabricated, as intolerable *latent content* is pushed into the shape of a much less disquieting *manifest content*. The task of dream analysis is precisely to attempt to reverse the process, to coax the latent content out from the clues offered by the manifest content present in the dreamwork. The presence of Sancho's Dulcinea at the level of manifest content does not, therefore, imply that Sobrina is not lurking at the latent level. It does indicate, however, that Don Quixote has successfully repressed (banished) Sobrina from just below consciousness to some deeper unconscious level. And that is a positive sign, for contrary to another widespread belief, repression is not evil but necessary and even good. Repression is the most common defense mobilized by the ego to protect it from unacceptable impulses. If the repression is successful, life goes on. It is only when repression is unsuccessful that we resort to more drastic defenses that sometimes culminate, as in Don Quixote's case, in flight into psychosis.

There are, alas, some not entirely positive aspects to the presence of Sancho's Dulcinea in our hero's dream. Don Quixote's encounter with her is generally unsatisfactory. She refuses to see him, preferring to work through an intermediary; she is needy; she asks for a loan against collateral in the form of a more or less intimate item of feminine apparel; and worst of all, Don Quixote is unable to satisfy her needs. The obvious interpretation of this last is that the money stands for sexual needs (hers) and prowess (his) and that his failure to produce the six *reales* requested is indicative of his fear of impotence.[13] This is a perfectly plausible interpretation and probably correct. It is also possible to interpret Dulcinea's need not as that for sexual gratification but as a need for being. She is incomplete, still Sancho's creation, and needs Don Quixote's active participation to make her whole. He literally "gives it everything he has," not the six reales requested but the four he has.

Thus, in the dream, he "invests" everything he has in the new Dulcinea, in both the obvious financial and the metaphysical psychic senses. That is, the money may be interpreted not simply as sexual prowess but as a metaphor for the psychic energy Don Quixote has at his disposal for the maintenance of the myth of

Dulcinea. His total resources fall short of the amount requested. This raises a nagging doubt to the effect that perhaps our hero just does not have it in him to accept completely a Dulcinea who is the product of someone else's imagination. If Don Quixote's all is not enough, then Dulcinea comes apart. She is no longer available to serve as a displacement for Don Quixote's real desires, and he is plunged again into an intolerable situation, except that now his psychic resources are depleted if not exhausted. In order to prevent this from happening he will have to invest massive amounts of psychic energy—as he does here—in an effort to make Sancho's Dulcinea truly his own. This in turn means that he will have less energy at his disposal to deal with whatever new crises may present themselves later.

At the end of this episode we can see more clearly the paradoxical effects on Don Quixote of Sancho's enchantment of Dulcinea in II, 10. On the one hand it frees him from the need to come face-to-face with her, with its concomitant of having to admit she is only a figment of his imagination. On the other hand, because she is now also the figment of someone else's imagination, his psychic efforts to accept her and make her his own threaten his relationship with Sancho and have a debilitating effect on our hero. In a very real sense *Don Quixote, Part II* is the story of the accumulation of such debilitating effects, until the will to sustain life itself is finally overcome and Don Quixote dies.

Identifying the main theme of our hero's dream and under-scoring its importance for the evolution of Dulcinea—and indeed of the remainder of the novel—does not begin to exhaust its content or its interpretive possibilities. If we stay with it a while longer we may be able to make some discoveries, or at least some reasonable inferences, about other, related aspects of Don Quixote's psychic life.

The dreamwork, briefly, is as follows. Don Quixote descends into the cave, is overcome by drowsiness, and falls asleep. When he "awakes" he finds himself in a beautiful meadow with a crystalline palace in the distance. An old man dressed in academic attire greets him. He is Montesinos. A discussion follows concerning whether Montesinos has used a dagger or a dirk to remove his cousin Durandarte's heart. Durandarte appears. He is laid out like a statue on a tomb, but he is alive. His hand is described as hairy, with broad veins and nerves. Montesinos tells him the story of his (Durandarte's) death, of the removal of his heart with either a dirk or dagger, and of how he cleaned it and salted it down to keep it fresh as he delivered it to Durandarte's widow, Belerma. He further tells how Durandarte's squire and Belerma's dueña were changed into bodies of water and how they have all been enchanted by Merlin. Durandarte then quotes a ballad that covers the same events, and equivocates as to whether a dagger or a dirk was used on his heart. Montesinos presents Don Quixote to him and suggests that he will be the agent of everyone's disenchantment. Durandarte replies that if he is not, he should have patience and deal another hand. He turns away.

Belerma makes her entrance with two columns of beautiful maidens, all dressed in mourning and wearing white turbans. Her turban is twice as tall as those of the others, and the hanging panels of her headdress (*tocas*) are so long that they touch the ground. Her eyebrows are close together; her nose is rather flat; her mouth is large, but her lips are red; and her teeth are sparse and poorly located, although white as peeled almonds. She carries Durandarte's heart wrapped in a cloth. Montesinos identifies her and observes that four days a week the maidens parade in this way. He goes on to say that if Belerma seems ugly and not as beautiful as tradition depicts her (she has dark circles under her eyes and a sallow complexion), it is due to the effects of enchantment. He reiterates that her dark circles and yellow skin are not the effects of a menstrual period, which she has not had for years. In fact, he avers, if she were not so destroyed by enchantment and grief, Dulcinea herself could scarcely equal her.

Don Quixote interrupts to direct Montesinos to "tell your story as you should," then upbraids him for suggesting a comparison between Belerma's beauty and Dulcinea's. Montesinos apologizes and this satisfies Don Quixote, calming "the great shock I received in my heart when I heard my lady being compared with Belerma." There follows a long interruption in which Don Quixote discusses various aspects of his adventures, principally their credibility, with Sancho and the Primo. Then he resumes his narration.

Montesinos shows him three farm girls leaping like goats over the greensward. He recognizes them as Dulcinea and her two companions from II, 10. Montesinos does not know who they are but presumes they must be three principal ladies under enchantment. They have arrived just a few days previously. He further observes that there are many enchanted ladies there, among them Queen Guinevere and the dueña Quintañona, who poured Lancelot's wine "when from Britain he came."

Here Sancho reacts, then invites Don Quixote to describe Dulcinea and report his conversation with her.

Don Quixote recognized her, he says, because she was dressed as they both saw her in II, 10. He tries to overtake her, but she runs away. Montesinos advises him to desist, because the time for his departure is approaching. Suddenly one of Dulcinea's companions appears at Don Quixote's side and with tears in her eyes first inquires after his health and then requests a loan of six reales, or whatever he can spare, against a cotton skirt of Dulcinea's. Don Quixote expresses incredulity and dismay at the spectacle of an enchanted princess in need. Montesinos assures him it is not uncommon and suggests that since the skirt appears to be a good one, Don Quixote should make the loan. Don Quixote refuses the collateral and gives the girl all he has—four reales Sancho gave him to use for charity. He then tells her to convey to Dulcinea that he wishes he were a German banker to help her economic necessity, that he is ill without her conversation and begs to see her, and that he has sworn to disenchant her. She replies, "All this, and more, you owe to my lady." She then takes the money and leaps more than ten feet into the air.

This dreamwork is long and complex, and to analyze it properly is impossible in this study. We can, however, observe a number of salient features. First off, I should note that what I identified as the major theme—the internalization of Sancho's Dulcinea—consumes much less space than the rest of the dream-work, which is concerned with Montesinos, Durandarte, and Belerma. We should therefore pay some attention to the major portion, if not the most obvious theme. We shall be concerned with the "chivalric" characters Don Quixote encounters (Monte-sinos, Durandarte, Belerma) and their relation to him.

Before we start it might be well to recall the processes by which a dream's latent content is transformed into the manifest content, the dreamwork reported by the dreamer. Briefly, these are distortion, displacement, symbolization, condensation, and secondary elaboration.[14] Of these, the least obvious, but still important for purposes of our analysis of Don Quixote's dream, is that of condensation. By condensation is meant simply that a number of facts, or persons from the dreamer's childhood, recent past, and contemporary experience, may be condensed into one, so that a single character in the dreamwork may in fact represent two or more individuals from the dreamer's life, including per-haps himself. For example, suppose we have three people: Mr. A., Mrs. B., Professor C., who all share a certain quality (Q). They may, for example, all be widows or widowers. The product of their condensation (P) is obtained according to the formula $P = A + B + C/Q$. In addition, each of the three people has a specific relation to the environment. Thus, for example: Aa = generous; Bb = living in a foreign country; Cc = famous teacher. In the dream, the individuals A, B, and C may become fused together in the picture of, say, B. The condensation could be expressed as B = a + b + c. The dreamer might report: "I see Mrs. B. [B] in Canada [b] in a mourning dress [Q] teaching children [c] of the poor [a]." In order to derive the latent content of the dream it is necessary to discover that Mrs. B. in the dream is simultaneously herself and Mr. A. and Professor C., and then to go on to discover the relationship between all of them and the dreamer.[15]

Armed with this knowledge, let us examine the characters, beginning with Montesinos. His scholarly appearance suggests he knows the answers to the questions Don Quixote brings to his cave, but in fact he does not. He cannot recall whether he used a dagger or a dirk, he does not know if Don Quixote is the one called upon to disenchant him, and he does not recognize Dulcinea. He appears to be at once a projection of Don Quixote's own uncertainties and, in all probability, a representation of his father or some other influential adult man from his childhood. Dreams about old people frequently involve a return to the dreamer's past, and an old man is most frequently the dreamer's father. If in Montesinos our hero conjures up his father, the father so constituted is not everything a father should be. He does not have the answers to Don Quixote's questions, and his principal achievement is the removal of Durandarte's heart with some kind of a knife.

In the case of Durandarte two facts stand out. First, he shares with Don Quixote the profession of knight. Second, Durandarte's hand is described by Don Quixote in his dream in a way that recalls his earlier description of his own hand to Maritornes and Palomeque's daughter in I, 43. Durandarte's hand is "somewhat hairy, with prominent nerves, a sign of the great strength of its owner" (II, 23). Don Quixote calls attention in his own hand to "the contexture of its nerves, the articulation of its muscles, the breadth of its veins, all signs of the strength of the arm behind it" (I, 43). In brief, Durandarte is easily identifiable with Don Quixote himself. Indeed, it has already been suggested that in his encounter with Durandarte our hero sees a prefiguring of his own death.[16]

Before we continue we should leave the categories of psychoanalysis for a moment and return to the more familiar ground of literary history. It is interesting to note that neither Montesinos nor Durandarte is known in the French chivalric tradition. They are rather of Spanish origin. Montesinos is a son born to parents wrongly sent into exile in a mountainous region (*Monte*-sinos) who as an adult returned to civilization and avenged his parents. Durandarte is originally the name of Roland's sword. Some Castilian bard must have misinterpreted his name as that of a person, another of Charlemagne's champions killed at Roncesvalles with Roland, and made up a story about him. This piece of information, in combination with our identification of Durandarte and Don Quixote, allows us to associate Durandarte the sword with the phallus in general through the normal process of symbolization, and in particular a sword-phallus rendered useless by bloody mutilation, and to refer all of this to Don Quixote himself. Conchita Marianella provides further food for thought as she identifies the source of the specific events of the Montesinos-Durandarte-Belerma story as the fifteenth-century *Demanda del Sancto Grial*, where its protagonists are our old friends Lancelot and Guinevere. Guinevere's last request before her death is that her heart be given to Lancelot. Although her doncella wishes to comply and carries the Queen's heart around in Lancelot's helmet, she never finds him.[17] We should recall, first, Don Quixote's obsessive interest in the Lancelot-Guinevere relationship and, second, the presence of Guinevere and her dueña Quintañona among the enchanted ladies who populate the cave of Montesinos in his dream. To say that Durandarte in the dreamwork brings together some of the most pervasive themes of Don Quixote's psychic life, with some of his most deep-seated fears about himself and his manhood, is to understate the case.

Having observed the presence of Guinevere and Quintañona, who are merely mentioned in passing, we should devote
some attention to the other "real" (that is, visualized) woman Don
Quixote evokes in his dreamwork, the noble lady Belerma. Like
Montesinos and Durandarte, she is unknown in French literature, and like them also, her physical appearance is described by
our hero in some detail. She is, in brief, old and not as beautiful as
tradition depicts her. Her description is a catalog of the ravages of
time: she is postmenopausal; she has dark circles under her eyes;
her complexion is sallow; she has lost many of her teeth. Her red
lips, in marked contrast, suggest a more youthful sensuality. It is
reasonable to suggest that she represents all the older women in
Don Quixote's life—his mother, grandmother, and perhaps an
aunt or two. The combination of advanced age and sensuality
suggests an oedipal attraction in our hero's past. Now, the only
older female relative he has mentioned in the text is his paternal
grandmother, in I, 49, where he associates her with the dueña
Quintañona. We also know, from his nocturnal fantasy in I, 16,
that he considers Quintañona an erotic object along with Guinevere. These associations suggest in turn that the grandmother is
the particular older woman from our hero's childhood most
readily identifiable with Belerma in his dream.

This identification does not exhaust Belerma's importance,
however. Her first identity, after all, is that of Durandarte's lady.
She has his heart but not his body. We have already observed the
identification of Durandarte with Don Quixote. Belerma is to
Durandarte as Dulcinea is to Don Quixote. We know, however,
that Dulcinea is a figment of our hero's imagination who conceals
his intolerable attraction to Sobrina. This evocation, moreover, in
the form of an older but still interesting woman suggests that
more archaic material, from Don Quixote's childhood, may also
have been present in the need to create Dulcinea at the beginning.
In turn this suggests a clue to whatever it was in his early life that

incapacitated him for normal relationships with women. The point of all this, we must keep in mind, is not to dredge up Don Quixote's childhood ourselves—an impossible task since he exists only in a book that begins when he is already fifty—but to insist on the fact that his behavior at age fifty-plus is so astonishingly verisimilar that it allows us to conceive of "early childhood" and "adolescent" experiences for him. Cervantes's genius projects Don Quixote's prehistory behind and beneath the moment we meet him in I, 1. It is this archaic, oedipal aspect of Belerma which explains Don Quixote's violent reaction to Montesinos's comparison of her beauty with Dulcinea's. It is not simply that Belerma is old and not as beautiful as tradition depicts her, for Montesinos is careful to ascribe her appearance to the effects of enchantment and grief. It is rather the idea that Belerma and Dulcinea have in common an identity as erotic objects. Don Quixote experiences their sudden rapprochement, the blurring of the differences between them, as intolerable because it brings the hidden relationship between them dangerously close to the surface.

Finally, Belerma is reminiscent of Don Quixote himself, in spite of the difference in their sexes. There are several points of contact. First there is the abandonment of at least a part of normal sexual functioning. Don Quixote is impotent, Belerma postmenopausal. There is also the matter of teeth or their lack. Belerma's are "sparse and ill-placed." Some of Don Quixote's are missing as well, as Sancho observed when he dubbed his master "the Knight of the Sad Countenance" in I, 19. Both Belerma and Don Quixote have sallow complexions. We have noted hers already, and Don Quixote himself mentions his to Don Diego de Miranda in II, 16, where he tells him not to marvel at "my armor, nor at the yellowness of my complexion."

Of what use is it to note that Don Quixote and Belerma share certain relatively minor physical characteristics and to conclude that she is a projection by him of himself? The identification of Belerma with Don Quixote leads to a larger one, namely, the fact that all three of the chivalric characters are projections of different aspects of our hero himself. He projects in Montesinos a number of more or less intellectual insecurities, in Durandarte his fears of castration and impotence, and in Belerma his concern for age and aging. All three have in common with Don Quixote their ages and the fact that their lives cannot go forward even though they are nominally alive. The enchantment suffered by the chivalric characters is the perfect analogue of Don Quixote's own arrested psychosexual development. It would be more accurate to say that the characters' enchantment is Don Quixote's projection of his unconscious realization of that most basic fact of his own situation.

Don Quixote's dreamwork leads not only to his concerns of the recent past and the present—his ability to internalize the new Dulcinea created by Sancho in II, 10—but points toward the remote past of childhood as well. The assimilation of Montesinos to a father who appears to be omniscient or at least knowledgeable but in fact is not, and who practices a bloody mutilation on a loved one identifiable as Don Quixote himself, is surely food for thought. Equally or perhaps more unsettling is the assimilation of Belerma to an older woman from his childhood, most probably his paternal grandmother but quite possibly also his mother. Her sensuous red mouth surrounding white teeth suggests the classic *vagina dentellata* of the castrating female, and this in combination with the emphasis on daggers and dirks—the instruments of mutilation—reiterates our hero's fear of castration and simultaneously suggests the most probable childhood cause of his chronic inability to interact successfully with women. The manifest content of the dreamwork—the chivalric characters and the institution of chivalry, together with Don Quixote's attitude toward it—does not begin to exhaust the importance of the dream. Analyzable by the criteria of psychoanalysis, Don Quixote's dream correlates amazingly well with what is revealed about him through his waking thoughts, words, and actions. It is truly a tribute to his creator.

Let us move on to a new series of adventures, those of the duke and duchess's palace which begin in II, 30 and continue through II, 57. Structurally this series of episodes is analogous to the adventures at Palomeque's inn in Part I, with some differences we shall observe shortly. There are three important real women and a couple of false ones present at the ducal palace, and we shall be concerned with all of them, beginning with the duchess herself.

She is first described by the narrator as a "beautiful huntress." Sancho approaches her with Don Quixote's compliments and she, having read Part I, expresses a desire to see him. Upon hearing this news, our hero "*se gallardeó*" in his saddle. The Spanish verb is usually translated as "drew himself up," but its literal meaning is "he made himself appear graceful, elegant, and brave." Arturo Serrano Plaja observes that Don Quixote's reaction to the duchess's desire to meet him, summed up in this eloquent verb, "demands an entire psychological treatise."[18] Since the present treatise is already overlong, I shall observe simply that Don Quixote's reaction is primarily if not totally erotic in nature. He reacts as a man to the presence of a real flesh-and-blood woman of beauty and breeding who has demonstrated an interest in him. She seems to have the same sort of appeal that Dorotea had in Part I, except that the threat of possibly having to marry her is absent here. Don Quixote so extends himself in praises of her beauty that her husband finally intervenes to observe that he has apparently forgotten Dulcinea! This brings our hero to heel, and from this time on he remains within the bounds of the institutionally defined relationship between them.

In II, 31 we make the acquaintance of a woman who turns out to be of much more immediate erotic importance for Don Quixote, the dueña Doña Rodríguez. She is one of the great minor characters created by Cervantes, and although she has been well studied indeed as the Cervantine evolution of a literary type, she has not really been dealt with as a middle-aged woman.[19] We meet her first through Sancho, who when he arrives at the palace, recalling the old ballad about dueñas seeing to Lancelot's horse, asks her to attend to his donkey. She angrily refuses, whereupon Sancho calls attention to what he perceives as her advanced age. At this she reacts most violently. "I shall account for my years to God, and not to you, you garlic-reeking bumpkin" (II, 31). The duchess comes to her defense, observing that "Doña Rodríguez is quite young, and her long headdress [tocas] is a sign of her authority, not of her age." The lady who reacts so violently to the suggestion that she is old most probably does so because she is in fact concerned about her age and its effects on her appearance. That the duchess comes to her defense suggests that she shares her servant's concern, that she too is worried about the ravages of age. In short, the two women present themselves not so much as dueña and duchess as they do as women "of a certain age," conscious of their fading beauty.

In II, 33 the duchess takes Sancho aside to ask him about Dulcinea, and in the course of their conversation she threatens to withhold the *ínsula* from him. Sancho reacts with a blitzkrieg of popular proverbs designed to convince himself and the others present that the governorship of the island means nothing to him. He concludes with a reference to the last Gothic king, Rodrigo, who was eaten by serpents, if (as he says) the old ballads do not lie. Doña Rodríguez, who has been silent for two chapters, is immediately attentive and volunteers more precise information concerning King Rodrigo's fate. Not only was he eaten by serpents, but, she continues, quoting the old ballad, the reptiles bit him first "where he had sinned most," that is, in the genitals. The unpleasant death is considered to be the monarch's comeuppance for having violated a beautiful young woman, the daughter of Count Julián—an event, incidentally, which supposedly triggered the

Muslim invasion of 711. Doña Rodríguez's continuation of Sancho's asexual reference to its culmination in Rodrigo's private parts suggests that she is a woman with sex on the brain. Her recollection of the king's punishment, besides indicating her general interest in sex, manifests her feelings towards the man who violated her daughter and who has gone unpunished. That affair will come up in her nocturnal encounter with Don Quixote in II, 48.

In II, 37, as the assembled company awaits the arrival of the "countess Trifaldi," Doña Rodríguez observes that "the duchess has in her service dueñas who could be countesses," an obvious reference to herself and her qualifications. She continues, insisting first that she is neither old nor a virgin and establishing a qualitative distinction between widowed dueñas and virginal dueñas. These apparently gratuitous remarks demonstrate her concern for her age and her sex life. The widowed dueña to whom she refers is obviously herself, whom she considers superior to the virginal dueña, who we learn later is Altisidora, her rival for the duchess's favor and, as it turns out, for Don Quixote's affections. These relationships are not clarified until II, 48. Here Cervantes is simply laying the groundwork, establishing Doña Rodríguez as a character and hinting at some of her problems.

When she appears in II, 48 late one night, unannounced, in our hero's bedroom, therefore, the reader is aware that she is a middle-aged woman—probably about Don Quixote's age—concerned for her appearance and desirability as a woman, with a marked interest in sex. Don Quixote, meanwhile, has been attracted to young Altisidora, who has pretended to be in love with him. When he hears his door being opened he believes it is Altisidora. When he discovers it is not, he assumes Doña Rodríguez must be there representing her. At this suggestion she reacts indignantly. "I am not so old, I still have my soul in my flesh, and all my teeth and molars, God be praised, except for a few that lie lost to the catarrh so common here in Aragón." She leaves the room to relight her candle, and while she is gone Don Quixote transfers to her the erotic anxiety he has been feeling on Altisidora's account. Doña Rodríguez is specifically identified in his soliloquy as a possible object of desire, perhaps the only woman capable of breaking down his chastity, and he is worried, to say the least. "Who knows," he begins, "if the Devil might do to me now with a dueña what he has never been able to do with empresses, queens, duchesses, marquises or countesses? Who knows if this solitude, this opportunity and this silence will awake my dormant desires and cause me to fall, after so many years, where I have never even stumbled before? And in such cases it is better to flee than to await the battle" (II, 48).

After this pathetically frank confession of his awareness of his history and the powerful attraction exercised by this woman, he falls back, as a defense, not on Dulcinea but on a series of popular anti-dueña clichés.[20] This is a marked departure from his usual reaction to the threat of physical intimacy. Normally he invokes his prior commitment to Dulcinea; here he attempts to convince himself that Doña Rodríguez is in fact unattractive. After thus assuring himself that she is totally incapable of arousing him, he jumps up and runs across the room to close the door so she will not be able to get back in!

Too late, it seems, for we next witness an extended discussion between the two of them in which they agree that they find themselves in a potentially explosive situation, and in which each agrees to respect the other's chastity.

She: Are we safe, sir? Because I consider your having arisen from your bed a bad sign for my chastity.

He: That is exactly what I should ask you, Madam, and so let me ask you if I am safe from being attacked and forced. . . . Because I am not made of marble, nor are you cast in bronze, nor is it ten o'clock in the morning, but midnight, and in a room more secret and enclosed than the cave where false Aeneas had his way with the beautiful and pious Dido.

They ceremoniously join hands—a disturbingly erotic sign of their pledge not to violate each other—and walk back to Don Quixote's bed. The Arab historian Cide Hamete Benengeli comments at this point that he would have given the better of two robes that he owned just to have seen the two of them holding hands like that and making their way across the room to the bed.

Don Quixote climbs back in bed, Doña Rodríguez takes a chair, and they sit there contemplating each other. The tension subsides, and Don Quixote opens the discussion of Doña Rodríguez's problem, which as it turns out concerns the recuperation of her daughter's honor.

On the surface, the sight of these two mid-lifers alone in Don Quixote's room in the middle of the night, each bundled up in several layers of clothing (and in Don Quixote's case in the bedclothes as well), both so preoccupied that their own sexuality would run away with themselves, both adopting exaggerated defensive postures, is ludicrous or embarrassing, analogous to the episode of "love in the old folks' home" in the Spanish film described earlier. This is probably why the human dimension of this episode has received scant critical attention, and this is certainly why Cide Hamete Benengeli makes fun of the two of them. One might inquire here why Cervantes goes out of his way to ascribe the ridicule to Cide Hamete and does not indulge in any himself in his capacity as principal narrator. Cide Hamete is an Arab, a Muslim. He conspicuously identifies himself as such when he swears "by Mohammed." According to a popular kind of anthropology current in the sixteenth century, Muslim Arabs have a different view of human sexuality than do European Christians. They are considered to be much less inhibited, free of the strictures stemming from the Christian belief that sex is evil. For Cide Hamete what is ludicrous is the couple's elaborate avoidance of sexual intimacy. For most Christian readers, I imagine, what is either ludicrous or embarrassing is that two senior citizens like Don Quixote and Doña Rodríguez should find themselves in a sexual situation at all. The characters are finally overcome by their *race, milieu,* and *moment.* The Arab narrator observes the scene from another, different perspective and finds it risible. There is a strong suggestion here that Cervantes, a fiftyish Christian like Don Quixote, turns the stated reaction to this scene over to Cide Hamete because he himself finds it not humorous, but pathetic. This is as close as Don Quixote ever comes to a relationship with any woman, and Doña Rodríguez is, furthermore, particularly appropriate for him in terms of her age and station. With her he could have outgrown, so to speak, the unresolved oedipal conflict hinted at in his description of Belerma in his dream, for he is now just as old as the lady in question, and what was "unthinkable" when he was a boy is now perfectly acceptable—except that now society considers both of them too old. Both of them are sensitive, to say the least, to their own sexuality and to the possibilities of the situation in which they find themselves. In this sense, their inability to become intimate is truly pathetic.[21]

The counterpoint to our hero's real but foiled opportunity for intimacy with Doña Rodríguez is offered by the machinations of the young, virginal dueña (as Doña Rodríguez describes her— she is more properly a doncella) named Altisidora, who for her own amusement, and that of the duchess, pretends to have fallen hopelessly in love with him. Both the duchess and Altisidora have obviously read *Don Quixote, Part I* attentively, and Altisidora constructs the situation and her performance as an expanded, deliberate version of the spontaneous series of events that led up to the farcical encounter with Maritornes in I, 16.

It is probably the duchess who first gets the idea of some public demonstration, for general amusement, of Don Quixote's middlescent libido. After Sancho departs for his governorship, Don Quixote is left without a servant. The duchess offers him "four of my most beautiful doncellas" to wait on him in his chamber (II, 44). Our hero instantly refuses the offer on the grounds that the presence of the attractive young women in his room would constitute a threat to his chastity. The duchess assures him that, now that she is aware of his great virtue, she will see to it that not even a fly, let alone a doncella, enters his room. Having discovered that Don Quixote is so fearful of his own sexual urges, a person like the duchess does not need to think very hard in order to conceive the project of putting his chastity to the test. So that very evening Altisidora falls passionately in love with him.

It is a hot night. Don Quixote is upset by Sancho's absence and by his discovery of a hole in his stocking—a convenient displacement of his feelings toward Sancho, without whom he feels alone and exposed. He feels exposed, of course, to the upsurge in his own libido, as the ensuing encounter makes clear. He cannot sleep and goes to the open window. In the garden below Altisidora and her friend Emerencia are talking (for his benefit, of course). Altisidora confesses her love for Don Quixote and her desire to serenade him. She has refrained, she claims in two splendid strokes of misdirection, because to do so would surely anger the duchess, and because she would be taken for a "fickle and loose" young woman. Which of course she is. She decides to go ahead and sing.

Don Quixote reacts to what he has heard. He recalls innumerable similar love adventures from his books. He imagines that one of the duchess's doncellas is in love with him and that chastity has forced her to keep her desires to herself. Suddenly, "he feared he might be overcome, and determined not to allow himself to give in" (II, 44). That is, his concern is immediately transferred from the lovesick girl to himself; he is afraid for his own chastity. He commends himself to Dulcinea, demonstrating again her function as a barrier between his own desire and its object, and then, incredibly, instead of closing the window and going back to bed, he sneezes to let the girls know he is there and leans forward the better to hear Altisidora's siren song. He reacts to

Altisidora and Emerencia just as he reacted to Miss Palomeque and Maritornes in I, 43.

The song contains enough mockeries of the rhetoric of Petrarchan love poetry to identify it—to us at any rate—as a parody, but Don Quixote takes it seriously. He heaves a great sigh and curses his luck, which causes every doncella to fall in love with him. Then he curses Dulcinea's luck: her man is persecuted by so many attractive women. He observes that for her only he is soft as sugar paste, for all the others hard as stone. He specifically recalls the episode of I, 16, indicating that the duchess and Altisidora have done their homework and know their man. "Let Altisidora weep or sing; let Madama on whose account I was beaten in the castle of the enchanted Moor be driven to the brink of suicide; I must belong only to Dulcinea." He slams the window shut and retreats to his bed, where, not surprisingly, he cannot sleep.

He appears the next morning dressed in a way that reveals the unconscious war raging inside him. He has armed himself with an enormous rosary, which Serrano Plaja has already identified as an attempt to bring his erotic urges under control by making himself look too pious to entertain any lascivious thought.[22] Don Quixote is also wearing his sword, the obvious symbol of precisely those impulses he is attempting to deny. The mention of the sword in this context is particularly significant because, as I have already observed, Don Quixote's sword is not emphasized, and is rarely mentioned at all, as an item of his knightly equipment. He appears here wearing not his heart on his sleeve but a statement of his desire and the instrument of its repression. When Altisidora sees him she pretends to faint, and Don Quixote observes that he knows why.

The next night he serenades her with a song designed to discourage her and to insist on Dulcinea's power over him. He is suddenly attacked by several cats and his face is scratched. Altisidora applies a bandage and as she does so berates him for his cruelty to her. Following the attack, Don Quixote stays in his room for six days. The narrator attributes this to the severity of the wounds he has suffered, but in fact only one cat scratched him at all, and that on his face, so he is certainly ambulatory. This extended convalescence is curiously at variance with his repeatedly demonstrated ability to bounce back after much more severe drubbings. I believe our hero stays in bed for practically a week simply to avoid Altisidora, for two contradictory reasons. On the one hand he does not want to see her and be aroused, and on the other he does not want her to see him looking less than his best, with his face swathed in bandages.

In II, 48, when Doña Rodríguez unlocks his bedroom door, he first believes she is Altisidora "come to overpower his chastity and cause him to betray the faith he owed to his lady." He responds to this threat precisely by invoking his faith in Dulcinea, be she transformed "into a farm girl smelling of onions, into a nymph of the golden Tagus wearing cloth of gold and silk, or held in thrall by Merlin or Montesinos wherever they will." Of the three visions of Dulcinea, two are the products of his recent experience and therefore easily explicable, but the "nymph of the Tagus" is not. She is derived from the Petrarchan love poetry of Garcilaso de la Vega. The threat posed by what Don Quixote thinks is the presence of Altisidora in his chamber is so powerful that, in addition to conjuring up the new "normal" images of Dulcinea, he reverts to behavior typical of Part I and invents a third image of her based on the clichés of literature, enclosing the whole in the quasi-religious concept of faith.

His reaction—the "trinitarian" evocation of Dulcinea—demonstrates the magnitude of Altisidora's effect upon him. One of the consequences of this effect is that Don Quixote attempts to regain control of the creation of Dulcinea by reverting to his old tactics from Part I and evoking Garcilaso's nymphs. The attempt will be for naught, as we shall see, but the detail offers an interesting glimpse into the workings of our hero's mind. He continues to need to create Dulcinea as a buffer in response to threats upon his chastity—that is, in a dialectical process. The Dulcinea so created now includes the new "official" version (Sancho's enchanted Dulcinea), his own imperfect internalization of this version, from his dream, and an image derived from his own imagination, reenergized by the threat posed by Altisidora.

Don Quixote's attempt to fight back and regain control of the creation of Dulcinea is doomed by the power and authority of the duke and duchess, first working directly on him and then on Sancho. In II, 32 the duchess asks Don Quixote to describe Dulcinea physically. He replies evasively, using pictorial art—an alternative to the clichés of poetry—as his standard. Then, possibly in order to relieve himself of the necessity to continue inventing her, and possibly because she is no longer his to invent, he announces that her appearance has been changed and that she is enchanted. He describes her as he saw her in II, 10. He then insists that the attack on her is an attack on himself because he lives through her—a recollection of the "Pauline" analogy from I, 29. Don Quixote's invocation of the new, enchanted Dulcinea may be seen as his first line of defense against the probings of the ducal couple. She makes the "old" one irrelevant. She is also a logical manifestation of his concern for the "truth" of the enchantment, a part of his campaign to internalize her begun in his dream in Montesinos's cave and continued in his interrogation of Master Pedro's monkey (II, 25). If the duke and duchess accept the new Dulcinea, the reality of her enchantment will be validated, for him, from another perspective.

The duke and duchess, however, are not satisfied. They bring Don Quixote back to the Dulcinea they know as readers of Part I, to see how—and if—he can keep her in existence in the face of their massive frontal assaults on her. The duke recalls that in Part I we are told that Don Quixote had never seen Dulcinea and that instead he had "engendered her and given her birth in his fantasy." Instead of springing immediately to her defense, our hero makes a kind of wistfully evasive answer in which he incorporates the lesson he learned at El Toboso in II, 9. "God knows if there is a Dulcinea in the world or not, or whether she is fantastic or not; and these are the kind of questions whose investigation must not be pushed to the limit. I did not engender nor give birth to my lady, but I do contemplate her as possessing the attributes appropriate and necessary to her fame."[23] The decadent aristocrats press on, inquiring after Dulcinea's lineage. Don Quixote retorts that she is the child of her own actions. Not good enough for the duchess, who recalls Sancho's image of her winnowing wheat. At this Don Quixote uses the recent enchantment of Dulcinea—her transformation into a coarse farm girl which he himself has witnessed—to explain the incongruous features of Sancho's narration in I, 32. She must have been enchanted then too!

Don Quixote is on very thin ice here, and he is saved by a complex reciprocal interplay of interests threatened and defended. The duke and duchess attack the Dulcinea they know from Part I. She could never have withstood their command of the facts as transmitted by the narrator. Don Quixote counters by declaring her irrelevant and superseded by the new Dulcinea of Part II, the one enchanted by Sancho. This tactic at once allows the myth of Dulcinea to continue and helps Don Quixote to continue his process of internalizing Sancho's Dulcinea, a process so necessary to his own continued existence. It helps counter the debilitating effect of her imposition from without. Alas, Don Quixote's tactic also allows the duke and duchess to invent new psychological tortures for him based on the new Dulcinea of Part II. Their scheme for her disenchantment will be, in the end, the most debilitating experience of all. But for the moment Dulcinea is safe, and Don Quixote's belief in her transformed state is strengthened.

In II, 33 the duchess takes Sancho aside and asks him about Dulcinea. He tells the story of his "enchantment" of her in II, 10. His candor is motivated at least in part by his desire to ingratiate himself with the duchess, who appears to have taken a liking to him, and to assure himself of the promised governorship. He proposes to accomplish this by demonstrating that although Don Quixote is mad, he, himself, is not, and that he is in fact cleverer than his master and perfectly capable of governing an island. After hearing Sancho's story the duchess informs him that he was mistaken, that Dulcinea really is enchanted, and in short requires him to believe in his own fabrication if he expects to exercise the function of governor he so ardently desires. Control of the creation of Dulcinea has now passed from Don Quixote to Sancho to the two decadent aristocrats.

Of all the acts of gratuitous cruelty perpetrated by the duke and duchess, this is the cruelest. They drive a wedge between Sancho and Don Quixote and pit one against the other by playing upon their respective vested interests with respect to Dulcinea. For Don Quixote, her existence is necessary to his own, so they point out the flaws and inconsistencies in his creation of her in Part I. For Sancho, the ruse of her enchantment is a proof of his own cleverness and fitness to govern, so they tell him he is not so clever after all and that she really is enchanted. It is highly significant that Don Quixote and Sancho are physically separated in these two chapters. But this is only the beginning. The method for Dulcinea's disenchantment devised and then imposed on them by the ducal couple has the effect of institutionalizing an adversary relationship between them which lasts until chapter 72.

Before proceeding to those matters I should pause to remark that in the duke and duchess's interrogation of Don Quixote based on their knowledge of Dulcinea from Part I, nowhere is there a reference to Aldonza Lorenzo as the "real woman" behind Dulcinea. Don Quixote and Sancho have already moved on to the new Dulcinea of Part II, and the duke seems to have been a much more attentive reader of Part I than he has been given credit for, because instead of referring to Aldonza, he suggests that Don Quixote engendered Dulcinea in his imagination; and as we shall see shortly, his idea of a physical representation of her is not based at all on Aldonza, but on someone most readily identifiable with Juan Palomeque's daughter, with whom Don Quixote fell in love in I, 16. Aldonza was not important in the beginning, and she continues to be unimportant here in the second part.

In II, 35 the duke and duchess assume control of "operation Dulcinea" and put their plan into effect. They stage an elaborate production featuring the Devil, Merlin (who has presumably been Dulcinea's enchanter), and Dulcinea herself, who appears in her "true" form as a beautiful maid in her late teens. The appearance here of Dulcinea in the flesh parallels that of II, 10, where she appears as a coarse farm girl. This new representation is presumably easier for Don Quixote to take, since this girl is more like the generally accepted ideals of beauty.[24] Like Sancho's, however, this Dulcinea is inauthentic in that she is not Don Quixote's creation but someone else's contrivance, who must be internalized and established in his psyche as the operative one. The net result of this process of internalization will be a drain on Don Quixote's psychic energy, leaving him correspondingly less prepared to deal with future crises.

The process of internalization is aided, paradoxically, by the characteristics of the two Dulcineas. Visually, and one supposes olfactorily, these two have nothing in common. One is rustic and ugly, the other courtly and beautiful. They are, however, quite similar in their rude treatment of Don Quixote and Sancho, whom they meet. The level of diction is different, but the underlying message is the same. Their respective attitudes being analogous, the idea that they are the same person under the skin is considerably strengthened. Unfortunately, the "implied person" so glimpsed is a haughty, arrogant little twit! This must surely place a strain on Don Quixote's psychic equilibrium, since he is supposed to be in love with this individual. There is further cause for alarm, for we recall Sobrina's arrogant attack on her uncle and his faculties in II, 5. "Dulcinea's" attitude is strongly reminiscent of her. Furthermore, this latest Dulcinea is described physically in terms that also recall Don Quixote's niece: "the face of a beautiful maiden, and the many lights upon her made it possible to distinguish the beauty of her years, which did not appear to reach twenty" (II, 35). In her speech to Sancho "Dulcinea" insists on her tender age: "I am in the flower of my youth, still in my teens, for I am nineteen and have not reached twenty." The repeated references to not having reached twenty recall the initial description of Sobrina in I, 1: "a housekeeper who had passed forty, and a niece who had not reached twenty."

The duke and his majordomo were probably thinking of Miss Palomeque when they envisioned Dulcinea as a maid in her late teens. Don Quixote can make that association, of course, and be upset by some reminiscence of his feelings for her. He can also be bothered, at a deeper level, by the unsettling resemblance between this latest incarnation of Dulcinea and the real, ultimate object of his affections, the niece whose intolerable propinquity he fled in I, 1. If Dulcinea is supposed to allow him to transfer to a by-definition unattainable princess the libidinous energy directed at Sobrina, this latest turn of events is unfortunate indeed, as it obliterates the distinction between them.

Nevertheless, a ray of hope may be discernible here. Don Quixote is in the midst of a series of encounters with young women who are reminiscent of Sobrina and who treat him shabbily. Miss Palomeque herself uses our hero ill during his second stay at her father's inn, and there is no exchange of soulful glances when he departs. The enchanted Dulcinea of II, 10 is verbally abusive and threatens physical violence. The Dulcinea in his dream refuses to see him and hits him up for a loan. This latest Dulcinea is arrogant and demanding. And finally, our hero is about to meet Altisidora, who willfully builds and expands upon his experiences with Palomeque's daughter, who pretends to be in love with him, and who will in the end humiliate him. It is possible that the total of these experiences, but most of all the deliberate, cruel deception practiced by Altisidora, will have a purgative effect on him to the point where he is honestly no longer attracted to women young enough to be his niece, including Sobrina herself.

For the moment, however, Dulcinea is no longer wholly Don Quixote's creation or Sancho's, but belongs to the duke and duchess. She is enchanted and she and Merlin have appeared precisely in order to specify how her disenchantment must take place. It is here that the gratuitous cruelty of the decadent aristocrats stands most fully revealed. Playing on Don Quixote's overweening desire to liberate Dulcinea from her enchantment, and playing on Sancho's overweening desire for the governorship of his ínsula as well as his desire not to be caught in his lie, they decree that Sancho must lash himself a total of 3,300 times, inflicting real physical pain, at the end of which experience Dulcinea will be restored to her former self. The disenchantment of Dulcinea creates and institutionalizes an adversary relationship between the two men. Sancho, of course, wants to avoid inflicting pain on himself, and for Don Quixote the most pressing obligation existing anywhere in the world is precisely that he do so. Their interests are thus diametrically opposed. From now on, every adventure, every interaction between them, will be dominated by the question of Sancho's lashes. The duke and duchess have transformed the relationship between them from one characterized by mutual support and reciprocally balanced interests to one of conflict and the necessity for choice. From now on Don Quixote's love for Dulcinea will be in conflict with his feelings for Sancho, and Sancho's interest will be divided between his love for and duty to Don Quixote and his desire to avoid physical pain. A triangle has been created, not exactly of the sort envisaged by

René Girard and Cesáreo Bandera,[25] but a more prosaic one not unlike that of the "Novel of the One Too Curious for His Own Good" in Part I. A woman comes between the love two men bear each other, and their relationship is jeopardized if not destroyed altogether.

Paradoxically, there is a ray of hope here as well, for the necessity to choose between Dulcinea and Sancho, coupled with the series of negative encounters with young women on whom our hero projects the imago of Sobrina, will have a therapeutic effect on him. If we recall that the time Don Quixote spends with Sancho is time not spent in the presence of Sobrina, we can better understand this paradox. The relationship between the two men is in general a substitute for the unthinkable one between uncle and niece. More particularly, Don Quixote will now be forced to make specific choices between the petulant young woman and Sancho, and he will ultimately come down on the side of the latter. These gains for Sancho are made at the expense of Sobrina-Dulcinea's appeal.

The leave-taking from the ducal palace is not without incident. Altisidora comes forward and subjects Don Quixote to a final, brief humiliation. After singing one of her patented songs in which the mention of pairs of places as contiguous when they should be widely separated signals a general context of insincerity and pranks, she accuses Don Quixote of having stolen from her some items of intimate apparel. The duke challenges our hero to single combat if the articles in question—a pair of garters—are not produced. At this crucial moment, when Don Quixote's reputation for honesty and chastity is hanging in the balance, Altisidora "discovers" she has been wearing the garters all along. The false accusation of the theft of intimate property is as old as the story of Joseph and Potiphar's wife. It is the weapon of the woman scorned. Here it appears to be employed more in order to embarrass Don Quixote than because Altisidora is really smarting from his rejection of her. Nevertheless, he has rejected her; she has in fact been scorned. The next and last time she and Don Quixote meet, in II, 70, her true emotions are much closer to the surface.

In II, 58 Don Quixote and Sancho discuss Altisidora's hopeless love for our hero. Don Quixote clarifies the relation as experienced by him. "Altisidora declared her desires; which aroused more confusion than pity in me." His reaction of confusion is indicative precisely of his strong inclination to reciprocate the girl's advances. Almost immediately thereafter, in II, 59, we witness an example of the friction between Don Quixote and Sancho as a result of the duke and duchess's scheme for Dulcinea's disenchantment. Here it is Sancho who prevails upon his master to allow Dulcinea to wait for a while. In II, 60 Don Quixote can stand it no longer and begins to beat Sancho while the squire is asleep. After subduing his master physically, Sancho reminds him that the lashes are to be voluntary, and he extracts from him a promise not to lay hands on him again. In II, 63, while they are touring the galley in Barcelona harbor, Don Quixote suggests Sancho subject himself to the boatswain's lash for a while, again with negative result. In II, 67 Don Quixote recalls that Altisidora seemed truly in love with him and interprets her insults upon his departure as signs of her love. This recollection calls forth the memory of Dulcinea and how Sancho continues to let her suffer the indignities of enchantment. Sancho remarks that the logic of the method of disenchantment escapes him, rather like anointing one's knee for a headache. Again Dulcinea must wait. In II, 68 Don Quixote awakens in the middle of the night and pleads with Sancho to lay on two or three hundred lashes, to no avail. In II, 69, when they have returned to the ducal palace and Sancho has "resuscitated" Altisidora by suffering physical pain, Don Quixote suggests this would be a good time for some lashes for Dulcinea. Again Sancho demurs.

There is a pattern discernible in this series of attempts by Don Quixote to motivate Sancho to lash himself. Don Quixote apparently has very little concern for Sancho's comfort. He is clearly much more concerned with Dulcinea. Something will happen in II, 71 to change this pattern, but for the present let us continue our chronology of events. In II, 62, when Don Quixote and Sancho are the guests of Don Antonio Moreno in Barcelona, their host's wife organizes a dancing party. Two of her lady friends are, although chaste, given to harmless pranks. They dance repeatedly with Don Quixote and pretend to be in love with him. He cuts a ridiculous figure on the dance floor, more clearly out of his element here than in any other setting in the novel. The women persist in their sweet nothings. Finally our hero exclaims, "Fugite, partes adversae!," invokes his fidelity to Dulcinea, and collapses on the floor. He is carried to his room to rest.

This is the kind of episode we have seen, with variations, beginning in I, 16, when Don Quixote believes Palomeque's daughter is approaching his bed. He feels his chastity under attack, feels his own desires mounting, and invokes Dulcinea to protect him, both from the woman and from himself. A good deal has happened since I, 16, however. Don Quixote has been on a kind of emotional roller coaster whose most recent revolution has been his powerful reaction to Altisidora. He has been forced to invest massive amounts of psychic energy in the internalization of the new Dulcinea. He is not as fresh, psychologically, as he once was. His collapse on the dance floor is the physical analogue of his emotional collapse, which does not occur in fact until later. Too exhausted emotionally to withstand the ladies' blandishments, he takes himself out of action. It is absurd to believe that a man as accustomed as he is to healthful outdoor exercise would be physically undone by a few dances. This psychically induced physical collapse is an indication of a general phenomenon that will be more and more important as the novel draws to a close: the debilitating effects of our hero's accumulated emotional experience here in Part II.

In II, 64 Don Quixote is defeated in single combat by the

Knight of the White Moon, thus bringing forcefully and irrefut-
ably to his attention the fact of his own vulnerability or, conversely, the end of one of his two sustaining myths: the belief in
his invincibility. He falls back on the other, the myth of Dulcinea.
The narrator describes him speaking from his position on the
ground, his voice "sounding as though it were coming from inside
a tomb" as he makes his most moving affirmation of Dulcinea's
beauty. In fact, this affirmation is apparently more important to
him than physical life itself. The stage is rapidly being set for his
willful abandonment of life ten chapters later.

A temporary and illusory revival occurs in II, 67 when Don
Quixote decides to turn his enforced retirement from the exercise of arms into a kind of literary-pastoral sabbatical. In this new
phase, of course, love will predominate. Although his name will
be changed to "the shepherd Quixotiz," our hero's identity will
remain the same, for he will still be enamored of Dulcinea, whose
name, significantly, will not change. Sancho joins his master in
imagining how it will be and suggests that his daughter Sanchica
can bring lunch out to them while they watch their sheep and sing
of their love. Then he remembers how attractive the girl is, and it
occurs to him that one of the "shepherds" might be tempted to do
her harm. He decides she should remain at home. Sancho's
expression of concerns so close to Don Quixote's—the daughter
grown into a desirable young woman—ruins the value of the
pastoral existence as a fantasy escape from intolerable reality, for
while it might liberate our hero from the unpleasant fact of his
recent defeat in combat, it would place him squarely back in his
original environment and evoke his central problem: the fear of
incest.

Two chapters later Don Quixote finds himself back at the
ducal palace and in the presence of Altisidora. The duke and
duchess have contrived one last exercise in gratuitous cruelty for
their own amusement, consisting again in the application of painful implements to Sancho's tender flesh. At the conclusion of the

performance, in which Altisidora is presumably brought back to life thanks to Sancho's self-inflicted torture, Altisidora joins Don Quixote in his room and reproaches him for his cruelty to her. Don Quixote decides to disabuse her once and for all of what he perceives as her hopeless infatuation with him. He insists, naturally, on his fidelity to Dulcinea. At this Altisidora, "appearing to lose her composure," tells our hero that everything has been a sham, that she could not possibly be in love with him, and she calls him all sorts of nasty names and, in short, brutally disabuses him of his misconceptions regarding her. Some writers have suggested that this angry speech is insincere in the sense that Altisidora has not been hurt by Don Quixote's latest rejection of her. Others, notably Unamuno and René Girard, believe that she has been stung and that the vehemence of her speech is the measure of the depth of her interest in Don Quixote. The duke too seems to think she is protesting too loudly, and he offers a proverb to the effect that the accumulation of insults is really the prelude to pardon.

All in all this is a most interesting and crucial episode. Don Quixote's attitude toward Altisidora seems finally to have changed, and he can now do spontaneously what he knew all along he ought to do but was able to accomplish only with great difficulty: reject her advances. This relative nonchalance is precisely what motivates her vituperation of him. In the course of his experiences with her Don Quixote has acted out his relationship with Sobrina, moving from forbidden desire imperfectly controlled to a realistic acceptance of the real and appropriate relation between them. This scene is the end of a process that began with Sobrina herself in II, 5, where she lashed out at her uncle in a series of insults concerning his age, appearance, and physical prowess. A striking verbal coincidence relates the two moments. Don Quixote remarks that Altisidora would be better occupied in making randas, for with her hands busy manipulating the bobbins, her mind will be similarly engaged and not busy with thoughts of illicit love. This is precisely what occurs to him following Sobrina's attack on him in II, 6, and these are the only two occasions in this massive two-volume novel on which the expression *menear los palillos de randas* occurs. In psychoanalytical terms, Don Quixote has made great progress, by an inadvertently therapeutic transference to Altisidora of the psychic energy (libido) directed at Sobrina, toward normalizing his relationship with Sobrina. Put less technically, we may say that the fires are beginning to go out.

Other things are changing as well. In II, 71 Don Quixote and Sancho come to a kind of showdown regarding their own relationship—can it or can it not be mediated by money—and their relationships to Dulcinea. Sancho begins by complaining that although the resuscitation of Altisidora had cost his backside dearly, she failed to reward him as promised with two new shirts. He compares himself to a physician, a professional who cures the sick for a fee. Don Quixote follows this idea up, and it is probably Sancho's fleeting identification of himself as a health services professional, as opposed to the squire of a knight-errant, which allows him to do so. He suggests in effect that he employ Sancho to lash himself at some mutually agreeable sum of money per lash. By placing in abeyance their normal, feudalistic, master-servant relationship and replacing it temporarily with a capitalistic one of employer and contract laborer, Don Quixote changes the dynamics of Dulcinea's disenchantment and provides an incentive for Sancho to lay on with a will. Immediately after a price is agreed upon and the lashings begin, however, Sancho reconsiders and demands double pay. Don Quixote agrees, and the self-inflicted punishment gets under way in earnest; not exactly in earnest, for Sancho, having discovered how painful a hearty whip stroke can be, steps out of Don Quixote's sight and begins to beat the trees and bushes, crying out every so often in feigned pain.

The fact of Sancho in pain, or his belief that Sancho is experiencing pain, forces Don Quixote to choose between his desire to set Dulcinea free and his love for his squire. As the episode progresses we can see Don Quixote's attitude evolving. At the beginning he is concerned lest Sancho beat himself so excessively that he render himself incapable of suffering the full measure of lashes. Clearly, at this point Sancho is merely the agent of Dulcinea's liberation. "Wait, my friend," he cries, "do not be so zealous that you run out of breath before the race is finished. By that I mean to say do not lay on so stoutly that life fails you before you reach the desired number." This same mentality is observable after the first thousand lashes, when our hero remarks, "Let there be enough for now, for the ass, speaking with your pardon, bears the load but not the overload." Sancho, however, caught up in the spirit of his new occupation, refuses to stop, and at this point Don Quixote makes his choice: Sancho and the love he bears him outweigh his interest in Dulcinea. "Let not the fates permit, Sancho my friend, that for my pleasure you lose your life, which should be spent in the support of your wife and family. Let Dulcinea await a more propitious moment, and I shall be content to hope for her release and wait until you have recouped your strength."

This is an important turning point in Don Quixote's life, comparable to that of the preceding chapter, in which he overcame his middlescent infatuation for Altisidora. "Let Dulcinea await a more propitious moment." The almost algebraic relation of Sancho and Sobrina becomes evident in these two episodes. As the coefficient of interest in Sobrina is reduced as a result of Don Quixote's ability to dominate his attraction to Altisidora, the coefficient of interest in Sancho is correspondingly raised and, finally, demonstrated to be greater than that of Don Quixote's interest in Dulcinea.

We should not conclude from this, however, that Don Quixote has lost interest in Dulcinea. In II, 72, in the space of two nights, Sancho completes the required 3,300 lashes. Don Quixote's reaction to this event is described as "extraordinary contentment," and he eagerly awaits the dawn "to see if he should meet his lady Dulcinea, now disenchanted, coming along the road." He scrutinizes every woman he meets in the hope that she will prove to be Dulcinea, "for he considered it impossible for Merlin to have lied."

Don Quixote appears to have abandoned himself to hope— hope that there really is a Dulcinea somewhere—and apparently expects to see Dulcinea at any moment. He does not seem to understand, as he did not understand in II, 9, that the worst possible course of action is to actively seek her out. He does not seem to perceive that, now that Sancho's lashes have been completed, the crisis of II, 9 has been re-created, but this time with no hope, no hope at all, of resolution. For one thing, the tried and true explanation for any unpleasant reality, a maleficent enchanter, has already been invoked by Sancho and successfully overcome by the master enchanter of all time, whom Don Quixote mentions by name in the passage just cited. For another, Don Quixote is simply not as fresh as he was when he and Sancho rode forth some sixty-five chapters earlier. His generative faculty, the ability to imagine the circumstances appropriate to a knight-errant's life and belief in his lady fair, has been seriously impaired by those around him who have wrested control of his environment—whether the creation of Dulcinea or the transformation of inns into castles—away from him. These include, principally, Sancho, who enchanted Dulcinea in II, 10, and the duke and duchess, who handed our hero everything he could possibly desire in the way of chivalresque ambience and adventures in II, 30–57. Moreover, his defeat at the hands of the Knight of the White Moon has sapped his confidence in his own strength.

Dulcinea is finished unless Don Quixote can hit upon some means of maintaining her as an unattainable ideal, and it is precisely at this point, when he and Sancho reach the outskirts of their village, with all it represents, that our hero mounts a last effort. Sancho, who has paused to drink in the sight of their native heath, begins a speech on the theme of the return of the prodigal son. Although Don Quixote should logically welcome any delay of the awful moment of homecoming and the inevitable encounter with Ama and Sobrina, he cuts Sancho short and tells him to get on into the village, "where we will let our imaginations run free, and plan out our exercise of the pastoral life." This sudden and apparently illogical insistence on the urgency of getting on with the exercise of the pastoral life is Don Quixote's last, desperate attempt to keep the myth of Dulcinea alive and intact, for the essence of the lovesick literary shepherd is precisely his absence from his beloved, frequently in combination with her failure to reciprocate his amorous sentiments. What Don Quixote proposes is the transformation of presumably disenchanted Dulcinea into a forever unresponsive literary shepherdess for whom he can pine away indefinitely.

At the entrance to the village an incident occurs which demonstrates a certain ambivalence on Don Quixote's part and reveals that he is only partially committed to the maintenance of the myth of Dulcinea. Two things happen in quick succession which convince him that he is never to see Dulcinea, with the implication that all is lost, that hopelessness—*desesperanza* (loss of the will to live) in Miguel Sabuco's technical sixteenth-century Spanish—is the appropriate response. First a hare pursued by some hounds takes refuge under Sancho's donkey. Don Quixote believes the animal symbolizes Dulcinea persecuted.[26] Next he overhears one boy tell another, "You will never see her again in all the days of your life." Don Quixote takes this as a reference to Dulcinea. Sancho undoes these "omens" with almost ridiculous ease. He picks up the frightened hare and presents it to Don Quixote. He demonstrates that the conversation beween the two boys referred only to a cricket, whose cage he buys and also presents to his master. Don Quixote refuses to be convinced. This behavior makes it apparent that in his intepretation of these famous "omens" our hero is projecting not his fear but his desire. Some part of him actually wants Dulcinea to be finished. This goes far beyond the attempt, immediately preceding, to convert her into an inaccessible shepherdess; that would allow Don Quixote to continue to be in love with her and offer a reason for living. What he seems to be seeking here is a reason for dying.[27]

Almost immediately he is plunged into his house, into the presence of Ama and Sobrina. The two women have overheard him discussing with Sansón Carrasco his new plan to embrace the pastoral life-style, and they deliver paired speeches in which each attempts to dissuade him from this new enterprise. We have come precisely full circle since the conversations of II, 6, when they tried, with the success we have seen, to keep him home from his third sally as knight-errant. Again, Sobrina attacks her uncle's advanced age, associating him, facetiously, with a ballad about a shepherd who is still a boy and then, brutally, with a proverb suggesting that he is too old now to learn anything new. Sobrina remains true to herself and unpleasantly similar to both Don Quixote's original fantasy of Dulcinea's haughtiness (I, 2) and the more recent incarnations as the strong-willed farm girl (II, 10) and the arrogant teenager portrayed by the duke's page (II, 35). Ama, for her part, eliminates the reference to Don Quixote's age while insisting on her own—"these fifty years that won't let me lie"—and on her master's delicate constitution. She further suggests that he "remain at home, administer the estate, confess frequently and give alms to the poor"—that is, that he adopt the repetitive, conformist life-style of Don Diego de Miranda, the country squire he met in II, 16. Her attitude toward him continues to be more reasonable, understanding, and supportive than Sobrina's, but the alternative she offers him—that he transform himself into a threadbare Manchegan version of the pompously smug Don Diego—is clearly unacceptable.

At this moment—at precisely this moment—Don Quixote reaches, or at least expresses, a momentous decision. He seems to sense that this is the time to choose between embracing the pastoral life-style, with maintenance of the myth of Dulcinea in a modified form, and abandoning it—along with his own existence—altogether. He chooses the latter. In the midst of his discussion with Ama and Sobrina he suddenly complains of feeling ill and asks to be put to bed. Perhaps the two women's observations have indeed convinced him that he is unsuited for the pastoral life he intended to adopt. More probably their comments act in concert with the recent series of reverses he has experienced—his defeat in combat, his realization that Sancho's lashes have served only to re-create an intolerable crisis—to produce this apparently sudden decision. Even more probably, the spectacle of Sobrina carrying on like Altisidora as well as like the more recent incarnations of Dulcinea has allowed him to put her, suddenly but not totally consciously, into proper perspective, to see her for what she is and to free himself, as he did with Altisidora, of his middlescent-incestuous desires. If this last is true, it means that he no longer needs Dulcinea and no longer needs to be Don Quixote.

In fact, this means that our hero is cured, in the sense of having come to terms with the realities of his environment. This important fact is demonstrated, I believe, in his exemplary death scene, where for the first time he refers to Sobrina by name— Antonia Quijana—and on two occasions at that, and assumes responsibility for her welfare. Conversely, there is no mention of Dulcinea or, naturally, of Aldonza.

Don Quixote has accomplished something akin to a working-through of his unacceptable desire for Sobrina by means of an unconscious transference of his feelings for her to Altisidora, which culminated in his matter-of-fact rejection of Altisidora's advances. This therapeutic process was aided by the coincidental incarnation of Dulcinea herself in unflattering terms that recalled Sobrina at her worst, in all her youthfully arrogant insistence on her uncle's age and physical infirmity. In the process, Sobrina herself has been rendered, finally, unattractive, and the proximate cause of our hero's retreat into psychosis in I, 1 has ceased to exist. Although this formulation is too neat (for long-standing psychic problems of the magnitude of Don Quixote's do not disappear completely overnight), it is substantially correct, and I might now profitably pose the question of why he prefers death over any attempt to reintegrate himself into the life of the village, see to his lands, give alms to the poor, and engage in the other "normal" activities Ama has suggested to him in her speech. I think first of all it must be clear that Don Quixote indeed chooses to die, that Kafka was right when he spoke of our hero's death as a suicide in disguise.[28] The multiplicity and nature of opinions expressed in II, 74 concerning the cause of his sudden illness demonstrate clearly that the malady is physiological in effect but psychological in its cause. Don Quixote has given up the will to live, and the question now becomes why.

The most widely held theory, I believe, is that expressed by Otis H. Green and based upon Huarte's application of humoral theory. In the latter chapters of Part II Don Quixote is subjected to a series of cruel disillusionments and humiliations which have the effect of dissipating his yellow bile (choler) and replacing what is lost with black bile (melancholy). This, aided by the sleep that restores moisture to his dried-out brain, swings his personality from the pathologically choleric to its opposite, the melancholic. This in turn results in his death, because melancholy, as I have remarked before, has the unfortunate side effect of constricting the heart. This physiological explanation is frequently linked to a discussion of how our hero comes to his senses, perceives the world around him correctly, "embraces holy humility," and "receives the supreme grace, the final mercy."[29] Don Quixote's renunciation of chivalry and of his life as a knight-errant, his reintegration into the established order, is thus seen as a triumph. At the opposite end of the spectrum is the "romantic" school headed by Unamuno which considers the knight's existence as a knight the only meaningful one he ever had and consequently regards his renunciation of it as a great tragedy. J. J. Allen and A. J. Close have concerned themselves with these extremes of interpretation, and it would be presumptuous of me to attempt to duplicate or even comment upon their work.[30] Rather than take a side in the debate, I should like simply to attempt to account for Don Quixote's choice of death in light of what we have learned about his psyche and observed about his actions.

Both Martine Bigeard and Louis Combet offer a variation of the "predominance of melancholy" theory that includes, besides what we have already seen, the idea that Don Quixote abandons his will to live, finally, when he returns home and realizes that he has come full circle, that he is literally back where he started, in his sterile and monotonous prequixotic existence.[31] This is an excellent starting point, but it does not seem adequately to account for the massive accumulation of experience, the experience of life we have observed through two thick volumes. Our hero's attitudes are presumed to be the same in II, 74 as they were prior to I, 1. I consider that prior to I, 1 Don Quixote's psychic life was dominated by his intolerable desire for his niece, and that by II, 74 he has freed himself from it vicariously through the transference to Altisidora. That is, his attitude is radically different.

Don Quixote's death for me is a result of his homecoming, but not of his return to the situation that produced the proximate cause of his retreat into psychosis. As we saw earlier, all the middle-aged resurgence of archaic libidinous drives, typical in normal men, is in Don Quixote's case complicated by the absence from his life of any relationship to any woman. That is, behind the attraction to Sobrina there are deeper problems either fought with or run away from but clearly never resolved in childhood and adolescence. I think it is this particular aspect of his sterile prequixotic existence which he finds so hopeless and to which he refuses to return. I further believe that the presence of the second woman in his house, Ama, and her appearance together with

195

Sobrina at the precise moment when he makes his great decision, is of crucial importance in this regard. Ama is a woman who except for her social class is eminently suitable for Don Quixote.[32] She is the right age, she sincerely cares for him, and she is not unintelligent. She is the kind of woman he should have courted and married but was unable to. Her presence in his house therefore becomes a kind of permanent reminder of his drastically stunted psychosexual development. Coming home in this context does not mean coming home to a certain environment and routine but coming home to himself, to the realization of who he is. In this sense, both the "romantics" and the "cautionary talesters" are right. Don Quixote dies when he comes to his senses, but his death is anything but a triumph. It is rather an admission of failure.

CONCLUSIONS

As I have been engaged in the preparation of this study over the past four years, I have been especially struck by a few things that I should like to offer here as closing observations. I do not propose to summarize the chronological evolution of Don Quixote's character and his encounters with women from his unnarrated but inferable prehistory to his death, because that has been the intent of the last two chapters. Rather, I should like simply to insist on three general principles—one thematic, one structural, one generic—that repeated readings and interrogations of Cervantes's text have forced me to accept.

First and foremost is the fact that this work is not a satire, not a cautionary tale, not an epistemological treatise, but a novel, a work of fiction. This means that this work's basic aesthetic criterion is that of verisimilitude, circumstantial and especially psychic. It means that the characters it portrays think and act as real people think and act, that their behavior, like ours, is overdetermined—that is, it responds to both conscious and unconscious motivation simultaneously—that they are sensitive, as we are, to life's pressures and mount unconscious defenses to deal with them, and that their "characters" are in part the result of the particular kinds of defenses to which they typically have recourse. This concept of character, which springs in turn from the principle of psychic verisimilitude, allows us as readers to perceive our own humanity in the work and engage in a vicarious experience of living. Don Quixote's bizarre and apparently illogical, unmotivated behavior is analyzable in human terms through the categories and criteria proposed by psychoanalysis, just as the behavior and motivations of all the rest of us are. In fact, they are analyzable only in these terms. Analysis shows our hero's behavior to be certainly bizarre, and frequently socially unacceptable, but by no means illogical or unmotivated. On the contrary, as I hope to have demonstrated in the foregoing chapters, his actions are almost always the result of multiple layers of motivations, both conscious and unconscious.

It is a tribute to the genius of his creator that we can observe Don Quixote's behavior and posit for him a plausible psychological prehistory in light of which those of his actions that comprise the artistic creation can be seen as parts of a larger, coherent whole, a verisimilar life of which the work presents a fictional slice. As I observed in chapter 3 and again at the end of chapter 5, Don Quixote's unnarrated prehistory is characterized by his flawed relation to the opposite sex. This in turn is divided into two aspects. There is first what I might describe as the basic situation, our hero's chronic inability to form relationships with women— in a word, his stunted psychosexual growth. On the basis of some offhand remarks Don Quixote makes in combination with his dream in the cave of Montesinos, we can make some reasonable inferences involving fear of castration and an unresolved oedipal conflict. This point is not to re-create his childhood but rather to observe that Cervantes's text allows us to posit a childhood and adolescence of a certain general nature, whose influence is observable in the thoughts, words, and actions of our fifty-year-old protagonist, in his paradoxical combination of strong desire coexisting with impotence. Second, Don Quixote responds in a more or less typical fashion to the resurgence of adolescent libido characteristic of men in mid-life. The passions kept under control by his repetitive, monotonous routine come dangerously close to the surface, and in a totally unacceptable form: incestuous desire for his niece. Progressively more drastic defenses are mobilized to keep them banished from consciousness, but all prove unsuccessful and a flight into psychosis, accompanied by a physical flight from the presence of his niece, is the result.

It is worth noting that a female "representative" of each phase of Don Quixote's psychosexual difficulties is present in his household. As I observed at the end of chapter 5, Ama is a woman of his own age who in fact cares for him, the kind of woman he should have courted and married but could not. She coexists in our hero's household with Sobrina, the teenaged object of his unspeakable middlescent desires.

In fact, Don Quixote repeatedly finds himself in situations with pairs of women who embody the two aspects of his own problems, especially in Part II. In Part I there is a series of young women—tentatively Marcela, especially Palomeque's daughter, possibly Dorotea—on whom he imposes the imago of Sobrina, and there are scattered references to older ones, principally his own paternal grandmother, whom he associates with the dueña Quintañona. The closest analogue in the real experience of Part I to the situation of his ménage and psychosexual difficulties is found in his misadventures at Palomeque's inn with the innkeeper's daughter and the servant Maritornes. There is an older woman—Palomeque's wife—in the background, but she is clearly not presented as an alternative to her daughter, as Maritornes is. Over and over again in Part I, however, Don Quixote's imagination demonstrates an obsession with a pair of women who fit the pattern neatly: the beauteous queen Guinevere and the dueña Quintañona, who for our hero, contrary to tradition, exists as an erotic object in her own right. We have already observed his assimilation of his paternal grandmother to her.

In Part II, Don Quixote's dream in the cave of Montesinos is populated by the young farm girl who represents Dulcinea enchanted, together with Belerma, the postmenopausal lady fair of

Durandarte. They are joined by Guinevere and Quintañona. At the palace of the duke and duchess Don Quixote has frankly erotic encounters with arrogant young Altisidora and with Doña Rodríguez, a woman of his own age who, like Ama, is the sort he might have courted and married had he been able to. The nocturnal encounter of the two oldsters is of crucial importance structurally, for it completes the symmetry of the middlescent infatuation with Altisidora.

Finally, at the beginning, in the middle, and at the end, there are Ama and Sobrina, related now to Quintañona and Guinevere, now to Doña Rodríguez and Altisidora, and always to Don Quixote's unconscious, embattled on two fronts.

Don Quixote's first plan of action involves simply escaping from his intolerable ménage to inhabit a fantasy world of knights and castles and giants. He escapes from women, alone, from I, 2 to I, 5. In his second sally he is still fleeing from involvement with women, but this time he does it in the company of another man. The relationship between Don Quixote and Sancho has been well and often studied, and I do not presume to offer anything like a detailed analysis of it here. I should like merely to make a few observations in the context of this book. First of all, there can be no doubt that, in human terms, this relationship is the most important, most valuable thing that ever happens to either man. It is with Sancho that Don Quixote reaches his maximum level of psychic maturity and learns how to be a person. They have in common virtually nothing at the beginning. Sancho is emphatically Old Christian; Don Quixote, probably of *converso* origin. Sancho is a pechero; Don Quixote, an hidalgo. Sancho falls into the role of servant; Don Quixote, of master. Don Quixote is well educated and a voracious reader; Sancho never does learn to read. One is married and a father; the other, a troubled bachelor. Both, however, sally forth from households dominated by women. In both households there is an older woman of appropriate age for the man and a younger one hovering between adolescence and womanhood. In Sancho's house the relationships are the obvious ones: wife and daughter. In Don Quixote's they are not quite so close, consisting in housekeeper and niece. They are obviously analogous, however. The reactions of all these women to their menfolk's wanderings are paired according to household in I, 52; II, 5 and 6; and II, 74.

Now, the idea of turning one's back on a house full of women to go off with another man suggests a relationship either overtly or latently homosexual. Some time ago Victor Oelschläger remarked simply that "Sancho falls in love with Don Quixote and all that he stands for."[1] More recently Louis Combet has offered an elaborate analysis of the relationship between the two men, in which he observes, for example, that their physical types are "long and phallic" and "round and vaginal" respectively and that both are indifferent to the opposite sex; he also makes much of Don Quixote's nocturnal attack on Sancho in II, 60, where he pulls down the squire's pants and attempts to whip his tender flesh.[2] For Combet the relationship is at bottom homosexual and sadomasochistic. I do not believe the events of II, 71 allow us to accept this reading, for on that occasion, as we have seen, the true nature of the relationship is finally defined. The encounter begins, it is true, rather negatively, highlighting an aspect of Sancho's penance I have not previously mentioned—namely, the function of the entire disenchantment scheme as a Cervantine-Erasmian attack on the institution of purgatory so stoutly defended by the Council of Trent. Sancho prepares to punish himself, for a fee, and Don Quixote proposes to count the lashes on his rosary. "I shall be standing to one side counting on this rosary of mine the lashes you administer. May Heaven favor you to the degree your worthy intention merits" (II, 71). We appear to be confronted with a grotesque combination of sadomasochism and perverted religious fervor. As the whipping progresses Don Quixote comes to place the human dimension of Sancho's suffering before his own desire to disenchant Dulcinea, and it is here that he exclaims, "Let Dulcinea await a more propitious moment," and orders Sancho to stop the beating. This is not the action of a man who enjoys inflicting pain. In fact it is the polar opposite, delineating a caring, loving, compassionate personality. This episode is crucial, for it is here that the relationship could degenerate into some kind of sick whips-and-chains affair, or it could be sublimated and restored as the original sexual motivation—the pressure of life in their respective households dominated by women—is subordinated to the men's psychic growth. It is almost as though Cervantes anticipated the thought of de Sade and other, more recent explorers of the dark side of our psyche and introduced and then consciously rejected it in this crucial episode.

If Don Quixote goes mad, as he does, to escape a situation he experiences as intolerable and which consists in a constricting social role in combination with an irrepressible forbidden desire for his niece, his defensive retreat into psychosis allows him to do many positive things that were impossible in his state of pre-quixotic sanity. He is free at least to attempt to act out and put into practice the noble ideals of chivalry, the altruistic actions denied him by his foreordained status as country hidalgo. It is instructive here to contrast him with another country hidalgo, Don Diego de Miranda, the "Knight of the Green Greatcoat" we meet in II, 16.

When the two men meet each presents himself to the other. Don Quixote, aware of the anachronistic figure he cuts, begins with his appearance, moves on to his profession and his accomplishments (which justify his strange appearance), notes the fact of his fame in "thirty thousand printed volumes," and then and only then names himself. His identity, like his appearance, is the result of his chivalresque exploits; or phrased another way, who he is is a function of what he does. Don Diego de Miranda presents himself first as a member of the nobility, an hidalgo, and then moves on to his place of birth (still his place of residence) and to his economic status. He is "more than fairly well off," he tells

Don Quixote. These qualities—lineage, birthplace, wealth—lead in turn to the identity as encapsulated in the name. In polar opposition to Don Quixote, Don Diego's identity has nothing to do with what he does, and it is really not even a function of himself, but of his forebears. He is what other people have made him. Having first established his identity, he then moves on to his accomplishments. What he describes is in fact not a series of deeds but a routine. He lives in a village with his wife and son. Like our prequixotic hidalgo, Don Diego is a hunter—but not of noblemen's game. Instead, he hunts partridge and hare, and only with the aid of a tame male partridge and a "bold ferret." He reads, but never romances of chivalry. He dines frequently with friends and acquaintances, and when it is his turn to invite them he offers an abundant table. He does not engage in idle gossip, nor does he pry into other people's lives. He hears mass daily, distributes alms to the poor without making an ostentatious show of charity, is devoted to our Lady, and trusts in the mercy of God.

By the most generally accepted social and even psychological standards, Don Diego's life is a success. He has succeeded in developing an enduring relationship with a woman, he has a son who is more interested in poetry than "serious pursuits" but who nevertheless is not estranged from his father, and his time is occupied by a round of socially useful and generally pleasant activities. In short, Don Diego is the sort of country hidalgo Don Quixote ought to have been but could not be. His life suggests an apparently effortless conformity with both the particular, historically determined values of his society and with those associated with contentment and mental health generally.

In this sense Don Diego is a successful human being and Don Quixote is a failure. Don Quixote cannot relate to women, he apparently cannot adjust to the demands of his social position, he seeks refuge in escapist literature, and he retreats, finally, into a full-blown psychosis. And yet something is present in Don Quixote's life which is lacking in Don Diego's. It comes out in II,

17 when both men meet a pair of lions on their way to the royal zoo. Don Quixote has stopped the cart and demanded that the keeper open the animals' cage so that he can confront them and thereby demonstrate his bravery. Don Diego attempts to dissuade him from an enterprise he regards as foolhardy in the extreme. Don Quixote retorts: "You run along, Sir Hidalgo, and see to your 'tame partridge' and your 'bold ferret', and let each man practice his profession. This is mine, and I know whether these lions are coming at me or not."

Don Quixote knows perfectly well who he is and that his existence depends on actions, and he also knows who and what Don Diego is, as his reference to the "tame partridge" and "bold ferret" reveals. Don Diego's life, successful as it is, lacks élan, zestful involvement in the challenge of facing the unknown. In fact, Don Diego appears to have been successful principally at insulating himself from risk: the unknown, the unpredictable, the unsolved problem. Don Quixote's life is of course devoted to the search for precisely this sort of encounter. Don Diego has made a success of his life, but the vacuousness of his existence in combination with his air of smug self-satisfaction has caused some of us to wonder if it was worth the effort. Don Quixote is a certifiable failure, a madman, yet in his madness he has come to something valuable.

In his psychosis, with the threat of Sobrina's sexuality removed, Don Quixote is free to enter into and develop a wonderfully positive and profound human relationship, of the type Leslie Fiedler has termed homoerotic, with Sancho Panza. This relationship, the love between the two men, is in human terms the most precious in a long work filled with intensely moving human experiences.

In short, Don Quixote's madness propels him backward into life. It enables him to have a life, to engage in purposeful and meaningful activity, and to enjoy a fulfilling, evolving relationship with another human being. That is, in the psychological as

well as the existential sense already observed by Unamuno, our
fiftyish hidalgo's only meaningful life is his life as the madman
Don Quixote. I believe that this is why all of us, even the most anti-
romantic cautionary talesters, are saddened by his recuperation
of sanity and his swift, inevitable death.

George Vaillant argues that mental illness in itself and in
general is an adaptive mechanism. "Let us entertain the possibility," he writes,

> that mental illness, like the symptoms of measles, reflects our
> efforts to adapt to pathologic conflict. Let us suppose that mental
> illness, like measles, is not a deficit state, that it is neither immoral
> nor imaginary, but instead that the symptoms of mental illness
> reflect an unconscious effort at mastery through an aggregate of
> defense mechanisms. Defenses can become the critical variables
> that determine whether environmental stress produces madness or
> something analogous to the process through which an oyster,
> confronted with a grain of sand, creates a pearl.[3]

In the case of Don Quixote, environmental stress has indeed led
to madness, but madness itself turns out to be a pearl.

NOTES

INTRODUCTION

1. Dave Smith, "Nailing Down a New Career—at 50," *Los Angeles Times*, Monday, March 13, 1978, Part IV, pp. 1, 6.

2. Paul Descouzis, *Cervantes a nueva luz* (Frankfurt a.M: V. Klostermann, 1966).

3. Dominique Auber, *Don Quichotte, prophète d'Israel* (Paris: R. Laffont, 1966).

4. Germán Arciniegas, "Don Quijote, un demócrata de izquierdas," *Revista de Occidente* 142 (1974): 85–100; Graciela Mendoza, "Don Quijote, un demócrata de izquierda," *Cuadernos Americanos* 197 (1974): 129–135.

5. Mauro Olmeda, *El ingenio de Cervantes y la locura de Don Quijote* (México: Atlante, 1958), pp. 246–254.

6. Francisco Sánchez Castañer, *Penumbra y primeros albores en la génesis y evolución del mito quijotesco* (Valencia: Universidad, 1948), pp. 184, 193.

7. Among the literary critics who share this view is Carlos Varo, *Génesis y evolución del Quijote* (Madrid: Alcalá, 1975).

8. Juan Bautista Avalle-Arce, *Don Quijote como forma de vida* (Madrid: Fundación March-Castalia, 1976), p. 99.

9. Américo Castro, *El pensamiento de Cervantes* (Barcelona: Noguer, 1972), p. 108 n. 4.

10. José Barchilon, M.D., and Joel S. Kovel, M.D., *"Huckleberry Finn:* A Psychoanalytic Study," *Journal of the American Psychoanalytic Association* 14 (1966): 776.

11. Ernst Kris, *Psychoanalytic Explorations in Art* (New York: International Universities Press, 1952), p. 17.

12. Maurice Molho, *Cervantes: raíces folklóricas* (Madrid: Gredos, 1976); Louis Combet, *Cervantès ou les incertitudes du désir* (Lyon: Presses Universitaires, 1980).
13. Barchilon and Kovel, "*Huckleberry Finn,*" p. 783 n. 6.

1. PSYCHIATRY AND DON QUIXOTE

1. Francis Johnson, "Elizabethan Drama and the Elizabethan Science of Psychology," in *English Studies Today*, ed. C. L. Wenn and G. Bullough (London: Oxford, 1951), pp. 111–119. This passage was quoted by O. H. Green, "El *ingenioso* hidalgo," *Hispanic Review* 25 (1957): 175–193, and the concept related to Cervantes, his public, and a particular theory of personality then current in Spain.
2. F. Alexander and S. Selesnick, *The History of Psychiatry* (New York: Harper and Row, 1966), pp. 101–102, quoted in P. E. Russell, "*Don Quixote* as a Funny Book," *Modern Language Review* 64 (1969): 313.
3. P. Bassoe, M.D., "Spain as the Cradle of Psychiatry," *American Journal of Psychiatry* 101 (1945).
4. Joaquín Fuster, M.D., "Origen y evolución de la asistencia psiquiátrica en el Instituto Mental de Santa Cruz," *Anales del Hospital de la Santa Cruz y San Pablo, Barcelona* 20 (1960): 173–332. As befits his professional status, Dr. Fuster is more concerned for the extent and quality of patient care than for simple chronological priority. This is why he omits the purely confinatory facilities, e.g., London's Bedlam (1337) and Florence's Bonifacio "dei Dementi" (1377).
5. See J. Delgado Roig, M.D., "Historia del hospital de inocentes de Sevilla," *Actas Españolas de Neurología y Psiquiatría* 16 (1941).
6. Quoted by Vicente Peset, M.D., in his Appendix to J. B. Ullersperger, *Historia de la psicología y psiquiatría en España* [1871], ed. V. Peset (Madrid: Alhambra, 1954), pp. 179–182. See also F. M. Torner, *Doña Oliva Sabuco de Nantes*, Biblioteca de Cultura Español (Madrid: Aguilar, 1935).
7. Available in a modern edition by Antonio Vilanova (Barcelona: Selecciones Bibliográficas, 1953). See also Juan Bautista Avalle-Arce, *Don Quijote como forma de vida* (Madrid: Fundación March-Castalia, 1976), p. 139.
8. The four humors, in their traditional roles as determiners of human personality, are the "scientific" basis for a recent treatise on the control of tension. See Tim LaHaye, *Spirit Controlled Temperament* (Wheaton, Ill.: Tyndale House, 1971).
9. Ullersperger, *Historia*, p. 89.

10. Ibid., pp. 90–91. On Alfonso Ponce de Santa Cruz see the doctoral dissertation of A. Escudero Ortuño, *Concepto de la melancolía en el siglo XVII* (Huesca: Imprenta Provincial, 1950).

11. Luis Astrana Marín, *Vida heroica y ejemplar de Miguel Cervantes Saavedra*, 7 vols. (Madrid: Reus, 1948–1958), 6: 383.

12. Noam Chomsky, *Language and Mind* (New York: Harcourt, Brace, Jovanovich, 1972), pp. 9–10, offers this summary of Huarte's three levels of intelligence. Because Huarte's theory of generativity anticipates important aspects of Chomsky's own thought, he plays down its basis in traditional humoral medicine. Huarte, however, insists repeatedly on the authority of Galen.

13. Mauricio de Iriarte, *El "Examen de ingenios" y "El ingenioso hidalgo": el Dr. Juan Huarte de San Juan y su "Examen de ingenios," contribución a la historia de la psicología diferencial* (Madrid: Consejo Superior de Investigaciones Científicas, 1948).

14. Peset in his Appendix to Ullersperger, *Historia*, pp. 166–178.

15. Green, "El *ingenioso* hidalgo," briefly summarized in his *Spain and the Western Tradition* (Madison: University of Wisconsin, 1966), 4: 61.

16. Cervantes, *The Ingenious Gentleman Don Quixote de la Mancha*, trans. Samuel Putnam, The Modern Library (New York: Random House, n.d.), Pt. I, chap. 1, p. 27. All subsequent citations are from this edition unless noted otherwise, and will henceforth be abbreviated in the text as follows: [Part] I, [chapter] 1, or I, 1.

17. C. P. Otero, "Introducción a Chomsky," prologue to his translation of Noam Chomsky, *Aspectos de la teoría de la sintaxis* (Madrid: Aguilar, 1970), pp. xxv–xxviii.

18. Iriarte, *El "Examen de ingenios,"* p. 242. The same point is made in another context by Leland Chambers, "Idea and the Concept of Character in *Don Quijote*," in *Studia Iberica, Festschrift für Hans Flasche*, ed. K.-H. Körner and K. Rühl (Bern/Munich: Francke, 1973), pp. 119–130.

19. Jacques Ferrand, M.D., *Erotomania or a Treatise . . . of Love or Erotique Melancholy*, trans. Edmund Chilmead (Oxford, 1640). See the excellent summary offered by Lawrence Babb in *The Elizabethan Malady* (East Lansing Michigan State University, 1951), pp. 128–130.

20. See Francisco Márquez Villanueva, *Personajes y temas del Quijote* (Madrid: Taurus, 1975), pp. 46–51. More recently, Michèle Gendreau-Massaloux has developed this theme and related it to Ferrand and other writers on melancholy in a paper presented at the Primer Congreso Internacional sobre Cervantes (Madrid, July 1978) entitled "Los locos de amor en el *Quijote*: psicopatología y creación cervantina."

21. Antonio Vallejo Nágera, M.D. (de la Real Academia de Medicina), *Apología de las patografías cervantinas* (Madrid: Instituto de España, 1958).
22. Carlos Gutiérrez Noriega, M.D., "Contribución de Cervantes a la psicología y a la psiquiatría," *Revista de Neuro-Psiquiatría* [Lima] 7 (1944), and "Cervantes y la psicología médica," ibid. 9 (1946); Antonio Vallejo Nágera, M.D., *Literatura y psiquiatría* (Barcelona: Barra, 1950) and *Tratado de psiquiatría* (Barcelona: Salvat, 1954)—both of which contain chapters on the *Quixote*—and *Apología*.
23. See, for example, John H. Kirschner, "Don Quixote de la Mancha: A Study in Classical Paranoia," *Annali del Istituto Orientale* [Napoli] 9 (1967): 275–282.
24. Vallejo Nágera, *Apología*, p. 9.
25. Martine Bigeard, *La folie et les fous littéraires en Espagne, 1500–1650* (Paris: Centre de Recherches Hispaniques, 1972), p. 161.
26. Gutiérrez Noriega, "Contribución de Cervantes," p. 154.

2. "NEL MEZZO DEL CAMMIN"

1. Daniel J. Levinson et al., *The Seasons of a Man's Life* (New York: Knopf, 1978), pp. 324–325.
2. Juan Huarte de San Juan, *Examen de ingenios para las ciencias* [1594], Biblioteca de Autores Españoles, 65: 424–425.
3. Attributed to Oliva Sabuco de Nantes, *Verdadera ciencia del conocimiento de sí mismo*, no. 44, in F. M. Torner, *Doña Oliva Sabuco de Nantes* (Madrid: Aguilar, 1935), p. 161.
4. Sabuco, *Conocimiento*, no. 45, in Torner, *Sabuco*, p. 164. The phrases in brackets were excised by the Inquisition.
5. See Levinson, *Seasons*, pp. 32–33.
6. Roger Gould, M.D., *Transformations: Growth and Change in Adult Life* (New York: Simon and Schuster, 1978).
7. George E. Vaillant, M.D., *Adaptation to Life* (Boston: Little, Brown, 1977).
8. Edmund Bergler, M.D., *The Revolt of the Middle Aged Man* (New York: Grosset and Dunlap, 1957), p. 9.
9. Barbara Fried, *The Middle Age Crisis* (New York: Harper and Row, 1967), p. 22.
10. L. A. Murillo, *The Golden Dial: Temporal Configuration in Don Quixote* (Oxford: Dolphin, 1975), p. 28. These ideas are also elaborated in the same author's "The Summer of Myth: *Don Quijote de la Mancha*

and *Amadís de Gaula,*" *Philological Quarterly* 51 (1972).

11. Elliott Jaques, M.D., "Death and the Mid-Life Crisis," *International Journal of Psycho-Analysis* 46 (1965): 504.

12. Gould, *Transformations,* p. 231.

13. Quoted in Fried, *The Middle Age Crisis,* p. 42.

14. David L. Gutmann, "An Exploration of Ego Configurations in Middle and Late Life," in *Personality in Middle and Late Life,* ed. Bernice Neugarten (New York: Atherton, 1964), p. 117.

15. Matías de los Reyes, *Dar al tiempo lo que es suyo* [Jaén, 1629], f. 1, v., quoted in C. B. Johnson, *Matías de los Reyes and the Craft of Fiction* (Berkeley, Los Angeles, London: University of California Press, 1973), p. 78.

16. Philippe Aries, *Western Attitudes toward Death* (Baltimore: Johns Hopkins, 1974), p. 44.

17. Jaques, "Death and the Mid-Life Crisis," p. 502.

18. Bergler, *Revolt,* p. 1.

19. Fried, *The Middle Age Crisis,* pp. 102–103.

20. See n. 7.

21. George E. Vaillant, M.D., "The 'Normal Boy' in Later Life," *Harvard* 80 (Nov.–Dec. 1977): 48.

22. *Adaptation to Life,* pp. 383–386.

23. Gutmann, "An Exploration," pp. 125–127.

3. DON QUIXOTE'S HOUSEHOLD AND THE ESCAPE TO DULCINEA

1. For a fuller discussion of this essential background to Don Quixote's historical situation, see José Antonio Maravall, *Utopía y Contrautopía en el "Quijote"* (Santiago de Compostela: Pico Sacro, 1976).

2. The classic study of this pattern is Earl J. Hamilton, *American Treasure and the Price of Revolution in Spain, 1501–1650* (New York: Octagon Books, 1934). Hamilton's positions have been refined and related to Don Quixote by Pierre Vilar, "Le temps du Quichotte," *Europe* (1956), pp. 3–16; idem, "Don Quichotte et l'Espagne de 1600, les fondements historiques d'un irréalisme," *Beiträge zur Romanischen Philologie* (1967), pp. 207–216. Vilar's *Crecimiento y desarrollo—Economía e Historia. Reflexiones sobre el caso español* (Barcelona: Ariel, 1976) is a fundamental collection of pertinent studies.

3. See Augustin Redondo, "Historia y literatura: el personaje del

escudero en el *Lazarillo*," in *La Picaresca. Orígenes, textos y estructuras*, Actas del 1º Congreso Internacional sobre la picaresca, Madrid, June 1976 (Madrid: F.V.E., 1979), pp. 421–435.

4. See, for example: Concha Espina, *Mujeres del Quijote* (Madrid: Renacimiento, 1930); Sadie E. Trachman, *Cervantes' Women of Literary Tradition* (New York: Hispanic Institute, 1932); Martha K. de Trinker, *Las mujeres en el Don Quijote de Cervantes comparadas con las mujeres en los dramas de Shakespeare* (México, 1938); Carmen Castro, "Personajes femeninos de Cervantes," *Anales Cervantinos* 3 (1953): 45–85; and Ann E. Wiltrout, "Las mujeres del *Quijote*," *Anales Cervantinos* 12 (1973): 167–172.

5. See Arturo Serrano Plaja, *Realismo "mágico" en Cervantes* (Madrid: Gredos, 1967), p. 39.

6. Daniel J. Levinson et al., *The Seasons of a Man's Life* (New York: Knopf, 1978), p. 45.

7. Martine Bigeard, *La folie et les fous littéraires en Espagne, 1500–1650* (Paris: Centre de Recherches Hispaniques, 1972), pp. 153, 162–163.

8. Teresa Aveleyra, "El erotismo de don Quijote," *NRFH* 26 (1977): 478.

9. Edward Dudley, "Don Quijote as Magus: the Rhetoric of Interpolation," *BHS* 49 (1972): 363; idem, "The Wild Man Goes Baroque," in *The Wild Man Within*, ed. Dudley and Novak (Pittsburgh: Pittsburgh University Press, 1972), p. 123.

10. Luis Andrés Murillo, "La espada de don Quijote (Cervantes y la poesía heroica)" (Paper presented at the Primer Congreso Internacional sobre Cervantes, Madrid, July 1978).

11. Miguel de Unamuno, *Vida de don Quijote y Sancho*, 14th ed. (Madrid: Espasa-Calpe, 1966), p. 195. My translation.

12. Let it be said that the sword-phallus correspondence is not only legitimate in a general sense, it is also used consciously by Cervantes himself. At the beginning of the *Casamiento engañoso y coloquio de los perros* [The deceitful marriage and the colloquy of the dogs] the protagonist, presented leaving the hospital where he has taken the cure for syphilis, is dragging his sword on the ground. As he has misused his sword (by not soldiering), so has he misused his phallus (by contracting venereal disease). The friend who meets him explicitly relates the two activities.

13. Maravall, *Utopía y Contrautopía*, p. 95.

14. Juan Bautista Avalle-Arce, *Don Quijote como forma de vida* (Madrid: Fundación March-Castalia, 1976), pp. 224–228.

15. John G. Weiger, *The Individuated Self: Cervantes and the Emergence of the Individual* (Athens: Ohio University Press, 1979), p. 35.

16. Luis Andrés Murillo, "Lanzarote and Don Quixote," *Folio: Papers on Foreign Languages and Literatures*, no. 10, Studies in the Literature of Spain, Sixteenth and Seventeenth Centuries, ed. M. J. Ruggerio (Brockport, New York: Department of Foreign Languages, SUNY Brockport, 1977), p. 64; also, Conchita H. Marianella, *"Dueñas" and "Doncellas": A Study of the "Doña Rodríguez" Episode in "Don Quixote,"* North Carolina Studies in the Romance Languages and Literatures (Chapel Hill: 1979), pp. 76–77.

17. On Gutierre de Quixada and his possible relation to Don Quixote, see the *Crónica de don Juan II*, in Biblioteca de Autores Españoles, vol. 68; F. Rodríguez Marín in his edition of *Don Quijote* (Madrid: Atlas, 1949), 10: 132–149; Varios, *Caballeros andantes españoles* (Madrid: Espasa-Calpe, 1967); L. Astrana Marín, *Vida ejemplar y heroica de . . . Cervantes* (Madrid: Reus, 1948–1958), vol. 4, chap. 45.

18. Quintañona is not mentioned in any of the chivalresque prose romances, only in the ballad "Never was there a knight / so well served. . . ." Even there she is not the go-between, only the pourer of Lancelot's wine before Queen Guinevere takes him to bed. In the materials Cervantes could have known there is no emphasis on Guinevere's marriage to Arthur and the consequent fact that she and Lancelot are committing adultery, although those facts were certainly known in Spain. The adulterous nature of the love affair is insisted upon in the *Demanda del Sancto Grial* (1515), which Cervantes surely knew. The anonymous *Lanzarote del lago*, which circulated widely in the sixteenth century, has an episode involving Lancelot and King Pelles' daughter. Lancelot arrives at the castle and, immediately after being disarmed, requests wine. The *dueña* Brisaina sends for wine, which is served to Lancelot by Brisaina's sister. Lancelot asks for Guinevere. Brisaina continues to ply him with wine, then, pretending to lead him to Guinevere, takes him instead to her own mistress's bed. Brisaina is "a *dueña* more than one hundred years of age." The word *quintañona* in Spanish denotes a woman of that age. Thus, by combining various Lancelot stories and telescoping Quintañona and Brisaina, the Quintañona of the ballad came to be perceived as an erotic figure, the intermediary in the adulterous relationship of Lancelot and Guinevere. See Marianella, *"Dueñas" and "Doncellas,"* pp. 84–91.

19. The Spanish text says: "socorriendo viudas, amparando doncellas, *favoreciendo casadas*, huérfanos y pupilos." The *casadas* (married women) are unaccountably omitted by Putnam.

20. Miguel de Unamuno, *Vida de don Quijote y Sancho*, p. 59. My transla-

tion. More recently our attention has been called to the fact that love—particularly the relationship between weak, masochistic men and cruel, domineering women, but love in any case—is the great theme of all Cervantes's works. This provocative thesis is advanced and argued by Louis Combet, *Cervantès ou les incertitudes du désir* (Lyon: Presses Universitaires, 1980). Combet's work will surely be attacked, and many of the applications of his theory need to be rectified, but its publication is an important event in the evolution of Cervantine criticism.

21. Letter dated 2 Nov. 1906. Published by Arturo Sergio Visca, *Correspondencia de Zorrilla de San Martín y Unamuno* (Montevideo: Instituto Nacional de Investigaciones y Archivos Literarios, 1955), p. 33. My translation. This letter was brought to my attention by my friend and colleague, Rubén A. Benítez.

22. Helene Deutsch, "Don Quixote and Don Quixotism," read at the 13th International Psycho-Analytical Congress, Lucerne, 28 Aug. 1934. Published first in *Psychoanalytic Quarterly* 6 (1937): 215–222. Reprinted in Deutsch's *Neuroses and Character Types* (New York: International University Press, 1965), pp. 218–225.

23. Donald D. Palmer, "Unamuno, Freud and the Case of Alonso Quijano," *Hispania* 54 (1971): 243–249. Salvador de Madariaga has also remarked our hero's basic timidity "in matters of the heart" in *Guía del lector del Quijote*, 6th ed. (Buenos Aires: Editorial Sudamericana, 1967), p. 98. Most recently, Helena Percas de Ponseti has included the "Unamuno hypothesis" as one possible explanation for the etiology of Don Quixote's madness in her *Cervantes y su concepto del arte* (Madrid: Gredos, 1975), 1: 65.

24. Carmen Castro, "Personajes femeninos de Cervantes," p. 49. A certain indefinable tone in this article leads me to suspect that Castro had somehow intuited the relationships I am attempting to articulate here, and that her unconscious insight fell victim to her equally unconscious internal censorship.

25. Avalle-Arce, *Don Quijote como forma de vida*, pp. 16, 30.

26. Luis Andrés Murillo, *The Golden Dial: Temporal Configuration in Don Quixote* (Oxford: Dolphin, 1975), p. 28.

27. Levinson et al., *The Seasons of a Man's Life*, p. 62.

28. George E. Vaillant, M.D., *Adaptation to Life* (Boston: Little, Brown, 1977), p. 225. The phenomenon of father-daughter incest, as it begins to emerge into the realm of popular sociological discourse, appears to be amazingly widespread. See for example Diane Elvenstar, "Incest: A Second Reality for a Child," *Los Angeles Times*, Monday, Oct. 22, 1979. Two weeks later, thanks to the miracle of

syndication, "Dear Abby" was sharing with readers around the country a number of letters from men who had been involved in this sort of relationship. See "Therapy Can Help Child Molesters," *Los Angeles Times*, Thursday, Nov. 8, 1979. Massive, readily available, empirical documentation of this particular phenomenon is now accumulating. See Florence Rush, *The Best Kept Secret: Sexual Abuse of Children* (New York: McGraw-Hill, 1980).

29. Roger Gould, M.D., *Transformations: Growth and Change in Adult Life* (New York: Simon and Schuster, 1978), p. 269.

30. Robert F. Peck and Howard Berkowitz, "Personality and Adj stment in Middle Age," in *Personality in Middle and Late Life*, ed. Bernice Neugarten (New York: Atherton, 1964), p. 19.

31. Carlos Varo, *Génesis y evolución del Quijote* (Madrid: Alcalá, 1968), pp. 71–80. The same class distinction, however, does not impede the satisfactory resolution of the Dorotea-Don Fernando romance.

32. Avalle-Arce calls attention, although not in this sense, to the possible parallel of Don Quixote and his niece to "that small-town gossip about the parish priest and his 'niece,'" in *Don Quijote como forma de vida*, p. 64. The "priest's housekeeper" is also a well-established character, at least in folklore.

33. Serrano Plaja, *Realismo "mágico" en Cervantes*, p. 202.

4. DULCINEA AND THE REAL
WOMEN: PART I

1. See Conchita H. Marianella, *"Dueñas" and "Doncellas": A Study of the "Doña Rodríguez" Episode in "Don Quijote,"* North Carolina Studies in the Romance Languages and Literatures (Chapel Hill: 1979), pp. 76–77.

2. It should be observed that the creation of Dulcinea is not the only thing at stake in this episode. The reader of 1605, especially the inquisitive, minoritarian reader to whom Cervantes typically addresses himself, would have little difficulty in recognizing the Toledan merchants as representatives of the New Christians (*conversos*), descendants of Jews, who conform to obligatory religious practices, totally devoid of real faith, simply in order to continue in business. These people, it was felt, would affirm any belief in order to avoid trouble with the authorities. Enforced religious conformism and its natural concomitant—hypocrisy—is the "1605 theme" of this episode. See José Gómez-Menor Fuentes, *Cristianos nuevos y mercaderes de Toledo* (Toledo: LGM, 1971).

3. See V. R. B. Oelschläger, "Sancho's Zest for the Quest," *Hispania* 35 (1952): 1–22; and more recently, Harry W. Hilburn, "Lo subconsciente en la psicología de Sancho Panza," in *Studia Iberica: Festschrift für Hans Flasche*, ed. K.-H. Körner and K. Rühl (Bern/Munich: Francke, 1973), pp. 267–280.

4. Louis Combet, *Cervantès ou les incertitudes du désir* (Lyon: Presses Universitaires, 1980), pp. 452–453.

5. Thomas Hart and Stephen Randall observe that Marcela's chaste retreat into nature is really an exercise in self-love, as Renato Poggioli had suggested earlier. See Poggioli, *The Oaten Flute: Essays on Pastoral Poetry and the Pastoral Ideal* (Cambridge, Mass.: Harvard University Press, 1975), p. 174; and Hart and Randall, "Marcela's Address to the Shepherds," *Hispanic Review* 46 (1978): 287–298.

6. See Jean Chrysostome, *La virginité*, texte et introduction critiques par Hubert Musurillo, S.J., introduction générale, traduction et notes par Bernard Grillet (Paris: Les editions du cerf, 1966), pp. 19–20, 26–30, 43–64.

7. See Sant'Ambrogio, *Opera*, a cura di Giovanni Coppa (Torino: Unione Topografica, 1969), pp. 42–56. Coppa remarks that besides sister Marcellina, Ambrose's older brother Satiro, a layman, also preferred to remain celibate, and that Ambrose had been raised in an atmosphere characterized by "verginale candore" (p. 548 n. 26).

8. I disagree with Helena Percas Ponseti, who maintains that Marcela is the polar opposite of a verisimilar literary character, and is actually a symbolic spokesperson for a particular set of values. Marcela may not be the most likable character in the work, and her speech to the shepherds may be a set piece, but her motivations are real. Professor Percas also makes reference to SS. Ambrose and John Chrysostom, but with respect to their positions on the gratuity of Divine Grace, and observes that Grisóstomo dies because he has in effect practiced a theology of works and expects "salvation" from Marcela as a reward for his efforts. See *Cervantes y su concepto del arte* (Madrid: Gredos, 1975), pp. 129–131. The carefully worked out names in this episode further suggest that Cervantes's choice of the name Anselmo for the "one who was too curious for his own good" (I, 33–36) may carry a reference to St. Anselm, who "proved" the existence of God with a syllogism. Anselmo in the story insists on demonstrating "scientifically" a proposition it is necessary to accept on faith.

9. Combet considers that because Marcela, like Don Quixote, is engaged in denying her sexuality, he sees in her "l'incarnation de son idéal feminin." *Cervantès ou les incertitudes du désir*, pp. 422–423.

10. The fact that El Toboso was a place populated principally by *moris-*

cos—indeed the polar opposite of the great families Don Quixote has enumerated—and the inference that the future of the society, at least as Don Quixote and probably Cervantes saw it, lay in the incorporation of the racially isolated minorities—moriscos and conversos—into the mainstream, is interesting and essential for the ideological dimension of the novel, but it is not germane to the present discussion, which is concerned with Don Quixote's efforts to liberate himself emotionally from Sobrina. See Américo Castro, "Cervantes y el *Quijote* a nueva luz," in his *Cervantes y los casticismos españoles* (Madrid: Alfaguara, 1966), p. 78.

11. Arturo Serrano Plaja, *Realismo "mágico" en Cervantes* (Madrid: Gredos, 1967), p. 206.

12. Teresa Aveleyra, "El erotismo de Don Quijote," *NRFH* 26 (1977): 471–477.

13. Miguel de Unamuno, *Vida de don Quijote y Sancho* (Madrid: Renacimiento, 1905), p. 98.

14. See Francisco Rodríguez Marín, ed., *Don Quijote* 10 vols. (Madrid: Atlas, 1948), 2: 237 n. 12.

15. See Luis A. Murillo, ed., *Don Quijote* 3 vols. (Madrid: Castalia, 1978), 1: 298 n. 19; also, Celina S. de Cortázar and Isaías Lerner, eds., *Don Quijote* 2 vols. (Buenos Aires: EUDEBA, 1969), 1: 189 n. 13, for the definition of this important term.

16. Michèle Gendreau-Massaloux, "Los locos de amor en el *Quijote:* Psicopatología y creación cervantina" (Paper presented at the Primer Congreso Internacional sobre Cervantes, Madrid, 7 July 1978).

17. See, for example, Francisco Márquez Villanueva, *Personajes y temas del Quijote* (Madrid: Taurus, 1975), pp. 46–51; Ruth El Saffar, *Distance and Control in Don Quixote*, North Carolina Studies in the Romance Languages and Literatures (Chapel Hill: 1975), pp. 54–61; and Juan Bautista Avalle-Arce, *Don Quijote como forma de vida* (Madrid: Fundación March-Castalia, 1976), p. 170. Avalle waxes nostalgic at the reduction by psychoanalysis of this episode's noble "gratuitous act" to a "vulgar association of ideas in the unconscious."

18. The word *desesperado* (suicidal melancholic) suggests the influence of Grisóstomo (author of the *Canción desesperada*) in addition to that of Cardenio.

19. *Vida de Don Quijote y Sancho*, pp. 101–102.

20. *Cervantès ou les incertitudes du désir*, p. 493.

21. Anthony J. Close observes that the language of I, 1 "clearly implies that Aldonza Lorenzo . . . is not now the object of his affections, nor a person in whom he is interested." In his discussion of this episode,

Close remarks that "setting out to prove that his love is platonic, the knight ends by demonstrating it is non-existent." For Close, the fact that Don Quixote is not at all in love with Aldonza is a manifestation of Cervantes's irony, here developed as a conscious parody of the attitudes and canons of courtly love. I believe that Don Quixote must be taken seriously as a lover—but not as Aldonza's lover. See A. J. Close, "Don Quixote's Love for Dulcinea: A Study in Cervantine Irony," *BHS* 50 (1973): 237–255.

22. Ramón Nieto observes that Dorotea is "beautiful and sensual, perhaps even provocative." "Cuatro parejas en el *Quijote*," *Cuadernos Hispanoamericanos*, no. 276 (July 1973), p. 499.

23. Cervantes, *La Galatea*, Bk. VI, ed. J. B. Avalle-Arce, 2 vols. Clásicos Castellanos, 2: 184.

24. Unamuno, *Vida de Don Quijote y Sancho*, p. 127; Manuel Machado's poem quoted by Francisco Sánchez Castañer, "La locura de don Quijote," in his *Homenaje a Cervantes* (Valencia: Mediterráneo, 1950), pp. 132–133; Carmen Castro, "Personajes femeninos de Cervantes," *Anales Cervantinos* 3 (1953): 59.

5. DULCINEA AND THE REAL WOMEN: PART II

1. See Fiedler's classic *Love and Death in the American Novel*, rev. ed. (New York: Stein and Day, 1966). The intense emotional bond between two men, instead of man and woman, that Fiedler finds so characteristically American might be considered equally characteristic of Spanish literature, at least prior to the eighteenth century. With the exception of Calisto and Melibea in *La Celestina* (1499), the great couples are Lazarillo and the Squire, Don Quixote and Sancho, Pablos and Don Diego.

2. Salvador de Madariaga, *Guía del lector del Quijote*, 6th ed. (Buenos Aires: Editorial Sudamericana, 1967), pp. 127–136.

3. With his accustomed perspicacity Avalle-Arce identifies the confrontation between niece and uncle as an example of the *puer-senex* topos. *Don Quijote como forma de vida* (Madrid: Fundación March-Castalia, 1976), pp. 278–280.

4. See Pierre Alzien, Y. Lissorgues, and R. Jammes, *Floresta de poesías eróticas del siglo de oro* (Toulouse: France-Ibérie Recherche, 1975), p. 89.

5. The use of eggs as a restorative and aphrodisiac is well documented.

See Miguel Garci-Gómez, "Huevos asados: afrodisíaco para el marido de Celestina," *Celestinesca* 5 (1981): 23–24, with pertinent bibliography.

6. *Pace* A. J. Close, who terms the idea that in Part II Aldonza is completely replaced by Dulcinea the "Romantic thesis" and suggests that Sancho's single communication to Teresa renders it untenable. The overwhelming preponderance of evidence, as we shall see, is on the other side. See A. J. Close, "Don Quixote's Love for Dulcinea: A Study in Cervantine Irony," *Bulletin of Hispanic Studies* 50 (1973): 252.

7. Louis Combet has also noticed our hero's reluctance to search seriously for Dulcinea, but he ascribes it to his fear of being overpowered by her, should he find her. How does Combet think Don Quixote is going to come face-to-face with a figment of his own imagination? See *Cervantès ou les incertitudes du désir* (Lyon: Presses Universitaires, 1980), p. 120.

8. See Carroll B. Johnson, "A Second Look at Dulcinea's Ass: *Don Quijote* II, 10," *Hispanic Review* 43 (1975): 191–198; also Combet, *Cervantès ou les incertitudes du désir*, pp. 121–122.

9. Richard L. Predmore, *The World of Don Quixote* (Cambridge, Mass.: Harvard University Press, 1967), p. 115.

10. George Devereux, *Dreams in Greek Tragedy* (Berkeley, Los Angeles, London: University of California Press, 1976), pp. xviii–xix. I find this formulation much more satisfying than that, for example, of Avalle-Arce, whose dread of modern psychology leads him to "remind" us that it was not Freud, after all, but Plato who discovered the mechanisms of dreams. The ideas being available in written form for Cervantes to read about, therefore, their presence in his work is justified. After remarking, unnecessarily, that he considers Freudian interpretations of literature to be of extremely limited value, he concludes: "But I do want to avail myself of the authority of fashionable language, and so I shall say that Don Quixote's dream is constructed by a free, subconscious association of ideas, which are sublimated as they rise to the surface. I am the first to confess that this tells us little or nothing." *Don Quijote como forma de vida*, pp. 191–193. My translation. Professor Avalle-Arce would doubtless be heartened by the striking parallels between Plato and Freud, their concepts of the structure of the mind and the nature of mental disorders, presented in Bennett Simon's splendidly humanistic study, *Mind and Madness in Ancient Greece: The Classical Roots of Modern Psychiatry* (Ithaca: Cornell University Press, 1978). See especially Chapter 10, "Plato and Freud." It seems to me that the mere fact that everyone, including Avalle-Arce, can agree that Don Quixote's dream is "true

to life" in this sense is the highest form of praise we can bestow on his creator. The central fact, which tends to escape us precisely because of Cervantes's apparently effortless genius, is that Don Quixote is *not* a real person, and that his existence is in fact circumscribed by the covers of a book.

11. Norman N. Holland, "Romeo's Dream and the Paradox of Realism," *Literature and Psychology* 13 (1963): 97–103.

12. I am by no means the first to call attention to these anomalies. Their presence has been pointed out by *inter alios:* T. E. Hamilton, "What Happened in the Cave of Montesinos?" *Proceedings of the Comparative Literature Symposium* 2 vols. (Lubbock, Texas: Texas Tech College, 1968), 1: 3–18; Manuel Durán, *La ambigüedad en el Quijote* (Jalapa, México: Universidad Veracruzana, 1960), pp. 210–228; Helena Percas de Ponseti, "La cueva de Montesinos," *Revista Hispánica Moderna* 34 (1968): 379–393; Avalle-Arce, *Don Quijote como forma de vida*, pp. 187–213. Most critics are concerned with the dream as a revelation of our hero's unconscious attitudes toward the chivalric ideal and its realization. Here I shall be concerned with what the dream can tell us about his attitudes toward women.

13. John G. Weiger is among several critics who offer this interpretation. See *The Individuated Self* (Athens: University of Ohio Press, 1979), p. 61. See also Louis Combet, *Cervantès ou les incertitudes du désir*, pp. 380–381.

14. See Emil A. Gutheil, M.D., *The Handbook of Dream Analysis* (New York: Liveright, 1951; 2d ed., New York: Washington Square Press, 1966), p. 94.

15. See Gutheil, *Handbook of Dream Analysis*, p. 111, for a concise discussion of all the dream processes.

16. Percas, "La cueva de Montesinos," p. 390.

17. Conchita H. Marianella, *"Dueñas" and "Doncellas": A Study of the "Doña Rodríguez" Episode in "Don Quijote,"* North Carolina Studies in the Romance Languages and Literatures (Chapel Hill: 1979), p. 87.

18. Arturo Serrano Plaja, *Realismo "mágico" en Cervantes* (Madrid: Gredos, 1967), p. 184.

19. I refer to the oft-cited *"Dueñas" and "Doncellas"* by Marianella, an indispensable source of information and numerous acute observations. Also see Luis Andrés Murillo, "Lanzarote and Don Quijote," *Folio: Papers on Foreign Languages and Literatures*, no. 10, Studies in the Literature of Spain, Sixteenth and Seventeenth Centuries, ed. M. J. Ruggerio (Brockport, New York: Department of Foreign Languages, SUNY Brockport, 1977).

20. The dueña as a type was a well-established object of masculine scorn.

Perhaps the best-developed image of her from this point of view among Cervantes's contemporaries is that offered by Quevedo in his *Sueño de la muerte* [Vision of death]. The portrait culminates in "a drop of mucous falling from her hooked nose and the stench of the cemetery." See also Marianella, *"Dueñas" and "Doncellas,"* p. 64.

21. Other critics have sensed the humanity and the eroticism of this encounter, but—apparently for the reasons suggested in the text— none has been willing to elaborate upon it, let alone make it the centerpiece of Don Quixote's erotic life. Conchita Marianella suggests that Doña Rodríguez's humanity is revealed in her foolish vanity (*"Dueñas" and "Doncellas,"* p. 127). Teresa Aveleyra remarks that Doña Rodríguez "stirs up a tempest" in Don Quixote and groups her with Palomeque's daughter as one of the two most important real women in his life. See "El erotismo de Don Quijote," *Nueva Revista de Filología Hispánica* 26 (1977): 475, 472 n. 4. Carmen Castro recognizes the genuineness of Doña Rodríguez's womanhood and the erotic potential of her nocturnal encounter with Don Quixote. See "Personajes femeninos de Cervantes," *Anales Cervantinos* 3 (1953): 80. Other than myself, the only man who has taken this episode seriously is Stelio Cro, who relates it to the nocturnal encounter with Maritornes in I, 16 and remarks that on both occasions Don Quixote's fidelity to Dulcinea is in danger. See "Cervantes entre Don Quijote y Dulcinea," *Hispanófila* 16 (1973): 56.

22. Serrano Plaja, *Realismo "mágico" en Cervantes*, p. 215.

23. This is the most overtly "Huartean" passage in the novel, and it incorporates the most advanced aspect of Huarte's theory of *ingenio*—the ability to generate a totally new reality. The duke's formulation suggests that he as well as Cervantes had read Huarte.

24. This girl is in fact a boy, a page recruited for the job by the duke's fun-loving majordomo. This fact—the representation of Don Quixote's love object by a male—has led Weiger and Combet to speculate concerning our hero's ultimate sexual preferences.

25. René Girard, *Mensonge romantique et verité romanesque* (Paris: Grasset, 1961); Cesáreo Bandera, *Mimesis conflictiva. Ficción literaria y violencia en Cervantes y Calderón*, Prólogo de René Girard (Madrid: Gredos, 1975).

26. E. C. Riley has offered a splendid analysis of the symbolism of the hare which is most pertinent to our hero's own psyche. The hare symbolizes at once rampant sexuality and chastity. Don Quixote's reentry into the oppressive atmosphere of village and home could not be accompanied by a more appropriate symbol. See E. C. Riley, "Symbolism in *Don Quijote* II, 73," *Journal of Hispanic Philology* 3 (1979): 166.

27. Louis Combet calls attention to the fact that at the precise moment when Dulcinea has become accessible, thanks to Sancho's efforts, Don Quixote chooses to abandon his madness and to die. See *Cervantès ou les incertitudes du désir*, pp. 124–126.

28. See Marthe Robert, *Sur de papier* (Paris: Grasset, 1967), pp. 12–13.

29. See Otis H. Green, *Spain and the Western Tradition*, 4 vols. (Madison: University of Wisconsin Press, 1966), 4: 70, 72. Green's final formulation also betrays the influence of A. A. Parker.

30. John J. Allen, *Don Quixote: Hero or Fool*, 2 vols. (Gainesville: University of Florida Press, 1969–1979; Anthony J. Close, *Cervantes and the Romantic Approach to "Don Quixote"* (Cambridge: Cambridge University Press, 1978).

31. Martine Bigeard, *La folie et les fous littéraires en Espagne, 1500–1650* (Paris: Centre de Recherches Hispaniques, 1972), p. 154; Louis Combet, *Cervantès ou les incertitudes du désir*, pp. 412–413.

32. Even the barrier of social class is not insurmountable. I have personally examined many documents from the sixteenth and seventeenth centuries which demonstrate that marriages between pecheros and hidalgos were by no means uncommon.

CONCLUSIONS

1. V. R. B. Oelschläger, "Sancho's Zest for the Quest," *Hispania* 35 (1952).

2. Louis Combet, *Cervantès ou les incertitudes du désir* (Lyon: Presses Universitaires, 1980), pp. 122–124, 245, 250–251, 284–286, 370–371.

3. George E. Vaillant, M.D., *Adaptation to Life* (Boston: Little, Brown, 1977), p. 238; idem, "The 'Normal Boy' in Later Life," *Harvard* 80 (Nov.–Dec. 1977): 48.

INDEX

Lucena, Luis de, 43
Luscinda, 109, 110, 111, 112, 113, 125, 153
Lust. *See* Sex

Machado, Manuel, 128, 217 n. 24
Madariaga, Salvador de, 3, 143–144, 213 n. 23, 217 n. 2
Madásima (Queen), 111
Madness: in Cervantine characters, 27; diagnosis of, 28; in Don Quixote, 3, 64, 76–77, 105, 109, 142, 194, 195, 199, 202, 204–205; sixteenth-century concepts of, 4. *See also* Psychosis
Magalona, 73
Magical mastery, 54. *See* Gutmann, David L.
Maiden daughter (of Juan Palomeque), 102–107, 108, 109, 125, 126, 127–131, 134, 135, 136, 151, 163, 175–180, 181, 182, 185, 199, 220 n. 21
Manifest content (in dreams), 157, 158, 162
Maravall, José Antonio, 67, 210 n. 1, 211 n. 13
Marcela, 94–97, 98, 99, 100–101, 102, 103, 104, 105, 108, 151, 153, 199, 215 nn. 5, 8, 9
Marcellina (sister of Saint Ambrose), 98, 215 n. 7
Marianella, Conchita, 164, 212 nn. 16, 18, 214 n. 1, 219 nn. 17, 19, 220 nn. 20, 21
Maritornes, 102, 104, 106, 107, 115, 126, 127–128, 129, 130, 134, 135, 136, 163, 173, 175, 199, 220 n. 21
Márquez Villanueva, Francisco, 208 n. 20, 216 n. 17
Marriage, 61, 93, 94–99
Master Pedro's monkey, 177
Melancholy, 16, 25, 194, 195
Mendoza, Graciela, 206 n. 4
Mercator, 48
Merchants from Toledo, 90, 101, 102, 108, 116, 124, 214 n. 2
Merlin, 160, 176; as Dulcinea's enchanter, 180, 182, 190

Micomicona (Princess), 109, 120, 122, 124, 125, 140, 147
Mid-life, 31, 32–55 passim; and adolescence, 42, 47–48, 49, 50, 54, 100; career change, 1–2, 92; crisis, 8, 35, 37–39, 82, 92; crisis of generativity in, 45–47; and Don Quixote, 44–45, 81, 82, 92, 189, 193, 195, 198–199; reactions to, 40–41; as replay of oedipal drama, 41–42; resurgence of instinctual drives in, 42, 44–45, 135, 141, 173, 174, 189, 193, 195, 198–199
Miranda, Don Diego de, 75, 166, 192, 202–204
Molho, Maurice, 6, 207 n. 12
Mondragón, Jerónimo de, 15
Montesinos, 156, 160, 161, 162, 163, 164, 165, 166, 167, 176
Moreno, Don Antonio, 185
Mozo. *See* Don Quixote's household
Murillo, Luis Andrés, 3, 39, 66, 81, 209–210 n. 10, 211 n. 10, 212 n. 16, 213 n. 26, 216 n. 15, 219 n. 19
Musurillo, Hubert, 215 n. 6

Neugarten, Bernice, 37, 210 n. 14, 214 n. 30
Nieto, Ramón, 217 n. 22
Noble. See *Caballeros; Grandes; Hidalgo; Títulos*
Nogales, Aldonza, 114
Nuclear conflicts, 36, 37, 46. *See also* Erikson, Erik

Ocho comedias y ocho entremeses, 23
Oedipal conflict, 41–42, 44–45; and Don Quixote, 44–45, 79, 83, 165, 173, 198; reenergized in mid-life, 47
Oelschläger, Victor R. B., 201, 215 n. 3, 221 n. 1
Olalla, 94–95
Olmeda, Mauro, 3, 206 n. 5
On Melancholy, 11
On Virginity, 97–98
Ordóñez, Count Garci, 92
Oriana, 67

Designer: Linda M. Robertson
Compositor: Trend-Western
Printer: Braun-Brumfield
Binder: Braun-Brumfield
Text: Baskerville
Display: Cartier